FINDING
LOST
SPACE

FINDING LOST SPACE

THEORIES OF URBAN DESIGN

ROGER TRANCIK

VNR VAN NOSTRAND REINHOLD COMPANY
——————————————— New York

For my parents, wife, and children

Printed in the United States of America

Designed by Karolina Harris

Van Nostrand Reinhold Company Inc.
115 Fifth Avenue
New York, New York 10003

Van Nostrand Reinhold Company Limited
Molly Millars Lane
Wokingham, Berkshire RG11 2PY, England

Van Nostrand Reinhold
480 La Trobe Street
Melbourne, Victoria 3000, Australia

Macmillan of Canada
Division of Canada Publishing Corporation
164 Commander Boulevard
Agincourt, Ontario M1S 3C7, Canada

16 15 14 13 12 11 10 9 8 7 6 5 4 3 2 1

Library of Congress Cataloging-in-Publication Data
Trancik, Roger, 1943–
    Finding lost space.

    Bibliography: p.
    Includes index.
    1. City planning—Philosophy.   2. Space (Architecture)
—Philosophy.   I. Title.
NA9031.T73   1986   711′.4′01   85-26297
ISBN 0-442-28399-7

Contents

PREFACE

This book is an introduction to the theory, vocabulary, and current issues of urban spatial design. Although intended primarily for designers and students of the city, the hope is that the concepts and examples will be useful in the professional office as well as the classroom. Theoretical and critical discussion is combined with the study of practical applications and strategies for correcting the problems of spatial structure in the modern city.

Through an examination of the nature of traditional urban space several fundamental principles of structure emerge. In most modern cities these have been lost, resulting in what is referred to as "antispace" or "lost space." The text looks at the reasons for this loss and suggests ways for the designer to restore traditional values and meaning to urban open space.

In the first chapter, the problem of lost urban space is introduced. Five major factors contributing to the problem are identified: the automobile, the Modern Movement in architectural design, urban-renewal and zoning policies, the dominance of private over public interests, and changes in land use in the inner city.

Chapter 2 first describes more fully the philosophy, evolution, and impact of Functionalist thinking and introduces some of the important critical reactions of recent years. The second part of the chapter discusses other factors that have eroded traditional forms of urban space. Within the city, the push toward verticality has destroyed the integrity of street space, while raised or sunken plazas and internalized malls have further undermined the traditional social function of the street. Also covered are attempts to provide alternatives to city life—garden cities, new towns, and suburbanization. The result of utopian dreams for a fusion of rural and urban existence, these alternatives have also directed energy away from the problems of urban space.

Chapter 3 discusses both important historic precedents of urban space and contemporary approaches. The distinction between "hard" and "soft" space is made, and the situations appropriate for each are described.

In chapter 4, the major theoretical and critical responses to the crisis of the modern city are grouped into three categories: figure-ground, linkage, and place theories. The strengths and weaknesses of each are identified and illustrate the need to integrate all three approaches for effective urban spatial design.

In chapter 5, different aspects of spatial structure, connection, and context are illustrated through studies of urban-design problems in Boston, Massachusetts; Washington, D.C.; Göteborg, Sweden; and the Byker area of Newcastle, England. In Boston, an evolved structure strongly identifies neighborhoods, but the connections between districts are problematic. In Washington, the grand master plan was intended to provide strong linkage to monuments within the city, but the urban fabric to reinforce these connections was never realized. Göteborg combines the tight pattern of the planned inner core and the strong identity of districts with problems of connection across the former wall. The reconstruction of Byker was primarily an experiment in how to retain community identity and historic references while redesigning the physical fabric of the neighborhood. In each case there are issues of figure-ground relationship, linkage, and place, but the emphasis varies according to the context.

The concluding chapter summarizes principles that can accomplish the goals of integrated design. Principles include lateral enclosure, bridging, and the fusion of outdoor and indoor space, while strategies include incrementalism and advocacy. The prognosis for the future is that a more efficient use of urban land will make necessary a tighter and more integrated urban form, and that this will offer the opportunity to recapture our lost space.

ACKNOWLEDGMENTS

Special thanks must go to Barbara Pulleyblank, who untangled the words and made them flow smoothly, Paul Hirzel, who insisted on a clear structure, Carol Brower, for her talented hand in graphics, and Roger Conover for his insightful editorial feedback. Help from the many people who provided illustrations, an important ingredient of this book is very much appreciated. Every effort has been made to credit sources appropriately in the captions, but apologies are due for any omissions or inaccuracies. All illustrations not specifically credited to an individual or group were supplied by the author.

Funds supporting the research were provided through grants from the Graham Foundation for Advanced Studies in the Fine Arts, Chicago, Illinois; The School of Architecture at Chalmers University of Technology, Göteborg, Sweden; and Cornell University, College of Agriculture and Life Sciences, Office of Instruction, Ithaca, New York.

Figure 1-1. Västra Frölunda, Sweden. Aerial Photograph. 1975.
In this example of twentieth-century European development, traditional qualities of urban space have been lost.
Buildings are isolated objects; spaces between them are vast and formless, without the coherent structure of historically
evolved streets and squares. High vacancy rates, social pathology, and boredom plague many such Functionalist
developments. (Courtesy: Göteborg City Planning Office. Photo by C-G Johansson)

CHAPTER

1

WHAT IS LOST SPACE?

THE PROBLEM OF URBAN DESIGN TODAY

In today's cities, designers are faced with the challenge of creating outdoor environments as collective, unifying frameworks for new development. Too often the designer's contribution becomes an after-the-fact cosmetic treatment of spaces that are ill-shaped and ill-planned for public use in the first place. The usual process of urban development treats buildings as isolated objects sited in the landscape, not as part of the larger fabric of streets, squares, and viable open space. Decisions about growth patterns are made from two-dimensional land-use plans, without considering the three-dimensional relationships between buildings and spaces and without a real understanding of human behavior. In this all too common process, urban space is seldom even thought of as an exterior volume with properties of shape and scale and with connections to other spaces. Therefore what emerges in most environmental settings today is unshaped antispace (fig. 1-1).

The approach proposed in this text falls between the design of site-specific buildings and that of the urban land-use plan. It is centered on the concept of *urbanism* as an essential attitude in urban design, favoring the spatially connected pub-

lic environment over the mere *master planning* of objects on the landscape. This approach calls for making figurative space out of the lost landscape. As professionals who permanently influence the urban environment, architects, urban planners, and landscape architects have a major responsibility to meet the challenge of redesigning lost spaces that have emerged over the last five decades or so in most major American and European cities. Understanding the concept of antispace as a predominant spatial typology is essential in contemporary urban-design practice.

Every modern city has an amazing amount of vacant, unused land in its downtown core—hundreds of acres in most major American cities (fig. 1-2). For instance in Pittsburgh, Pennsylvania, there are 4,930 acres of industrial land, 260 acres of underutilized railroad land, and 17.5 miles of riverfront available for redevelopment today within the city boundaries.[1] As the movement to suburbia during the fifties and sixties drew industry and people to the periphery, previously viable downtown land became desert. Over the past few years, radically changing economic, industrial, and employment patterns have further exacerbated the problem of lost space in the urban core. This is especially true along highways, railroad lines, and

1

Figure 1-2. Fort Point Channel, Boston, Massachusetts. Aerial Photograph. 1985.
In almost every American city there are hundreds of acres of underused space within the downtown core.

waterfronts, where major gaps disrupt the overall continuity of the city form. Pedestrian links between important destinations are often broken, and walking is frequently a disjointed, disorienting experience (fig. 1-3). It is important first to identify these gaps in spatial continuity, then to fill them with a framework of buildings and interconnected open-space opportunities that will generate new investment. Identification of the gaps and overall patterns of development opportunities should be done before any site-specific architec-

ture or landscape architecture is designed and as a key element in urban land-use planning.

Designers of the physical environment have the unique training to address these critical problems of our day, and we can contribute significantly toward restructuring the outdoor spaces of the urban core. Lost spaces, underused and deteriorating, provide exceptional opportunities to reshape an urban center, so that it attracts people back downtown and counteracts sprawl and suburbanization.

Figure 1-3. Syracuse, New York. Interrupted Pedestrian Space. 1984.
Roads and parking lots often interrupt pedestrian connections within the city; walking is frequently an unpleasant and disorienting experience. (Photo: James R. Chrisfield)

LOST SPACE DEFINED

What exactly is lost space and how does it differ from positive urban space, or "found" space? Lost space is the leftover unstructured landscape at the base of high-rise towers (fig. 1-4) or the unused sunken plaza (see fig. 1-13) away from the flow of pedestrian activity in the city. Lost spaces are the surface parking lots that ring the urban core of almost all American cities and sever the connection between the commercial center and residential areas. They are the no-man's-lands along the edges of freeways that nobody cares about maintaining, much less using (fig. 1-5). Lost spaces are also the abandoned waterfronts, train yards, vacated military sites, and industrial complexes that have moved out to the suburbs for easier access and perhaps lower taxes. They are the vacant blight-clearance sites—remnants of the urban-renewal days—that were, for a multitude of reasons, never redeveloped. They are the residual areas between districts and loosely composed commercial strips that emerge without anyone realizing it. Lost spaces are deteriorated parks and marginal public-housing projects that have to be rebuilt because they do not serve their intended purpose (see Pruitt-Igoe, fig. 1-17). Generally speaking, lost spaces are the undesirable urban areas that are in

Figure 1-4. Hancock Tower Coporate Plaza, Boston, Massachusetts. 1984.
The most characteristic type of designed open space in the modern American city is the plaza at the base of a high-rise corporate tower. Rarely do these function as effective social spaces—in general they are unpopular and suffer from a lack of "thereness" (see also fig. 2-19).

need of redesign—antispaces, making no positive contribution to the surroundings or users. They are ill-defined, without measurable boundaries, and fail to connect elements in a coherent way. On the other hand, they offer tremendous opportunities to the designer for urban redevelopment and creative infill and for rediscovering the many hidden resources in our cities.

THE CAUSES

There are five major factors that have contributed to lost space in our cities: (1) an increased dependence on the automobile; (2) the attitude of architects of the Modern Movement toward open space; (3) zoning and land-use policies of the urban-renewal period that divided the city; (4) an unwillingness on the part of contemporary institutions—public and private—to assume responsibility for the public urban environment; and (5) an abandonment of industrial, military, or transportation sites in the inner core of the city.

The Automobile

Of all these factors, dependence on the automobile is the most difficult to deal with, since it is so

Figure 1-5. Syracuse, New York. Lost Space at the Edge of the Freeway. 1983.
The automobile has had a major impact on the city of the twentieth century. Along the edges of freeways acres of wasted space have been created. (Photo: Carol A. Brower)

deeply ingrained in the American way of life. It has resulted in an urban environment in which highways, thoroughfares, and parking lots are the predominant types of open space.

Mobility and communication have increasingly dominated public space, which has consequently lost much of its cultural meaning and human purpose. A staggering percentage of urban land in major modern cities is devoted to the storage and movement of automobiles—in Los Angeles and Detroit as much as 75 to 80 percent. Partly because of this, buildings are separated, encompassed by vast open areas without social purpose. Streets, no longer essential urban spaces for pedestrian use, function as the fastest automobile link, regardless

of social cost. At the outskirts of the city the street has become the "strip," the square a parking lot framed by unrelated buildings (figs. 1-6, 1-7).

In the 1940s, the federal government launched a massive road-building program. The nationwide Interstate Highway System was motivated both by the needs of military defense and by the desire to foster economic growth. (As an historical aside, Baron Georges-Eugène Haussmann's boulevards through Paris were carved out in the 1870s to afford quick military access to disband crowds in times of social unrest as well as to allow light and air into working-class areas.) The United States Interstate System was meant to link the major ur-

Figure 1-6. Washington, D.C. Aerial Photograph. Valuable urban lands are often given over to the excessive movement and storage of automobiles. (Courtesy: Marvin I. Adleman)

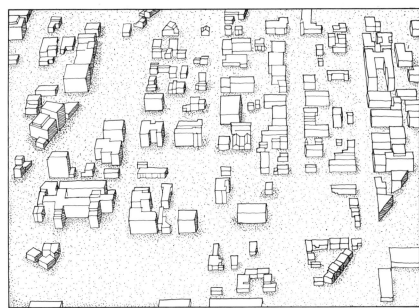

Figure 1-7. Washington, D.C.
Diagram of the same site above, showing how roadways and parking lots have destroyed the consistency of the urban fabric. Without the paved surfaces buildings have little if any relationship to one another.

ban centers of the nation. As these highways cut through the cities, they created huge areas of lost space. Like urban renewal, the highway projects forced tens of thousands of people to relocate, creating profound traumas resulting from social disorientation. Mobility, motion, and the auto-

mobile became tools for isolation (figs. 1-8, 1-9).

The Interstate System also created the need for a complex pattern of connector roads within the city. To disperse traffic from the major highways into the narrower network of streets, the street systems of most cities were drastically altered. The

Figures 1-8, 1-9. Cambridge, Massachusetts. Site for the Proposed Interstate Highway.
Highway extensions through urban areas such as this were common in the fifties and sixties. Successfully prevented by neighborhood opposition, the highway would have destroyed an established community and created an inpenetrable barrier through the city. Unfortunately such projects were rarely halted; therefore most cities have experienced major disruption caused by interstate highway systems. (Courtesy: Harvard Urban Design Program)

artery replaced the avenue and the street lost its social meaning as a multipurpose space. Neighborhoods and districts no longer interacted, but became isolated, homogeneous enclaves. In the end the desire for order and mobility has undermined the diversity and richness of urban public life.

Fortunately, in some cities public protest stopped this wholesale destruction of the urban center, with people literally taking to the streets in an expression of dissent that pointed up the disparity between planners' concepts and real public interests. Far too frequently it was too late.

Modern Movement in Design

Also contributing to lost outdoor space was the Modern Movement in architectural design. At its

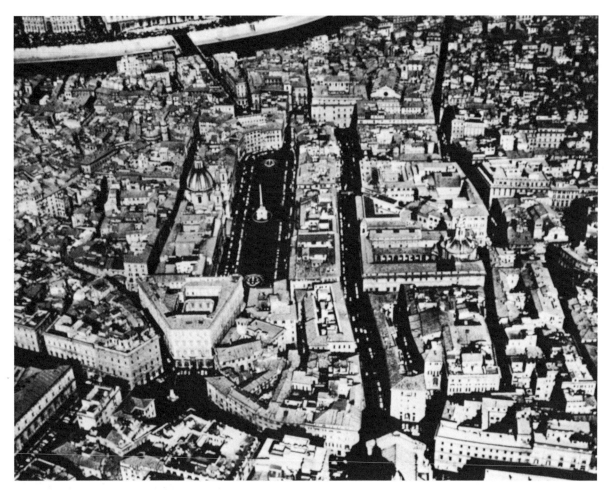

Figure 1-10. The Piazza Navona, Rome. Aerial View.
In the compact, evolved form of traditional European cities, streets and squares are carved out of the dense mass of
building. The public space has structure and meaning. (From Benevolo, History of the City. *Courtesy: MIT Press)*

zenith from 1930 to about 1960, this movement was founded on abstract ideals for the design of freestanding buildings; in the process it ignored or denied the importance of street space, urban squares and gardens, and other important outdoor rooms. Stanford Anderson's book *On Streets* contains a paper by the Institute for Architecture and Urban Studies that includes the following statement:

One of the problems with planning and archi-

tecture today is that the spaces between buildings are rarely designed. This is especially true in the case of this century's Modern Movement in architecture. In contrast, planning in the seventeenth and eighteenth century was concerned with total composition and organization (whether for utilitarian, aesthetic, iconic, defensive, or, as in most cases, a complex of such reasons). In the nineteenth century, as buildings became more utilitarian in their organization, the notion of function was gradually displaced from the external space to the organization of internal space. A building tended to become, in itself, more of an object, separate from its context.[2]

In a recent issue of the *Harvard Architectural Review,* Steve Peterson writes:

Modern space is, in effect, anti-space; the traditional architecture of streets, squares and rooms created by differentiated figures of vol-umetric void is by definition obliterated by the presence of anti-space . . . [which] leads to the erosion and eventual loss of "space," and the results of this can be seen all around us.[3]

In the Piazza Navona District of Rome (fig. 1-10), streets and squares are carved out of the building mass, giving direction and continuity to urban life and creating physical connections, meaningful places. In Houston, Texas (fig. 1-11), on the other

Figure 1-11. Houston, Texas. Aerial photograph. 1985.
In the city of twentieth-century America, individual buildings unrelated in scale or architectural style stand out as objects among unformed spaces. (Photo: Harper Leiper Studios, Houston)

hand, the urban form consists of separate buildings floating among parking lots and roadways. An identifiable ring of lost space encircles the urban core and spatially segregates surrounding residential areas—a typical pattern of most American cities (fig. 1-12).

How did this happen? Designers and builders influenced by the Modern Movement abandoned principles of urbanism and the human dimension of outdoor space established in the urban design of cities of the past. The profile of the Medieval or Renaissance city, our most important historic urban-design models, is generally low and horizontal, and there is usually a close connection between life inside the buildings and activity on the street. With the advent of the mechanical elevator and new technologies of construction, the modern

city has become an environment of high-rise towers removed from street life. Activities on the streets of Manhattan have little to do with the functions of the high-rises above.

The social and commercial role of the traditional street has been further undermined by such Modern Movement design features as enclosed malls, midblock arcades, and sunken or raised plazas (fig. 1-13). These have siphoned shopping and entertainment off the street, which no longer functions as a gathering place. The modern city dweller is forced to create a social life on personal, controllable territory instead of engaging in a communal existence centered around the street. As a consequence, individual attitudes toward the use of urban space have been radically altered.

With the loss of a collective sense of the mean-

Figure 1-12. Diagram of the Form of the Typical American City.
The high-rise core (hatched area) is surrounded by a belt of parking lots and highways created during urban renewal (stippled areas)—a ring of lost space that segregates downtown from residential neighborhoods. This diagram is based on the form of downtown Syracuse, New York.

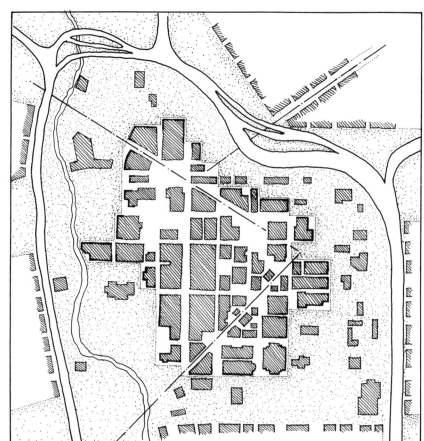

Figure 1-13. 1633 Broadway, New York, New York.
Urban space has been eroded by sunken plazas, enclosed malls, midblock arcades, and raised plazas. Not only do such spaces usually have a negative impact on the street, they also rarely function as successful gathering places. (Photo: William H. Whyte)

ing of public space, we have also lost the sense that there are rules for connecting parts through the design of outdoor space. In the traditional city, the rules were clear. Buildings were subordinate to the more powerful collective realm—to an implicit vocabulary of design and a deference to the larger order of things. The "manners and rules of a place" gave instructions on how to connect.[4] One of the challenges to urban design in our times is to redevelop a sense for the rules and, in doing so, to bring back some richness and variety to public life—important ingredients in cities of the past.

In criticizing the form of the modern city, the intention is not to imply that the architecture and urban design of the last half-century has been an utter failure or that the works of many great designers should be rejected out of hand. Functionalism, which laid the groundwork for our loss of traditional space, became obsessed with efficiency, but, like any great historical movement, it was most concerned with meanings and the problem of giving man an existential foothold. The ethics of modernism have proved inadequate, and its synthetic vision and preemptive dogma no longer constitute the dominant frame of reference in city design. Renewed interest in historicism and the traditional city, which were neglected by the Modernists, has reintroduced the grammar of ornament, metaphor, and style, which can reunite the many aspects of building as an art responsive to the larger issues of contemporary society.[5]

Zoning and Urban Renewal

The loss of traditional qualities of urban space has also been the result of zoning policies and urban-renewal projects implemented during the 1950s and 1960s. These closely allied approaches to planning were well-intentioned, if ultimately misguided, responses to urban decay. The impulse was to clear the ground, sanitize, and promote human welfare through the segregation of land uses into discrete zones and the substitution of high-rise towers for ground-level density. Urban-renewal projects rarely corresponded in spatial structure to the evolved community pattern they replaced, nor did they respond to the social relationships that gave meaning to community existence (figs. 1-14, 1-15). Zoning legislation had the effect of separating functions that had often been integrated. Discrete districts segregated living space from working space. Isolated "superblocks" formed by urban-renewal plans closed off historic streets, drastically affecting the scale of the city. Abstract notions of compatible uses created urban areas that could no longer accommodate physical or social diversity, and that therefore were no longer truly urban. Both zoning and urban renewal substituted functional for spatial order and failed to recognize the importance of spatial order to social function.

Zoning legislation was drafted to protect citizens under the slogans of "health, safety, and welfare"—as perceived by the planners. The result has been cities subdivided into homogeneous districts separated by traffic arteries. Areas between districts are usually major lost spaces in the urban fabric. The social impact has been to ban "nonconforming" activities from each district, thereby excluding the variety that gives life to the traditional, preindustrial city. Bureaucratic rigidity forbids Mom and Pop from living above their shop. Zoning operates under normative assumptions about human welfare and happiness. The complexity of social and functional relationships in the urban setting was incompatible with Modern Movement planning, which required aesthetic completeness for visual and graphic effect. The "messy vitality" that is the essence of urbanism has been sterilized by holistic planning models. Whatever could not be drawn in plan was omitted.

The massive urban renewal projects implemented in the 1950s and 1960s also responded to a concern for social hygiene and have had a profound impact on the centers of our cities. Whereas Functionalism had its origins in Europe, its full impact was realized under federally funded urban renewal in this country. Many European cities were devastated by bombs during the Second World War; America razed its own cities, destroying entire sections with bulldozers and urban-renewal money—"starting from zero" on a grand scale. Viable neighborhoods were declared blighted and summarily eliminated. Boston (fig. 1-16), Philadelphia, San Francisco, and virtually every other sizable city tore down great sections of their cores, accepting the values of architectural Modernism and political utopianism—both of which were used to justify the most extraordinary excesses. As a result, vehicular and pedestrian systems became confused, relationships of scale were ignored, and undeveloped space was given over to parking lots in wait for development. Urban renewal worked together with suburbanization to replace the "City Beautiful" of early twentieth-century America with the noncity of isolated objects. Under urban renewal the additive framework of public space consisting of street, park, and commons was lost.

The value system imposed by urban renewal rejected the elements of the old town that were physically structured around a network of street-level public spaces. A social commitment to the cleansing of city life sounded visionary and progressive, but soon resulted in environments that were unlivable. The physical environment designed to satisfy this commitment to society brought with it the stigma of "the projects" for working-class people. The standardized, prefabricated boxes offered by the housing authority were considered unacceptable. High vacancy rates, vandalism, and abandonment were (and are) commonplace.

The attitudes of the Federal Urban Renewal Program of the 1950s were epitomized at the no-

Figures 1-14, 1-15. Boston, Massachusetts. The Development of the Prudential Center. 1959.
This massive urban development introduced a new and alien physical structure between two residential neighborhoods. Zoning and urban renewal have frequently become a tool for the segregation of functions, destroying connections between areas in the city and contributing to the loss of viable urban space. (Courtesy: The Prudential Insurance Company of America)

torious Pruitt-Igoe Housing Project in St. Louis, Missouri. The buildings at Pruitt-Igoe won numerous architectural awards, but turned out to be so inhumane and poorly placed on the site that the St. Louis Housing Authority evacuated the units and demolished the buildings with sticks of dynamite—a price that is sometimes paid to repair the damage (fig. 1-17). Tom Wolfe's provocative critique of modern architecture, *From Bauhaus to Our House,* tells the Pruitt-Igoe story in this way:

Figure 1-16. Facing page: *Boston, Massachusetts. The Central Business District During Urban Renewal. Aerial View. 1973.*
Under the urban renewal schemes, vast areas of cities were demolished to make way for high-rises and highways. In Boston, for example, many tightly knit communities were torn down, to the detriment of traditional urban continuity. (Courtesy: Aerial Photos International Inc.)

In 1955 a vast worker-housing project called Pruitt-Igoe was opened in St. Louis. The design, by Minoru Yamasaki, architect of the World Trade Center, won an award from the American Institute of Architects. Yamasaki designed it classically Corbu, fulfilling the master's vision of highrise hives of steel, glass, and concrete separated by open spaces of green lawn. On each floor of Pruitt-Igoe's fourteen-story blocks there were covered walkways, in keeping with Le Corbusier's idea of streets in the air. Since there was no other place in the project in which to sin in public, whatever might ordinarily have taken place in bars, brothels, social clubs, pool halls, amusement arcades, general stores, corncribs, rutabaga patches, hayricks, barn stalls, now took place in the streets in the air. Millions of dollars and scores

of commission meetings and task-force projects were expended in a last-ditch attempt to make Pruitt-Igoe habitable. In 1971, the final task force called a general meeting of everyone still living in the project. They asked the residents for their suggestions. It was a historic moment for two reasons. One, for the first time in the fifty-year history of worker housing, someone had finally asked the client for his two cents' worth. Two, the chant. The chant began immediately: "Blow it . . . up! Blow it . . . up! Blow it . . . up! Blow it . . . up! Blow it . . . up!" The next day the task force thought it over. The poor buggers were right. It was the only solution. In July of 1972, they blew up the three central blocks of Pruitt-Igoe with dynamite.[6]

There are many lessons to learn from Pruitt-Igoe, the most important of which is to design the spaces between buildings so that they work for the people who inhabit them.

Privatization of Public Space

The sanctity of private enterprise has also contributed significantly to lost space in our urban centers. While the economic health of a city

Figure 1-17. Pruitt-Igoe Housing Project. St. Louis, Missouri.
Pruitt-Igoe was perhaps the most notorious of failed urban renewal housing projects. The disaster was the result of inappropriate design, misunderstood social needs, and poorly conceived public spaces. After only seventeen years, the only solution remaining was demolition. (Photo: St. Louis Post Dispatch)

Figure 1-18. Facing page: *Federal Reserve Bank, Boston, Massachusetts.*
Throughout American cities, corporations compete to create unique and identifiable images on the skyline. The results are cities of diverse and often clashing architectural styles and a constant push toward greater verticality. Note the suburbanlike landscape forms at the base of the building. (Photo: Edward Jacoby, Architectural Photography)

strengthens its downtown, it also creates a heavy demand for floor space in the center, thereby pushing toward the vertical city. A byproduct has been the appropriation of public space for private expression. Each site is seen as a place for "image" buildings as a potential corporate flagship (fig. 1-18). The very idea of modestly fitting into the collective city is antithetical to corporate aspirations and the chest-beating individualism of the American way.

We have transformed the city of collective spaces into a city of private icons. Regulations intended to define the broader urban vocabulary and to govern individual projects are regularly waived if they do not suit the whims of the particular developer. The continuities of streets are broken by ill-placed buildings, height ordinances are frequently violated, and varied materials and facade styles compete stridently for attention. The city becomes a showplace for the private ego at the expense of the public realm.

In cities of the past, the designs for streets, squares, parks, and other spaces in the public realm were integrated with the design of individual buildings. "Standards for the integration of architecture and urban spaces were set by the patrons and builders of the Renaissance—that model society architects should take as their most important precedent."[7] But in the modern city, each element is the responsibility of a different public or private organization, and the unity of the total environment is lost. Various development and urban-renewal projects are, by and large, put together separately, without an overriding plan for public space. The result is a patchwork quilt of private buildings and privately appropriated spaces, usually severed from an historical context.

As government has become more departmentalized and private interests more segregated from public, the feeling that there is a framework of common concern has been lost. Competition between a fragmented system of government decision making, bureaucratic regulations, community participation, and the sacred cow of private money, together with a mayoral scramble for limited federal tax dollars, has made a shambles of the orderly interrelationship of a city's buildings, open spaces, and circulation. Further, the institutional neglect of the public realm is a monumental problem both because of minimal investment in maintaining public space and a general lack of interest in controlling the physical form and appearance of the city. In any redesign of urban space the conflict between public good and private gain must be resolved.

Changing Land Use

The final major cause of lost space has been the pervasive change in land use in most American cities over the past two decades. The relocation of industry, obsolete transportation facilities, abandoned military properties (fig. 1-19), and vacated commercial or residential buildings have created vast areas of wasted or underused space within the downtown core of many cities. These sites offer enormous potential for reclamation as mixed-use areas, especially since the exodus from the inner city seems to be reversing. The obsolete shipping or rail yard frequently occupies a desirable waterfront site. The abandoned warehouse, factory, or wholesale outlet may have attractions as centrally located, architecturally interesting, and relatively inexpensive housing. Vacant land can be temporarily used for productive urban gardens, commercial horticulture, or neighborhood playgrounds. For the developer, advantages in reusing such sites are obvious; however, the contribution that well-conceived spatial changes might make to the urban fabric of the entire city offers social advantages that go far beyond those of economic gain.

Figure 1-19. Charlestown, Massachusetts. Former Naval Yards.
Abandoned military sites, industrial plants, or railyards exist in the heart of many cities. These offer major opportunities for reclamation as residential, recreational, and retail areas. (Courtesy: Boston Redevelopment Authority)

REDESIGNING LOST SPACE

The five factors we have discussed—the highway, the Modern Movement in architecture, urban renewal and zoning, competition for image on the part of private enterprise, and changing patterns of land use in the inner city—have, then, together created the dilemma of modern urban space. Most striking has been the unwillingness or inability of public institutions to control the appearance and physical structure of the city. This has resulted in the erosion of a collective framework and visual illiteracy among the public. The government must institute strong policies for spatial design, the public must take part in shaping its surroundings, and designers must understand the principles underlying successful urban space.

In order to address the lost-space question, de-signers should create site plans that become generators of context and buildings that define exterior space rather than displace it. In a successful city, well-defined outdoor spaces are as necessary as good buildings, and the landscape architect, in concert with architects and planners, should contribute to their creation.

The history of city design shows that exterior urban space, if conceived of as figural volume rather than structureless void, can reverse the unworkable "figure-ground" relationships between buildings and open spaces of the modern city (see chapter 4). A lesson we can learn from traditional, preindustrial, cities is that exterior space should be the force that gives definition to the architecture at its borders, establishing the walls of the outdoor room. People's image of and reaction to a space is largely determined by the way it is enclosed.

People like rooms. They relate to them daily in their homes and at work. This probably explains why tourists and residents enjoy the structured urban rooms of Europe in cities such as Rome, Venice, and Paris or the garden rooms of Villa Lante, Vaux-le-Vicomte, and Versailles.

In urban design the emphasis should be on the groups and sequences of outdoor rooms of the district as a whole, rather than on the individual space as an isolated entity. Special attention should be given to the residual spaces between districts and the wasteland at their edges. We need to reclaim these lost spaces by transforming them into opportunities for development; infill and recycling can incorporate such residual areas into the historic fabric of the city. Existing public plazas, streets, and parking lots that are presently dysfunctional and incompatible with their contexts can be transformed into viable open spaces. These design and development strategies can also provide the impetus to attract people back to the center. By identifying lost spaces in the city as opportunities for creative infill, local governments can allocate funding to stimulate private investment through "enterprise zones" and other community-development programs.

One of the major requirements therefore is to design environments in which individual buildings are integrated with exterior public space so that the physical form of the city does not fall victim to separation caused either by zoning or by a dictatorial circulation system. How can we do this—how can we give structure to our urban spaces so that they provide a unifying framework for groups of buildings of disparate architectural form and style? In order to find the answer, we should look closely at the traditional city, particularly at the principle of enclosure that gives open space its definition and connection, creating workable links between spaces (fig. 1-20). We need to return to the theories and models of urban space that worked in the past and to develop a design vocabulary based on these successful precedents for today's cities. Maybe we "finally have to understand that history and environment are the two faces of

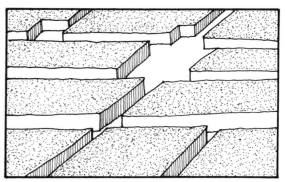

Traditional City Form

Modern City Form

Figure 1-20. Traditional and modern urban form. These drawings illustrate the spatial structure of traditional cities (above) and the fragmentary form of the modern city (below). *In the traditional city, urban blocks direct movement and establish orientation; in the modern city, the fragmentary and confused structure creates disorientation. (Drawing based on diagrams by Rob Krier)*

architecture, that no building stands alone";[8] "and that architectural solutions however brilliant cannot overcome the limitations of the urban fabric in which they are placed."[9]

We have introduced the importance of the outdoor environment as a social and physical space and some of the causes of its decline in the modern city. The most basic act in urban landscape design should be to establish the spatial framework of public design "rules" for streets, squares, and open spaces prior to the design of individual buildings. This code of rules should accommodate a diversity of building styles and forms. It should also express the rules of scale and character for making

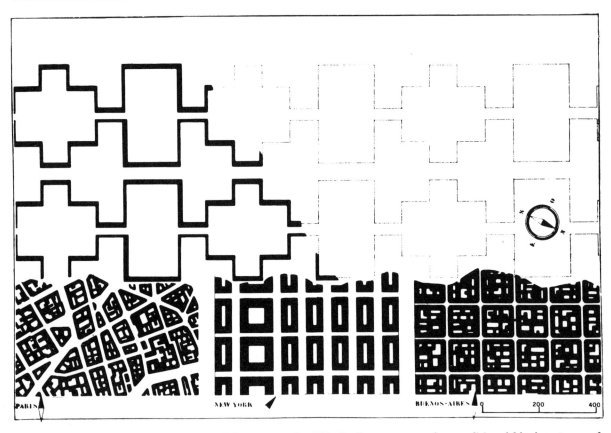

Figure 1-21. Le Corbusier. Figure-ground diagram on the Ville Radieuse compared to traditional block patterns of Paris, New York, and Buenos Aires. Le Corbusier's diagram dramatically illustrates the contrast between the traditional density of evolved cities and the freeflowing spatial structure advocated by Functionalist theorists. (Courtesy: Foundation Le Corbusier/SPADEM)

coherent, visible connections between new and old uses, buildings, and activities. It takes more than good architects and landscape architects to create good cities; it takes good rules—rules that may not guarantee quality in every instance, but that help prevent disasters.[10] In the end, the streets and squares of our cities should once again become spaces for social discourse, taking precedence over the movement and storage of automobiles.

The points stressed most strongly here are that an expertise in urban design can only be developed by: (1) studying historic precedents and the way in which modern space has evolved; (2) developing an understanding of the underlying theories of urban spatial design; and (3) developing skills in synthesizing and applying these in the design process. The following chapter looks in greater detail at the evolution of twentieth-century space and the significant movements in design and physical planning that were influential in its development, including those of the Modernists (fig. 1-21). Subsequent chapters will illustrate historic precedents, theories of spatial design, case studies, and strategies for implementing design principles.

2

DEVELOPMENT OF TWENTIETH-CENTURY SPACE

The evolution of twentieth-century space can be traced by studying the works of several important designers and design theoreticians, their writings and projects, and the professional and academic movements they generated. The most influential of these movements fall under the rubric of "functionalism."

FUNCTIONALISM

Twentieth-century urban space is closely related to the almost universal acceptance of the Functionalist program for architecture and landscape architecture—a program based on ideals of pure forms and unbounded, democratic, or flowing space (fig. 2-1). Functionalism originated as the dream of a small group of idealists in Germany, Austria, the Netherlands, and France during the 1920s. The movement spread with increasing impact after World War II and has been the guiding force behind most European and American urban development since. No doubt there were issues of expediency as well as aesthetic and moral concerns. Functionalism would never have had its overwhelming impact had it not offered fast and economical construction and had it not become conveniently allied with the technology of the high rise.

The prevailing attitude of the Functionalist Movement was to start from a clean slate. In the triumph of Modernism, regionalism and environmental identity were ignored. The very term "International Style" suggested that "buildings in the Nubian Desert in Sudan and Northern Canada had much in common."[11] Architects and landscape architects reduced the conditions to formal, abstract considerations, resulting in exciting designs on paper, but yielding segregated urban buildings and spaces. Somehow, without any conscious intention on anyone's part, the ideals of free-flowing space and pure architecture have evolved into our present situation of individual buildings isolated in parking lots and highways. Public urban space merely serves the utilitarian function of accommodating roads to get one quickly from A to B with little regard for the quality of the trip.[12] Sigfried Giedion, the enthusiastic spokesman for the Functionalists, expresses their almost mystical fascination with the freestanding building in his *Space, Time and Architecture*[13]—presenting this approach as the sine qua non of modern architecture and urban planning.

Figure 2-1. Le Corbusier's City Governed by the Course of the Sun. Drawing.
Le Corbusier's sketch of his concept for the City of the Twentieth Century expresses the Functionalist ideal of purified vertical architectural forms, low ground coverage, and a landscape of flowing, democratic space. (Courtesy: Foundation Le Corbusier/SPA-DEM)

But, over the past decade or two there has been a growing chorus of dissent. Rob Krier, for example, points out in his book, *Urban Space* that, "The erosion of urban space is an ongoing process which has been with us for the last fifty years in the guise of a democratic society."[14] From a somewhat different point of view, Christian Norberg-Schulz describes the problem as a negation of the need for the security of enclosure:

Spatially the new settlements do not any more possess enclosure and density and usually consist of buildings freely placed within a park-like space. Streets and squares in the traditional sense are no longer found and the general result is a scattered assembly of units. This implies that a distinct figure-ground relationship no more exists; the continuity of the landscape is interrupted and the buildings do not form clusters or groups. Although a general order may be present, particularly when the settlement is viewed from a plane, it usually does not bring about any sense of place.[15]

The image of the ideal city represented by Lud-

Figure 2-2. Ludwig Hilberseimer. The Ideal City. 1920.
Hilberseimer's drawing represents the Modernist utopia of high-rise buildings in straight, parallel rows. Traffic systems are rigidly separated, and functions are carefully zoned. (Courtesy: Dr. Franz Stoedtner and the Museum of Modern Art, New York)

wig Hilberseimer's drawings of the twenties (fig. 2-2) has become a reality in many modern communities. Buildings in straight, parallel rows dominate the new functionalist developments. For example, in the new town of Gårdsten, built in 1970 at the outskirts of Göteborg, Sweden (fig. 2-3), the traditional sense of scale is lost in high-rise buildings that bear a striking similarity to Hilberseimer's images. As a comparison, the Gårdsten site is the same size as the entire urban core of Göteborg, a city of a half-million people, yet contains only one-fifth the floor area. This represents a very different attitude toward traditional urbanism and the distribution of solids and voids. From an aerial view, Gårdsten, like Västra Förlunda (see fig. 1-1), is an environment that is not urban, suburban, or rural, and in which the traditional scale relationship between buildings, open spaces, and people seems irretrievably lost. The challenge is to reverse this relationship and redefine the kind of space that gives structure to urban environments,

environments in which connective space—instead of individual buildings—knits together the city fabric.

Three major European movements jointly created the Functionalist program of design: the Bauhaus in Germany, De Stijl in Holland, and the French urban-design movement led by the famous architect Le Corbusier.

The Bauhaus

Functionalism was the architectural expression of the intellectual and aesthetic revolution of the early twentieth century—a revolution that reverberated through all forms of creativity. The most influential force in defining Functionalism was the Bauhaus, a collective training school formed in 1918 under its first director, Walter Gropius, and located first in Weimar, then in Dessau, Germany (fig. 2-4). The aim of the Bauhaus was to unite art and technology under a purified aesthetic that removed all ornament and articulation from form

Figure 2-3. Gårdsten, near Göteborg, Sweden.
Many communities have been constructed on the principles expressed in Hilberseimer's images. Both traditional fig-ure-ground relationships of clusters or groups and the accommodation of building to human scale are lost in such environments. Realizing the magnitude of their error, the Swedish government has decided to begin dismantling these communities, many of which have been vacated, and to reassemble the parts in more appropriate physical forms closer to downtown.

and stressed the beauty of expressed function. There was a strong political ideology behind the teachings of Walter Gropius, Marcel Breuer, and Josef Albers (among other important figures of the movement)—ornament was considered a bour-geois decadence, if not an actual crime. As a pre-cursor of Gropius, the Viennese architect Adolf Loos in 1908 wrote a milestone essay entitled *Or-nament and Crime.*

As happened in other avant-garde movements in the arts, Functionalism suffered from overtones of intellectual elitism. The Functionalists made a clear distinction between ''architecture'' and

''building''—the former the language of the in-group, the latter the plebeian language of the ''boors.'' As a socialist, Gropius imagined that the

Figure 2-4. Facing page: Walter Gropius. The Bauhaus. Dessau, Germany. 1926.
Through the collective training school at the Bauhaus, the birthplace of Functionalist design theory, Gropius and his associates developed their highly influential aes-thetic of ''pure,'' unornamented architectural forms, exposed structure, and the ''honest'' expression of ma-terials. (Courtesy: Busch-Reisinger Museum, Harvard University. Photo by Lucia Moholy-Nagy)

architectural vocabulary of exposed structures and honest materials reflected the aspirations of the working class. However, the question of what the working class might really aspire to was pushed aside, as in Le Corbusier's apartment complex in Marseilles, where the inhabitants quickly filled the functional interiors with traditional ornaments.

The formal components of the Bauhaus, its white stucco walls, exposed concrete, glass cladding used particularly at corners, and flat roofs, became a set of motifs that could be applied anywhere, without consideration of indigenous traditions, climate, or natural setting. The word "context" was missing from the vocabulary of the Bauhaus; the assumption was that although people might have sentimental attachments to forms of ornament and historic references, given time and education they would come to appreciate the higher principles of aesthetic purity. In the words of Tom Wolfe:

> [The Bauhaus] rejected all things "bourgeois" and "functionalism" became one of several euphemisms for non-bourgeois. . . . at the heart of functional, as everyone knew, was not function but the spiritual quality known as non-bourgeois.[16]

In Germany, Bauhaus design was manifest in numerous early projects, including the long, straight blocks referred to as the Zeilenbau. Taken up by Gropius at the CIAM (Congrès Internationale d'Architecture Moderne) and implemented in Berlin in the twenties, Zeilenbau was a new image of life in urban residential neighborhoods. The Zeilenbau idea was further developed by Mies van der Rohe for the 1927 Werkbund Exhibition at Weissenhofsiedlung in Stuttgart (fig. 2-5). The intent of Zeilenbau was to establish a hierarchy of open spaces responding to user needs, but in fact the rigid layout of the site plan failed to meet human requirements for outdoor space. As building form was no longer determined by external design, public places lost their function. This model, applied to several international projects, led to undifferentiated linear space as a generator of urban form.

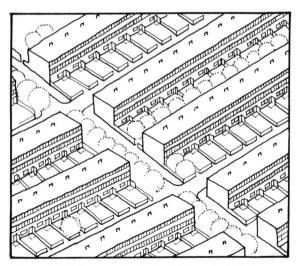

Figure 2-5. Mies van der Rohe. Weissenhof Siedlungen. Stuttgart, Germany. 1927.
One of the spatial concepts developed in the Bauhaus was the Zeilenbau (linear block). Mies van der Rohe attempted to apply this concept to workers' housing in Stuttgart. Although intended to provide hierarchies of spaces for occupants, such projects led to an environment of undifferentiated linear space.

Social idealism based on a concern for the masses was an ideological underpinning of the Bauhaus. Curiously, however, their architectural program largely ignored problems of social interaction outside the private domain. This asocial interpretation of how public spaces were actually to be used was also characteristic of Le Corbusier's studio in Paris and De Stijl in the Netherlands.

De Stijl

De Stijl in particular had formal objectives very similar to those of the Bauhaus. As in the Bauhaus, members of De Stijl were involved in all areas of design and the fine arts, from painting and architecture to furniture and coffeepots. The principal figures behind the Dutch movement of the twenties were the already well-known painter Piet Mondrian, the fierce design critic Theo van Doesburg, and the architects J. J. P. Oud, Gerrit Rietveld, and Mart Stam. Although equally pristine and geometric, the products of De Stijl are recognizably more decorative than those of the Bauhaus. Bright, primary colors are common, as are corners articulated by cross pieces rather than simply abutting.

But, as in the Bauhaus, the underlying motive of De Stijl was the pursuit of social renewal through ideal abstraction. The quest for social revolution and human self-improvement through art and design was a byproduct of the rise in utopian collectivist thinking and a recoil from the horrors of World War I. The designers of De Stijl looked to abstract forms for inspiration instead of the real needs of daily life. A fine example of this is the noncontextual design work of Gerrit Rietveld, especially his exemplary Schröder house in Utrecht, 1923, which synthesized the "high art and low craft" characteristics of De Stijl. Rietveld and his colleagues have had a profound effect on spatial attitudes of Western culture in the twentieth century.

Le Corbusier

The third major contributing force to the development of twentieth-century space was Le Corbusier and his followers. Le Corbusier dominated modern architecture in the period from 1920 to 1960. No other architect during this period has had more influence on modern attitudes toward design both in the actual architecture of individual buildings and at the scale of urban design. Many CIAM and Team 10 architects of Europe, including those who emigrated to the United States during World War II, adopted Corbusian principles of urban space. These European architects, many of whom became leading educators in American architectural schools, spread these design principles throughout the United States. Corbusier's large-scale urban projects, including the Plan Voisin in Paris of 1925, La Ville Radieuse of 1934, and his master plan for Algiers from the thirties, had an indirect but significant impact on site planning and urban design throughout the world.

There were three important principles behind Corbusier's influence on modern urban space:

1. The linear and nodal building as a large-scale urban element—a principle applied physically to define districts or social units (fig. 2-6).
2. The vertical separation of movement systems—an outcome of Le Corbusier's fascination with highways and the city of the future (fig. 2-7).
3. The opening up of urban space to allow for freeflowing landscape, sun, and light (fig. 2-8).

Even though Corbusier's urban works have received more criticism than praise in recent years, they are still a major contributing factor in modern design thinking.

As expressed in Le Corbusier's landscape of the modern city "governed by the course of the sun," developed around 1930 (see fig. 2-1), the Modern Movement ideal of light and air and flowing, parklike space, democratic and boundless, was intended to liberate man from the dense inner evils of the dying city organism. As an intentional departure from the tight block patterns of existing urban areas and public space for pedestrians, the city in a park was meant to give a newfound freedom to the urban dweller. Translated into physical form, however, this ideal had the reverse effect in many cases:

Rather than yielding a green park-like city, it produced in case after case, a central city that was a wasteland; cities pockmarked with the results of scavenger development, appeared more like bombed-out ruins than images of a twentieth-century utopia.[17]

The idea of the freestanding building in the round where all sides are equal, set on a wide, open plaza or green space, has been a pervasive concept in Functionalist architecture. Often abused and misunderstood, Le Corbusier's landscape of the modern city has resulted in buildings as isolated objects floating freely on useless plazas and unattractive parking lots.[18] At the edge of the city, too, massive housing projects have been built with the same ideals of liberation through open space, and the results have generally been as inhuman and alienating (see fig. 1-1).

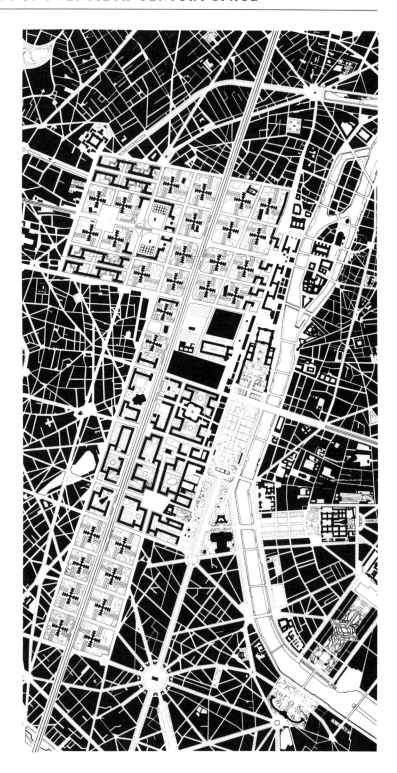

Figure 2-6. Le Corbusier. Plan Voisin. Paris, France. 1925.
Corbusier's Plan Voisin designed in the 1920s, but never constructed, illustrates the contrast between traditional urban density and the urban design of Modernism. Linear and nodal buildings define districts or social units over an open ground plane. (Drawing: Stuart E. Cohen and Steven W. Hurtt)

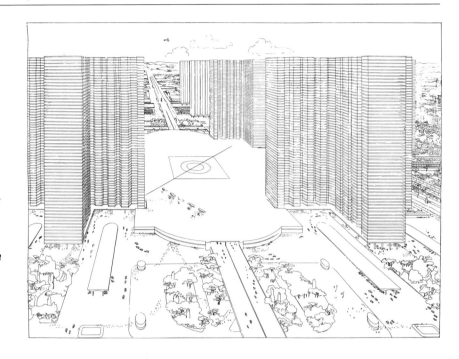

Figure 2-7. Le Corbusier. Ville Contemporaine. 1922. Perspective.
Le Corbusier's advocacy of vertical towers with low ground coverage has had a profound influence on modern urban design. Like Hilberseimer, he was fascinated by the idea of segregated traffic systems and with the emerging transportation technologies of the twentieth century. Ville Contemporaine is predecessor to Plan Voisin and La Ville Radieuse. (Courtesy: Foundation Le Corbusier/SPADEM)

Figure 2-8. Le Corbusier. La Ville Radieuse. Perspective Sketch. 1930.
Le Corbusier's concept for the city in the park was an intentional departure from the tight block patterns of the traditional European city. Meant to give new freedom and open space to the urban dweller, the city of towers has more often produced instead of a part setting an inhumane environment of out-of-scale buildings set among roadways and parking lots. (Courtesy: Foundation Le Corbusier/SPADEM)

Together then, these three movements have had a major role in shaping modern urban space. In many cases the actual architecture has been masterly, but the problem lies in the emphasis on the individual building at the expense of the space around it, a problem that has been exacerbated by the technology of high-rise construction and by the demands of the automobile. This problem became particularly manifest when Gropius arrived at Harvard in 1937. His vocabulary of pared-down form was combined with the skyscraper and with the need for a vastly expanded highway system. The result has been a fundamental change in the structure and social meaning of our cities. This marriage of form and technology has been dramatically reexported to Europe and to the urban form of developing countries, with the sad result that all settlements have begun to look alike (in an amazing sort of déjà vu), and almost every city has its core of lost space.

THE FUNCTIONALIST GRID

We have briefly discussed the Functionalist attitude toward the expression of building form and materials through the works of the Bauhaus, De Stijl, and Le Corbusier. Through a curious equation of social and formal idealism, the Functionalists assumed that there was a relationship between platonic solids and human happiness. It seems odd now that anyone would have thought that banishing ornament from buildings and utilitarian objects could be a source of social and individual well-being, except from the point of view of cheaper mass production. Nevertheless this was the concept behind not only Functionalist architecture but also most of the artistic movements of the early twentieth century. Perhaps the most extreme expression of this concept was, appropriately, the Russian Constructivist Movement of 1918 to 1923, represented by the stripped-down paintings of Kazimir Malevich and Eliezer Lissitzky.

It was a Dutch painter, Piet Mondrian, however, who expressed most consistently the other significant design principle inherent in Functionalism—the obsession with the grid. The resemblance between his paintings and the grid of contemporary cities is particularly manifest in his *Broadway Boogie-Woogie*.

The purified facade, the geometry of squares and cubes, was linked to a preoccupation with a regularized ground-plane: a system into which elements could be plugged at will. The joint power of these design principles from the early twentieth century has had a major influence on urban design well into the 1970s. What we have witnessed is a disciplined geometry of flat surfaces intersecting at right angles—the geometry of base planes—which runs counter to the flowing lines of nature and the human frame. We end up with furniture that is uncomfortable to sit on, houses that are uncomfortable to live in, and public spaces that are uncomfortable to be in.

The grid has functioned as an easily applied mechanical method for organizing separate parts. Le Corbusier's aphorism for the house was a "machine for living" in which all elements without a direct purpose were eliminated, an approach severely criticized by Friedrich Holderlin and Gaston Bachelard in *La Poétique de l' espace*.[19] Le Corbusier's remedy for the clogged streets of the dense inner city was "the right angle," which he declared was far superior to the other angles and represented the sum of forces to keep the world in equilibrium. If the analogies of the machine and the right angle were applied to the ordering of exterior space, the resulting grid could be used as a method for eliminating accidental and random juxtapositions.

As an ordering system the grid has a long history, especially in this country. In the late eighteenth century the entire nation west of the Ohio River was laid out on a consistent grid pattern of 64-mile-square parcels subdivided into townships of equal size. New York City's grid goes back to the 1830s. While the grid has the advantage of flexibility and expandability and is not inherently bad as an ordering device, it can contribute to a

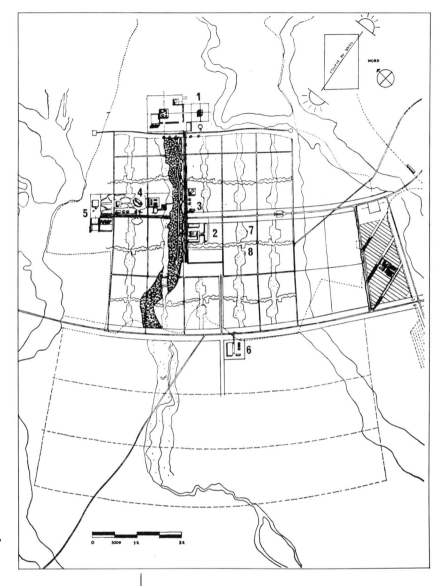

Figure 2-9. Le Corbusier. Plan of Chandigarh, India. The Functionalists tended to use the grid as a means of segregating activities into defined zones. In Le Corbusier's plan for Chandigarh, for example, government is physically set apart from the city. Another problem with the rigid application of the grid is that there is no logical way to establish a center. (Courtesy: Foundation Le Corbusier/SPADEM)

Key:
1. *The Capitol*
2. *Commercial Center*
3. *Hotels and Restaurants*
4. *Museum, Stadium*
5. *University*
6. *Market*
7. *Open Spaces with Schools, Clubs, Sports Facilities*
8. *Shopping Street*

loss of spatial containment, especially when the lines of the grid become superhighways and the spaces between become "prairies strewn with factories and other centers."[20]

The effectiveness of the grid as an organizing system really depends on whether it is used to connect or separate different elements. The Functionalist approach was to use it to differentiate places and activities. In Le Corbusier's Chandigarh or in Frank Lloyd Wright's Broadacre City, each urban element is given its own identity as a separate part of the composition. This is especially so at Chandigarh (fig. 2-9), where the government center is set apart from the grid, not integrated into the rest of the city. Although Chandigarh unites principles of city planning from the past and present and

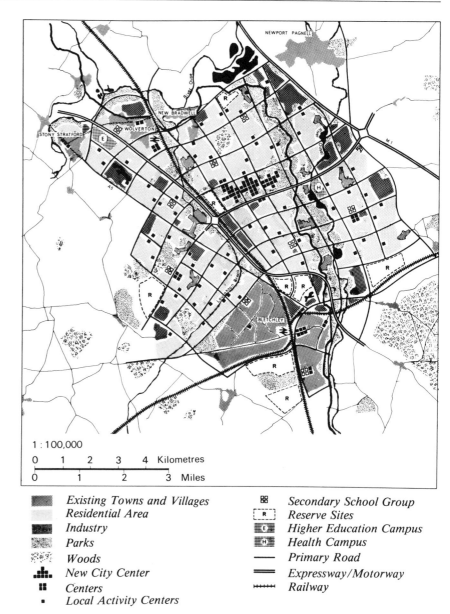

Figure 2-10. Milton Keynes. New Town. England. 1970. In the new community of Milton Keynes, England, a uniform grid of roadways is intended to give maximum flexibility for growth and change. However, the lack of hierarchy among the roadways and the low density of housing make this development closer in spirit to an American suburb than to a traditional English town. (Courtesy: Milton Keynes Development Corporation)

1 : 100,000

| 0 | 1 | 2 | 3 | 4 | Kilometres |

| 0 | | 1 | | 2 | | 3 | Miles |

Existing Towns and Villages
Residential Area
Industry
Parks
Woods
New City Center
Centers
Local Activity Centers

Secondary School Group
Reserve Sites
Higher Education Campus
Health Campus
Primary Road
Expressway/Motorway
Railway

represents a most convincing synthesis of order and freedom, one fundamental quality is lacking: the open-space configuration is a flowing continuum that refuses to accept a true "inside."[21] Hence it indicates a disdain for the historic evolution of urban form.

The new city of Milton Keynes, England, developed in 1970 (fig. 2-10), represents another contemporary application of the Functionalist grid to urban design. Milton Keynes is designed entirely around a uniform grid of roads spaced at one-kilometer intervals and indicates a nonspatial attitude. Within each cell of the grid there is room for approximately 500 dwelling units. The new city plan calls for an ultimate population of 250,000 and is intended to offer maximum growth and flexibility for change since the grid has no formal hierarchy and provides an even distribution of transportation access to all sectors of the town. Milton Keynes's low density and strong auto orientation create a suburban quality that is more American in character than British. Like Chandigarh, it suffers from the lack of exterior spatial definition, and the retail core is a large shopping mall reached primarily by car. The planners of Milton Keynes wanted a low, horizontal profile that would eventually become concealed by trees in order to relate (metaphorically) the new city to the rural countryside that it displaced.

A very different treatment of the grid is found in the eighteenth-century plan for Savannah, Georgia (fig. 2-11). Here the regular patterns of streets and blocks serve to organize a three-dimensional system of continuous space, integrating buildings into the fabric of the city. Because the block system was built up incrementally, the grid was not a system of zoning but allowed for a variety of uses close to one another. Savannah will be further discussed in chapter 3.

In recent studies at Columbia University, three

Figure 2-11. Savannah, Georgia. A View of In-progress Construction. 1734.
In contrast to the separatist zoning typical of the Functionalist grid, the design of Savannah demonstrates how the grid can serve as an integrating and unifying urban form. As each ward was constructed, varied uses were accommodated around a public open space. (See also fig. 3-22).

approaches for inserting viable public space for human use within the contemporary American grid were proposed:[22]

1. Building-by-building changes within the existing block configurations.
2. The introduction of new circulation systems that run counter to the orthogonal grid (such as diagonals similar to those Haussman designed for Paris).
3. Establishment of public monuments to define urban voids.

The first approach is smaller in scale and incremental in nature; the others tend to be monumental. Combinations and permutations of these types of intervention are required to transform the modern American grid into a system of public space for human use.

In general, however, the American grid has been

Figure 2-12. Herrington, Kansas. 1887.
In the American West the grid was applied carte blanche as an ordering system. Dispersed and piecemeal development was encouraged by this uniform application, and cities rarely developed the compact, organic form of evolved European towns. (Courtesy: John Reps)

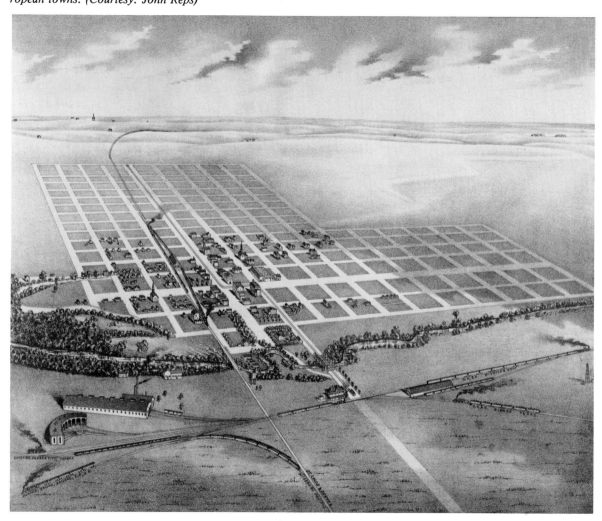

a mechanical ordering system, applied carte blanche to city plans throughout the nation regardless of topography (fig. 2-12). Thus San Francisco's hills are overlaid with a rectilinear system of streets, as are prairie towns. The grid was preferred over more complex types of planimetric organizations (radial, concentric, diagonal), because right-angled buildings were cheaper, faster, and easier to construct. To a large extent the adoption of the grid has predetermined the type of exterior space in which Americans live. In contrast to the density and diversity of the historic European city, almost every American city has an open-ended grid principally serving its economic life. In fact, most cities in this country were not conceived as cohesive spaces for all aspects of human life, but as orderly arrangements for economic independence. From the very beginning the physical pattern of the typical American city did not reflect a collective, centralized concept of public space that might serve as a focus for group meeting and interaction.[23] The difficulty in identifying the center of a grid has promoted a notion of nonhierarchical, repetitive spatial structures.

CRITICAL REACTIONS

Recent criticism has clearly documented the impact of European Functionalist thinking on the architectural forms of single buildings. Functionalist thinking has also had great impact on the entire public exterior environment and has contributed to the current problem of urban space.

In the 1950s a young group of second-generation European Modernists attempted to redefine the underlying principles and formal expression of urban space. With a loosely formulated charter and through periodic meetings Alison and Peter Smithson, Jacob Bakema, Aldo van Eyck, Giancarlo de Carlo, and several others formed Team 10 to readdress the Modernist failure to take account of human needs and activities in space. The published document of the group's philosophy, *Team 10 Primer,* outlines their attitudes about place definition and issues surrounding the design of urban space in response to the rules and disciplines of the existing community context (fig. 2-13). A key word in their vocabulary was "humanism."

Since Team 10 there have been several groups of architects who have critically examined the assumptions of Functionalism. Fortunately Europe is generating not only a strong critique of the Modern Movement aesthetic, but also some hopeful new forms of architectural expression. One of the more recent movements is Rationalism, headed by Aldo Rossi of Italy, Ricardo Bofill of Spain, and the brothers Leon and Robert Krier of Luxembourg. A reconstructed Functionalism, Rationalism promotes a concern for public open space over a preoccupation with individual buildings (fig. 2-14). It looks at historic models for inspiration. The movement has a strong political com-

Figure 2-13. Candilis, Josic, Woods. Frei Universität. Berlin, Germany. 1964.
The innovative scheme for the Free University of Berlin physically expresses the Team 10 philosophy of humanism and was an attempt to respond to both the urban context and the user's needs, and to redirect the course of Modernist thinking. The plan features a layering of urban spaces, courtyards, and pedestrianways organized around low-rise buildings. (Courtesy: Alison and Peter Smithson)

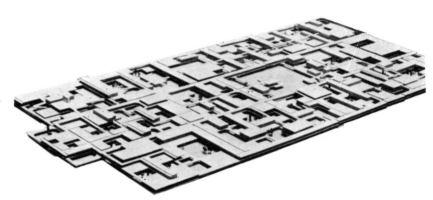

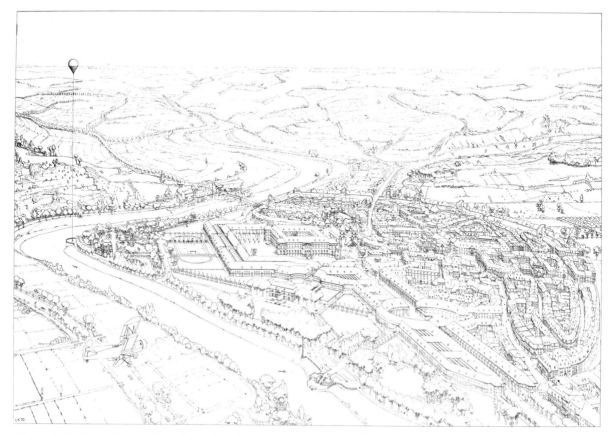

Figure 2-14. Leon Krier. Abbey Extension, Echternach, Germany. 1969.
Krier's design intervention at Echternach includes the addition of a long classical boulevard leading up to the Abbey (from the lower right to the center of the drawing), which restructures the old railyards and creates a new spatial edge to the village and river park. The principles adopted for this design are part of the social, economic, and cultural history of Echternach. (Courtesy: Leon Krier)

ponent, criticizing capitalism for polluting both architecture and urban space. The Marxist ideology of the movement is directed at undoing the problems of lost space caused by the marriage of Functionalism and private enterprise.

Leon Krier, a born polemicist whose drawings and writings represent the most provocative voice of the counter-movement, asserts:

The iconographic and symbolic emptiness of modern architecture can, of course, be explained by the fact that it never belonged to architecture. Rather, it belongs to packaging and in its most ambitious examples, it might have

been the art of packaging. . . . After the darkest and most destructive period of European urban history—including the two World Wars—the building crises leave us today to contemplate the damage which has been caused to the cities and countryside.[24]

In this country one of the most influential voices has been that of Robert Venturi, whose *Complexity and Contradiction in Architecture* came out in the mid-1960s followed by *Learning From Las Vegas* in the 1970s. Venturi's work has set the stage for the Postmodern movement. His self-termed ''gentle manifesto'' (in fact one of the most potent manifestos of our time) addresses particularly the absence of context and open space in modern architecture and urbanism, summing up in these words:

> An architecture of complexity and contradiction has a special obligation toward the whole—its truth must be in its totality or implications of totality. It must embody the difficult unity of inclusion rather than the easy unity of exclusion.[25]

Venturi recognized that most outdoor space created by the Modern Movement was exclusive space, or lost space isolated from its total surroundings. According to Venturi, inclusive space is the opposite, a representation of an integrated unity including the suburban and commercial strip environment. Venturi reinterpreted the popular Modern Movement phrase "less is more" coined by Mies van der Rohe to read "less is a bore," emphasizing that everyday, ordinary space should not be stripped of its cultural meaning. His point of reference is somewhat different from most urbanists, because he sees lost space in commercial strips and suburbs as inevitable—and, in fact, as a positive expression of American society for designers to build upon. Even though the subjects of his own design work are quite often the everyday suburban environment, an area that many designers will not touch, his theories and attitudes toward space are very scholarly and firmly founded in well-researched historical precedent. Venturi's books literally opened the floodgates for a wave of inquiry and reexamination of architectural language and urban-design theory. Examples of Venturi's work are illustrated in the case studies of Boston and Washington, D.C. (see figs. 3-25, 5-49, 5-50).

Colin Rowe, a leading urban-design educator, theoretician, and essayist also took issue with the freestanding building in the city and termed it the "predicament of texture."[26] By "texture" Rowe refers to the composite urban pattern of streets, buildings, and open spaces—the "fabric" of the city. He raises the predicament of the building as a freestanding object and its disruptive effects on the continuity of these urban patterns. Rowe's urban-design work is based on cubist geometries and historic models of urban fabric, especially Rome, Florence, and other similar settlements where buildings as articulated solids are designed to create positive voids (fig. 2-15).

The tide is turning in the right direction but much more needs to be done, especially in defining and designing exterior open space in the cities. As Christian Norberg-Schulz so compassionately writes:

> After the Second World War most places have been subjected to profound changes. The qualities which traditionally distinguished human settlements have been corrupted or have got irretrievably lost . . . in new towns and existing cities. . . . As a consequence, nodes, paths and districts lose their identity and the town as a whole its imageability. Together with the loss of the traditional urban structure, the landscape is deprived of its meaning as comprehensive extension and reduced to rests within the complex network of manmade elements.[27]

PHYSICAL MANIFESTATIONS

In retrospect we must ask the rhetorical question, "What price have we paid for progress?" Are urban areas that have escaped the impact of modernization better off than those that have not? Now is the ideal time to address this issue. As indicated, architects are reevaluating the assumptions behind the Modern Movement; economic conditions have tempered the construction of massive new housing and development; and planners and investors are looking with renewed interest at the center of the city as a reusable resource.

In this chapter we discussed among other topics the impact of the Functionalist aesthetic and ideological concerns of the modern city. Bypassing local historic traditions and needs, the new architecture was a conscious departure from the past,

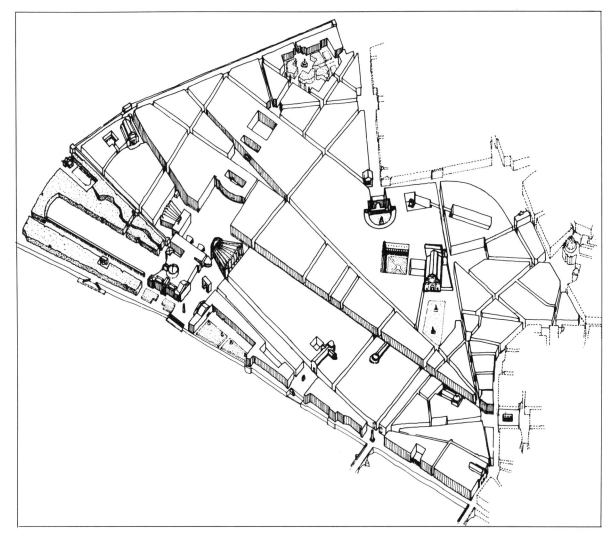

Figure 2-15. Cornell Studio of Colin Rowe. Proposal: New Quarter Del Prato, Florence, Italy. 1980.
Colin Rowe has looked closely at historic urban spaces, particularly those of Rome and Florence, in order to un-
derstand the values and expressions inherent in successful urban form. He stresses the need to fit individual buildings
into the larger urban fabric, as well as continuous ground coverage and the effectiveness of powerful geometric
patterns. (Courtesy: Department of Architecture, Cornell University)

generated by the vision of a humanized, democratic purity of form and openness of space. Under the banner of the International Style, the social
utopianism of Le Corbusier, Gropius, and the
CIAM cleared the palette for a heroic, technically
competent architecture that would establish a universal, man-imposed order, but that was funda-
mentally antiurban.

As Francois Barré writes in ''The Desire for Urbanity'':

The founders of the Modern Movement brutally
purged the city of its former urbanity, but at the
same time hoped it would announce a new era
and man's progress in an industrial civilization.
Urbanity relates the city, establishes its relation-

ships and congruities. It weaves the link while telling the tale.[28]

But it is not simply the Functionalist ideology that has produced the lost space of the contemporary city. Ideals of social hygiene through the abandonment of the city—the garden city/new town/ suburban concepts—also directed attention away from the central city. As manifestations of ideas for social hygiene, the urban-renewal projects of the 1960s were undertaken with the idea that only by starting from scratch could the ills of the inner city be resolved. Zoning ordinances also destroyed the integrity of urbanism by separating functions that had traditionally been integrated into the total urban way of life. The needs of the automobile, furthermore, have become dominant—one cause of growing suburbanization and increased mobility. The high-rise as an emblem of corporate success, furthermore, has produced cities of competing towers instead of cities of integrated spaces.

Modern Streets and Squares:
The Threat of the Vertical

The streets and squares of the modern American city rarely have either the unity to create a satisfying framework or the flexibility to accommodate the varied activities of the traditional street. One of the difficulties is the predominance of the vertical city, a manifestation of Functionalism that needs to be given serious pragmatic consideration in discussing the problems of modern urban space. With the exception of a few fantasy projects such as the futuristic city of towers proposed in 1914 by Saint Elia, the characteristic European urban form has historically consisted of horizontal blocks disposed in a regular pattern with a few dramatic projections above a predetermined cornice line. The occasional well-conceived church spire rises as an accent over the horizontal mass, reminding us of the low physical profile of the city and the importance of government and religion to society. This exhilarating contrast between low and high is exploited in the Italian hill town of San Gimignano, where the narrow towers make the medi-

eval town seem to soar into the sky. Unfortunately the traditional low-rise pattern is being violated in modern cities throughout Europe.

The modern tower in America began about a century ago when the Chicago School, led by Louis Sullivan, Daniel Burnham and John Root, and several others, exploited new techniques of steel-frame construction. In conjunction with the mechanical elevator, builders were now able to go vertical. The charcoal drawings of Hugh Ferriss from the early 1920s capture something of the excitement of the towers at San Gimignano and reveal the sense of power and conquest that the possibility of new technology gave to architects and builders. The skyscraper, furthermore, afforded private enterprise the unprecedented luxury of stacking floor area as a banner of success in the free world.

Today, with the exception of Washington, D.C.—the only major city in the United States to maintain its horizontal profile through strict height controls—the core of a typical American city is for all intents and purposes vertical. The central issue becomes that of how the directional continuity and enclosure of streets and squares can be preserved in an urban environment where the solids are vertical objects that leave unformed voids at their bases. Raymond Hood illustrated the problem in his 1927 "City of Towers" (figs. 2-16, 2-17), where a district of low-rise streets and blocks is diagramatically compared to the same district of towers. What Hood proposed was a constant ratio between the volume of building and the area of the street—the greater the height the more ground space required for light, air, and traffic, resulting in increased vertical stacking of floor area instead of horizontal site coverage. As developers tried to maximize volume, the buildings became as tall and thin as possible, a city of sheer, freestanding needles surrounded by lost space.

The only way the integrity of the street can be preserved in the city of towers is by making clear transitions from high to low building elements. In essence two separate building types are needed within one envelope—a low type that responds to the street-level public realm and a high-rise level

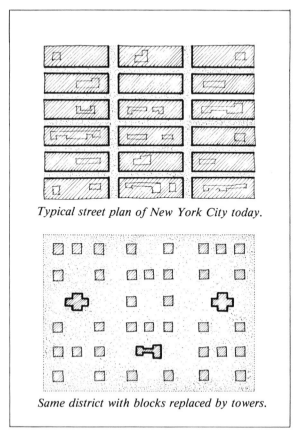

Typical street plan of New York City today.

Same district with blocks replaced by towers.

Figures 2-16, 2-17. Raymond Hood. City of Towers. 1927.
In the vertical city, density at street level must be severely reduced. The problem then becomes one of preserving directional continuity and sufficient enclosure. (Diagrams based on work of Rem Koolhaas)

Figure 2-18. Louis Sullivan. Concept for a City of Setback Skyscrapers. 1891.
As Sullivan realized almost one hundred years ago, transitional layers between low- and high-rise levels are needed to maintain the integrity of the street when the predominant urban form is the vertical tower.

Figure 2-19. Facing page: I. M. Pei & Partners. John Hancock Tower, Boston, Massachusetts. 1973.
From a distance the Hancock Tower is an exquisite building. At street level, however, it is less desirable (see fig. 1-4). Without significant transitional elements, the building simply disappears into the ground and makes no acknowledgment of the public surroundings. (Photo: Gorchev and Gorchev)

Figure 2-20. Sert, Jackson and Gourley. Peabody Terrace. Harvard University. Cambridge, Massachusetts. 1964. Like the Hancock Tower, Peabody Terrace is impressive from a distance. However, the complex is also effective at ground level. Transitional levels accommodate the vertical towers to human scale and create a network of streets and squares. (Photo: Laurence R. Lowry)

that steps back to accommodate private needs above the city. This is not a major breakthrough in urban design; Louis Sullivan proposed a similar idea as early as 1891 in his setback skyscraper (fig. 2-18). There are also numerous older high-rise buildings in Manhattan that more or less follow this concept of sculpted building tops designed to maximize sunlight and views. However, for some reason it has been difficult for more recent designers to incorporate this feature into their architecture. A case in point is the Hancock Tower in Boston (fig. 2-19), discussed later in reference to Copley Square. An exquisite building seen from a distance, the Hancock Tower is less than successful at street level where the narrow, vertical form simply disappears into the ground without acknowledging its immediate public surroundings. The entrance and ground plane at the tower's base become lost space. In contrast, Josep Lluis Serts's Peabody Terrace housing complex in Cambridge, Massachusetts (fig. 2-20), also exquisite at a distance, created formal transitions and adjustments in the towers as they approached the ground. The architect made a conscious effort to create streets and squares with the buildings. Moving through the exterior spaces on foot is profoundly satisfy-

ing, as is the experience of viewing it as distant architecture across the Charles River.

If we are to create successful streets in the city of towers, we need to separate layers of architecture to form continuous public spaces at ground level, a layer distinct from the free-enterprise architecture that rises above. The floor area ratio (F.A.R.), a legal density regulation governing the relationship of site area to building square footage, dictates the scale and bulk of the architectural envelope in most cities. Within the F.A.R. regulation, lower floors should spread out at the base, giving human-scale definition to streets and plazas; upper floors should step back before they ascend. The relatively recent Hötorget City in Stockholm, built in the early 1960s, is a successful example of this approach (figs. 2-21, 2-22). Varied street activities occur on all sides of this linear

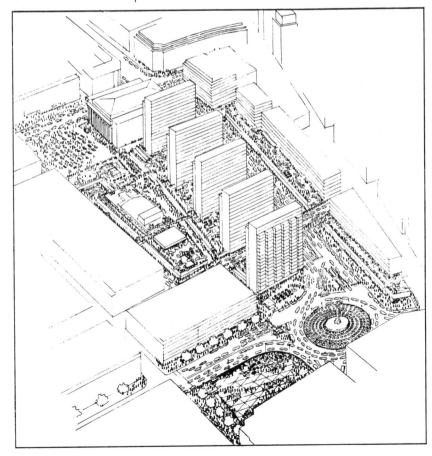

Figure 2-21. City Planning Office, Hotorget City, Stockholm, Sweden. 1958. Axon.
This project is a successful example of how the public life of the street can be integrated with private activities in offices above. Shopping arcades, restaurants, and open spaces occupy a transitional level between the street and the towers. (Drawing: David Hellden)

Figure 2-22. Hotorget City at Street Level.
Active, well-formed social spaces give life to the lower levels of the complex.

composition, which links the Old Hay Market to Sergels Torg at several levels, where office, retail, and transportation converge.

Main Street

Another manifestation of the pervasive disregard for urban space is the neglect of the smalltown main street. America has glorified the smalltown main street as the monument to commerce, but has at the same time neglected it in favor of the suburban-style shopping center at the fringe. In town after town we are confronted with vacant buildings and indeterminate public space on Main Street. Often elegant turn-of-the-century facades line these streets, but much of this history is concealed behind signs, plastic veneer, and aluminum

Figure 2-23. Nantucket, Massachusetts. Main Street.
Nantucket's village main street is in many ways an idealized model of American public space. Influenced by Jefferson's attitudes of an egalitarian form of landscape and urbanism (see also fig. 3-38), the tree-lined public center "gathers" the private parts registered on its perimeter. It is important to revive this uniquely American spatial typology.

trim of more recent vintage, marking the descent of Main Street to the suburbanized strip. A rebirth of the prototypical village main street as a *figural space* in an egalitarian landscape is necessary if small towns in America are to survive. In the past, Main Street was the focus of community life maintained as high-quality spatial experience. Its diversified commercial activities and close proximity to residential neighborhoods made it the physical and social center of the community. These notable traits (such as those seen in Nantucket Village, fig. 2-23), along with the unique scale and character

particular to the American context, must be revived as a future urban spatial typology.

Sunken Plazas and Internalized Malls

Also affecting the quality of public space in recent years have been sunken plazas and internalized malls. It is safe to say that with few exceptions both have had a significant and negative influence on the extent and flow of street activity. In the case of the sunken plaza, whether it be 1633 Broadway in New York City (see fig. 1-13) or Copley Square in Boston (see fig. 3-24), the problem is not exclusively its physical form but also its location in defiance of the street. Unless they become drawing cards as outdoor theaters for public events, such as Rockefeller Plaza (fig. 2-24) or Washington, D.C.'s, Pershing Park (see fig. 5-51), depressed plazas are anomalies in the natural structure of urban form, and seldom generate enough energy to be vital, inviting places in themselves. Too often they simply become spatial holes below grade that are lifeless and difficult to maintain.

The tendency of the urban interior mall is also to drain activity and economic vitality from the street. Interior malls can be seductive, comfortable shopping environments, but they conflict with the commercial habits and urban form that exists in the public realm of the memorable cities of the world. The Galleria Vittorio Emmanuele in Milan and the Quincy Markets in Boston (fig. 2-25) are exceptional examples of urban markets that are physically apart from the street but function in a traditional way as major gathering places for varied activities. In Milan, the Galleria "maintains and reinforces the city grid, providing a connection between two existing anchors, the Duomo and La Scala opera house."[29] The linear layout of the

Figure 2-24. Facing page: Rockefeller Plaza. New York, New York.
Rockefeller Plaza is an exception to the rule that sunken plazas removed from the street rarely function well. Probably its success owes much to its location and the fact that it operates as a constantly active theater for "people watching." (Courtesy: Rockefeller Center, Inc., Impact Photo)

Quincy Markets also continues the form of Boston from the heart of the city core to the waterfront. The exterior spaces between the three long buildings of the Quincy Markets unify instead of separate the shopping and entertainment on the inside and outside of the complex. Fortunately for contemporary Boston, the historic form of the Markets had originally evolved from concepts of marketplace and street and offered an ideal existing framework for modern revitalization and adaptation to new commercial needs. The Milan and Boston examples offer the contemporary designer important successful models to follow as expressions of good urban form.

In contrast to these two successful examples, the negative potential of the enclosed mall is revealed at Detroit's Renaissance Center (fig. 2-26). The so-called Ren Cen complex has very exciting interior architecture, as well as dramatic exteriors, but the development envelope is cut off from its urban environments. It illustrates what Daralice Donkervoet criticizes in her essay, "The Malling of the Metropolis." She describes the urban mall as "exclusivist, homogenous and utterly banal" and points out the tendency toward introversion, which allows for "total environmental control and complete separation of indoors and out that excludes all undesirable urban elements." She continues:

> Contemporary urban malls are both arbitrary and anti-urban and threaten to destroy both the scale of the side streets and the integrity of the urban grid. The small attempts to recreate the street by isolating it in the interior and destroying any sense of continuity with the city fabric—its simplistic front door/back door relationship to the street—is in sharp contrast to the complex weave of Rockefeller Center.[30]

In Detroit, the designers went so far as to ring the internalized complex with fortresslike walls housing the mechanical systems—creating an architecture of paranoia and fear in this hardpressed, industrial city. For the pedestrian, access to the Ren Cen and the riverfront on the other side is constrained if not totally blocked off. The style

Figure 2-25. Benjamin Thomson Associates. Renovation of the Quincy Markets, Boston, Massachusetts.
In this important example of building rehabilitation, the traditional market function of the historic complex was successfully revived. Despite its isolation from the street system of Boston, the market works well as both a retail venture and a social gathering place. (Courtesy of Boston Redevelopment Authority)

of architecture is more suited to Florida or maybe California than to Detroit, Michigan. Moreover, the massive economic revitalization of downtown that the project was to create has not been realized.

Toronto's Eaton Centre (fig. 2-27), on the other hand, is an attempt to recreate the celebration of light and space of Paxton's Crystal Palace of over a century ago. The interior design is almost a direct copy of Gum Department Store in Moscow

Figure 2-26. The Renaissance Center. Detroit, Michigan.
Parking lots and mechanical equipment present an impenetrable obstruction between the Renaissance Center and the rest of Detroit's downtown area. The whole complex blocks pedestrian access to the riverfront.

(see fig. 6-6). The volume of the interior glassed-in space is magnificent to the point of being overwhelming, but unlike the Renaissance Center, the designers also attempted to respond to Yonge Street by locating small-scale shops along the outside edge of the complex and tried to retain the physical continuity of the city grid with a new street wall. There has been a turnover in retailers along the opposite side of Yonge Street since the Eaton Centre was constructed, but many local shops still remain, and there is a marked difference between the rich diversity of street life out-

Figure 2-27. The Eaton Center along Yonge Street. Zeidler Partnership. Toronto. 1979.
Eaton Center's new wall along Yonge Street tries to retain the continuity of the city grid and channel activity to the street from inside the center. Small-scale shops and midblock passageways were designed to preserve Yonge Street's urban qualities.

side and the controlled, predictable modern version of urban commerce inside. Rather than drain activity from the street, the Centre tends to channel more life into it.

Garden City, Suburbia, and New Towns

The change in building scale and ground coverage, the neglect of Main Street, and the trend toward sunken plazas and internalized malls have been accompanied by various tendencies to abandon the city as an environment for living.

The normative values implicit in Functionalism had their counterpart in other movements from the late nineteenth century to the midtwentieth century, including the Garden City concepts of Ebenezer Howard, the New Towns of both Europe and America, and the suburb as an expression of the American Dream. Architects of the Modern Movement based ambitious utopian plans on a limited set of assumptions about human needs and feelings. The Ville Radieuse of Le Corbusier, the Città Nuova of Saint Elia, Buckminster Fuller's Dymaxion World were all examples of attempts to predict and direct the future utopia according to explicit norms. In many ways they were too successful; we are coming to realize that the range of norms was too limited. One of the lessons of our

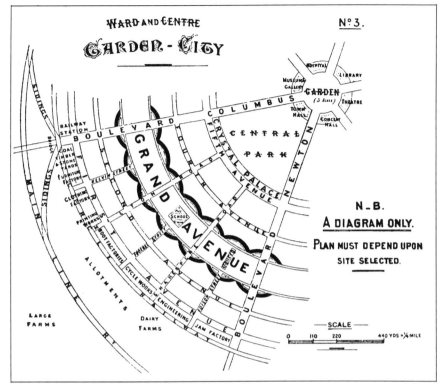

Figure 2-28. Ebenezer Howard. Diagram for the Garden City. 1898.
Another response to the decay and density of the post-industrial city was the Garden City concept originally proposed by Ebenezer Howard in the 1890s. Howard's concept was for a town of limited size surrounded by agricultural lands and clearly delineated open spaces within. The benefits of urban and rural existence would be balanced in a self-contained, self-sufficient community. (From Howard, Garden Cities. *Courtesy: MIT Press)*

century, learned slowly and at some cost, has been that when planners try to convert living cities into utopias they always make them worse. The famous words of the American officer in Vietnam, "We had to destroy that village in order to save it," are their epitaph.[31]

From a different but related point of view the antiurban utopianism of Ebenezer Howard, Clarence Stein, and Henry Wright and the development of suburbia have had their impact on the form of modern cities. The garden city and modern new-town movements began as early as 1898 with Sir Ebenezer Howard's milestone book, *Garden Cities of Tomorrow,* which, as Lewis Mumford writes, "has done more than any other single book to guide the modern town planning movement and to alter its objectives."[32] Howard's garden-city idea (fig. 2-28) was founded on the integration of town and country attributes. His goal was to devise the ideal plan that would bring

these polarities into harmony. Howard's formula, the "town-country magnet," consisted of 1,000 acres of urban land surrounded by 5,000 acres of agricultural land. This area would support a population of 32,000 people. The radial concentric plan focused on a central park and was organized around a series of landscaped boulevards and avenues. Factories ringed the perimeter of the "town estate," outside of which was located the "agricultural estate." The garden city was situated on an intermunicipal railway. Howard went to great lengths in establishing the municipal revenue and administrative operations of his garden city, based to a large extent on principles of socialism. While most of the twentieth-century new towns of Europe and America bear some resemblance to Howard's utopia, Letchworth, England, 1905, and Welwyn Garden City, England, 1922 (fig. 2-29) are the purest examples.

Howard's concept of parklike, soft space in cit-

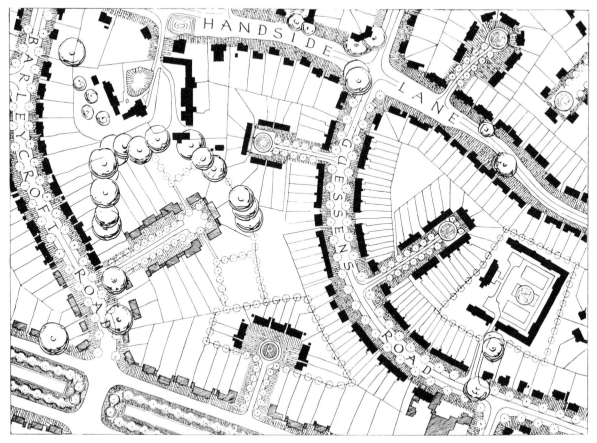

Figure 2-29. Welwyn Garden City. England. 1920–26.
Howard's ideas greatly influenced numerous new-town and surburban developments of this century. Welwyn Garden
City was among the purest realizations of the concept, which included well-designed community spaces and a public
landscape of major amenity areas. Buildings run parallel to streets, greens, village squares—creating clear boundaries
that define the community landscape. (Plan: Louis De Soissons)

ies was soon adopted by many planners of the early twentieth century, including Clarence Stein and Henry Wright in America. Stein and Wright applied Howard's principles in numerous important projects, including an urban prototype at Sunnyside Gardens, Queens, New York City, in 1924 (fig. 2-30), where the town-country concept was adapted to the New York City grid, and in Radburn, New Jersey, in 1929, a suburban development. In the Stein and Wright community, parkland formed the backbone as a continuous greenbelt. The residential superblocks were wide enough to trap open space within, a departure from the narrow rectangular blocks of their predecessors. Roads were also designed in a special way—as a hierarchy to accommodate one use instead of all uses—including specialized service lanes, secondary collectors, main through streets, highways, and parkways. Pedestrian and automobile traffic was separated by overpasses and underpasses. Stein and Wright also departed from the traditional orientation of the houses and turned them so that sleeping and living rooms faced the gardens and service rooms the access roads. The

Figure 2-30. Clarence Stein and Henry Wright. Sunnyside, Queens, New York. 1926.
There were also attempts to incorporate communal open space into the existing urban environment. At Sunnyside,
Stein and Wright (later responsible for the influential Radburn Idea) organized housing around open green space,
reversing the traditional orientation toward the street. (Photo: Gottscho-Schleisner, Inc.)

impact of Stein and Wright's design work was considerable. In 1951 Lewis Mumford wrote:

> Like Olmsted, Stein and Wright dared put beauty as one of the imperative needs of a planned environment: the beauty of ordered buildings, measured to the human scale, of trees and flowering plants, and of open greens surrounded by buildings of low density.[33]

It is interesting that Mumford equates Stein and Wright with the work of Olmsted, as one can clearly see certain philosophic if not physical parallels. Frederick Law Olmsted's major works in America occurred at about the same time that

Howard generated the garden city concept in England. There is no record of any communication between Olmsted and Howard; however, their emerging ideals were amazingly similar. Olmsted shared Howard's notion of the merger of town and country and designed one of America's first suburbs at Riverside, Chicago. In several enormously successful public-space-structuring efforts at the turn of the century, Olmsted transformed American urban neighborhoods, districts, and lost space into attractive parks, boulevards, and promenades. He brought the romantic landscape of the English countryside to the American city to relieve overcrowded local conditions and to offer a pastoral escape from the hard edges of the manmade environment. Olmsted's open spaces, which were woven into the fibers of the larger city, were conceived and implemented as tools for collective social reform. His works in New York, Boston, and Chicago, aimed at improving the lives and living conditions of urban residents, represent some of the most significant public-space transformations in the United States (see fig. 3-35).

Following the frontrunners of the garden-city movement and during Franklin Delano Roosevelt's New Deal of the late 1930s, suburbanization began expanding at an accelerating rate. Developers took advantage of the first comprehensive federally sponsored Housing Act in America, and prospective home buyers pursued the American Dream of a freestanding house on a plot with a fenced-in backyard and clean air. After the brief interlude created by World War II, suburban developments took off from coast to coast. Repetitive environments like Levittown (fig. 2-31), a departure from Stein and Wright, seemed to ap-

pear in short order, all having similar characteristics of minimum building coverage and maximum open land for streets, yards, sidewalks, and occasionally a park. There was a noticeable indifference to spatial definition of the public environment and marked emphasis on private space. The integration of social values and flowing countryside espoused earlier in the century soon became principles of the past.

Active suburban sprawl continued in America for about twenty years between 1945 and 1965 as the downtown core, neglected and underused, deteriorated. It was not until President Lyndon Johnson in the mid-1960s decided to do something about the "urban dilemma" and announced the New Communities Program that any action was taken. He said that the nation was in need of at least twenty new cities containing over 200,000 persons each to channel the suburbanization and relieve urban congestion. These would take the form of new towns-in-town, urban-expansion dis-

Figure 2-31. Levittown, Pennsylvania. 1952–58. Aerial Photograph.
The social idealism of early reformers and advocates of the Garden City disappeared with the rapid suburbanization following World War II. Repetitive environments like Levittown grew up all over America, with emphasis on maximum private space at the expense of communal green space. (Courtesy: William J. Levitt, Inc.)

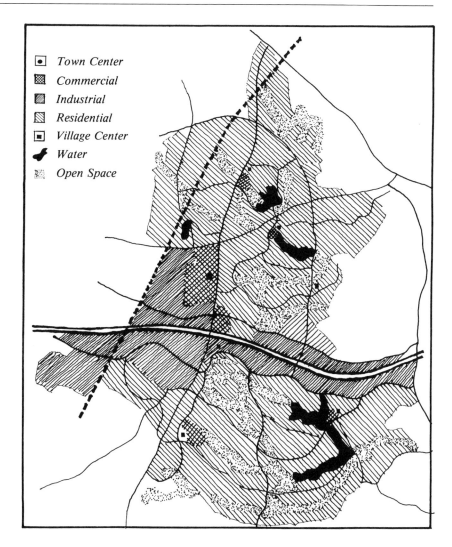

⊡	Town Center
▨	Commercial
▨	Industrial
▨	Residential
▪	Village Center
➤	Water
▨	Open Space

Figure 2-32. Robert E. Simon, developer. Reston, Virginia. 1962.
During the 1960s there were several attempts to revive Howard's goals. Reston, Virginia, and Columbia, Maryland, are the best-known of these new towns. Public open space provides the organizational core of the community. However, such new towns have not been able to create an economic base to become self-sufficient, mixed-income communities.

tricts, and self-contained new cities. At the same time, two privately sponsored new towns in Columbia, Maryland; and Reston, Virginia (fig. 2-32), were underway as attempts to revitalize Howard's ideal, which was lost in the suburbanization process. Columbia and Reston were meant "to create a social and physical environment which works for people and nourishes human growth."[34]

Excitement over the new communities and in starting from scratch immediately spread through architecture schools during the transitional period between the megastructure era and a new movement in social advocacy and applied behavioral design. This unusual combination of philosophies, from the most utopian and idealistic to the most pragmatic, set the tone for massive studies like the HUD-sponsored New Communities Project at Harvard and the Experimental City at the University of Minnesota. The Harvard study of 1968, led by a preeminent team of European architects including Josep Lluis Sert, Jerzy Soltan, and Wilhelm von Moltke, was a year-long multidiscipli-

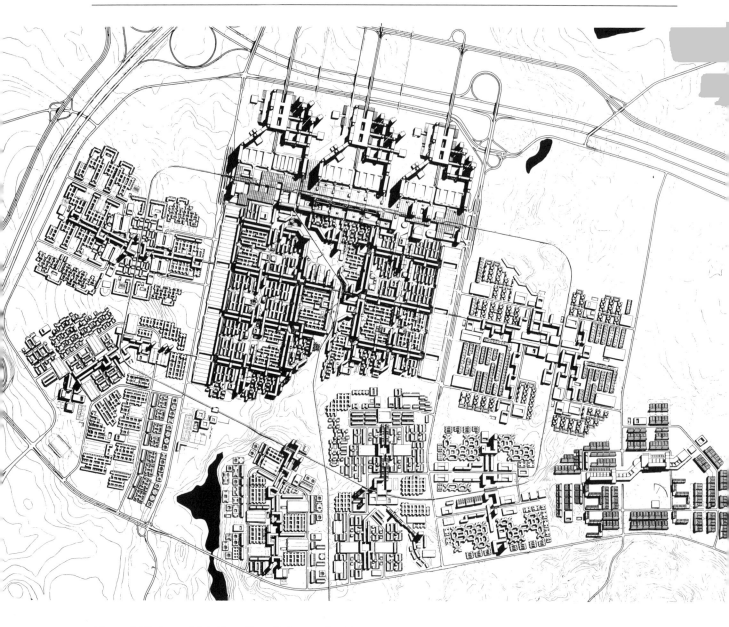

Figure 2-33. Josep Lluis Sert, Jerzy Soltan and Wilhelm von Moltke et al. New Communities Project. Harvard University. Cambridge, Massachusetts. Plan. 1968.
During the 1960s a wave of excitement at the idea of creating new towns "from scratch" spread through architectural schools. Sponsored by HUD, the New Communities Project at Harvard was an experiment in utopian alternatives to both the city and the suburb. All income groups would be accommodated in a setting that united urbanity and responsiveness to the natural site. Sophisticated technology would create an infrastructure that eliminated the need for the automobile. (Courtesy: Harvard Urban Design Program)

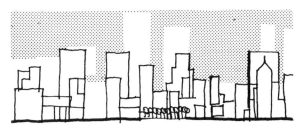

A. Central or Core City: high density with empty pockets (parking).

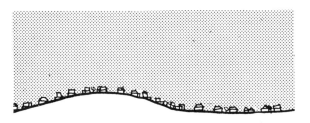

B. Suburban: low density sprawl—destruction of vast areas of land.

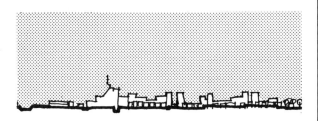

C. Compact Community: intensive use of land.

Figure 2-34. Sert, Soltan and Von Moltke. New Communities Project. Diagrams.
The goal of the New Communities Project was to create a compact environment based on intensive land use without the sprawl of the suburb or the inefficient planning of the core city. (Courtesy: Harvard Urban Design Program)

nary project that tried to incorporate the ideals of the socially responsive utopia (fig. 2-33). They declared that the city core, with its high density, pockets of lost space, and political and social problems, was unsuited for modern living for both rich and poor. The suburbs were equally undesirable, as low-density sprawl destroyed vast areas of land and did not allow for the richness of the urban experience (fig. 2-34). The compact new city open to all income groups was the answer. Here, the infrastructure systems of roads, utilities, and open spaces would be coordinated and urbanity would be put in balance and harmony with the ecology of the site. Here, lost space would be eliminated and a composite city structure would provide positive urban space in a variety of formal configurations. The city would become a place for learning, and residents would participate in change and control their own environment. All facilities would be within walking distance or accessible by moving sidewalks or monorail. The car would not be needed! Unfortunately, the government's program fell apart and monies went dry. The Harvard New City could have worked in a growth economy—not as an alternative to the real city, but most certainly as an alternative to suburbia. But things changed quickly during the late sixties following the sociopolitical upheaval, urban riots, and Vietnam. Attention moved back to smaller plans and working within the givens of the existing city, instead of abandoning it and escaping to the hinterlands. The country's lessened growth rate and faltering economy had a sobering effect on the New City Movement, and the need for reuse and adaptation of existing urban resources has been a reality for the past fifteen years.

As America confronted numerous problems with financing and getting things built under its New Communities Program, Great Britain, Scandinavia, and continental Europe proceeded with rapid new-town construction in the fifties and sixties. During this period the Europeans implemented more new communities than anyone else in the world.

What has made such communities as Vallingby, Sweden; Tapiola, Finland; or the "Mark 2" New Towns of England successful has been their strong response to the land, open space, and social structure (fig. 2-35). As manifestations of Howard's Garden City ideal, they have to a large extent achieved a healthy interface between man and nature (fig. 2-36).

Figure 2-35. Tapiola, Finland. Plan of Typical Residential Area.
The plan for Tapiola is circumstantial in layout, responding to natural features of the site rather than imposing a
preconceived notion of form and spatial order. (Courtesy: Tapiola Development Corporation)

However, planning for most new communities from an urban-space-design viewpoint has had mixed success. Often the buildings have a cookiecutter monotony, and the spaces between them are equally banal and unformed. Many New Towns are virtually indistinguishable from suburbs; most have not been able to attract the economic base to make them viable, independent communities. About planned communities architect Aldo Van Eyck writes, "Instead of the incon-

Figure 2-36. Tapiola, Finland. Typical Residential Area.
During the 1950s and 1960s several successful new towns were constructed in Europe. Tapiola in Finland is an especially significant example of how careful integration of architecture into the natural environment can create a strong sense of place.

venience of filth and confusion, we have now got the boredom of hygiene. . . . we have only to look at the new towns or recent housing developments to recognize to what extent the spirit has gone into hiding.''[35] Creating the spirit in a new, totally designed environment is essential, yet one of the most difficult tasks of the designer. In the development of twentieth-century outdoor space we have seen that designers were optimistically searching for a new spirit of the modern age and in this search abandoned historic precedents. It seems appropriate at this point to turn to precedent as a means of furthering our understanding of spatial design theory.

CHAPTER

3

URBAN SPACE PRECEDENTS

We have many examples of successful urban open space—the traditional cities of Europe and Asia offer numerous places that work wonderfully well. Therefore we should not be afraid or ashamed of borrowing principles from Venice or the ancient city of Peking—an approach *verboten* by the Bauhaus and the International Style. History cannot only inspire and justify design, it can become an effective tool for communication. By demonstrating the intention of a design through example, a designer can provide an immediately recognizable image, a familiar ambience that explains the goal of the proposal.

In most disciplines, whether scientific or artistic, current work and research are founded on precedents, on an accumulated body of knowledge. In science, for example, experimental procedure is generally founded on the results of previous work. However, the Modern Movement in architecture, as we have seen, deliberately broke with the past, seeking to recreate the wheel for each new project (although in fact establishing its own form of Academicism). As Jean Paul Carlhian puts it:

> Until the creation of the International Style and the establishment of Bauhaus-inspired schools

of architecture (both based on the rejection of precedent), architects continually searched the past for sources of inspiration. There is, however, a world of difference between borrowing and imitating, with the former bearing all the attributes of a creative act and the latter presenting all the characteristics of a fail-safe attitude, one that no architect can ever condone.

Carlhian proceeds to the artistic aspects of borrowing from history:

> It is not the mere accumulation of borrowed features that achieves a successful relationship of old to new; the greatest chance of success comes from a combination of efforts—a healthy respect for the site, careful analysis of the existing building or group of buildings, accurate determination of their essential characteristics and the weaving of these data into an uncompromisingly contemporary design concept. Such a task can be achieved successfully only by a true artist.[36]

Historic models of urban space can provide both formal and conceptual guiding principles during the design process. The adaptation of these models to contemporary needs, however, should not be an exercise in straight copying, but should involve at least "a 45-degree twist in the mind or eye."[37] In a rapidly changing world, the validity of preserving style for purely nostalgic reasons must be seriously questioned.

However, for many students trained under Functionalism, the option of borrowing or adapting from historic precedents was unavailable. One of the most neglected aspects of design education both in and out of school was the formation of a working knowledge and design vocabulary of principles derived from urban-space precedents. The design of successful new urban spaces depends on a critical understanding of examples, good and bad, of spaces that have been tested by users and analyzed by designers. The following text discusses numerous examples of historic and modern urban space.

The examples fall into two primary types: "hard" spaces and "soft" spaces. Hard spaces are those principally bounded by architectural walls; often these are intended to function as major gathering places for social activity. Soft spaces are those dominated by the natural environment, whether inside or outside the city. In the urban setting they are the parks and gardens and linear greenways that provide opportunities for recreation or retreat from the built environment. Emphasis has often been placed only on hard space as appropriate to the city. Urban designers, however, must look at both types of space for inspiration, as urban functions exist that are better served by soft space.

HARD SPACE

One of the most important factors in hard space is the creation of enclosure. As Venturi pointed out over twenty years ago, the problem is not the lack of open space in the city, but its openness:

> Residual space in-between dominant spaces with varying degrees of openness is not unknown in our cities . . . the open spaces under our highways and the buffer spaces around them. Instead of acknowledging and exploiting these

characteristic kinds of space we make them into parking lots or feeble patches of grass—no-man's lands between the scale of the region and the locality.[38]

More recently, Steven Peterson attempted to define, through numerous examples, the physical properties that differentiate space and "antispace." He describes space as conceivable and antispace as inconceivable volume.[39] Space can be measured; it has definite and perceivable boundaries; it is discontinuous in principle, closed, static, yet serial in composition. Antispace, on the other hand, is shapeless, continuous, lacking perceivable edges or form. The Piazza del Campo, Siena, is space, while Le Corbusier's St. Dié, the towers in the park at the Ville Radieuse, or the Las Vegas strip, are antispace. The Piazza San Marco in Venice, Bernini's Piazza and Colonnade at St. Peter's, or Michelangelo's triangulated Campidoglio in Rome are outstanding historic examples of space (fig. 3-1 through 3-10). Peterson's distinctions apply to hard urban spaces; soft space does not require the same degree of enclosure or defined boundary.

A review of precedents reveals three important components of successful hard urban space: (1) the three-dimensional frame; (2) the two-dimensional pattern; and (3) the placement of objects in space.

The *three-dimensional frame* defines the edges of the space, the degree of enclosure, and the characteristics of the spatial wall. Transparency, opacity, openings, and surface ornament have significant impact on the character of space, as does the relationship of vertical mass to horizontal space. The scale of the wall in relation to human scale and the way this frame meets the ground plane are also major factors in the definition of the three-dimensional edge.

The *two-dimensional pattern* refers to the treatment and articulation of the ground plane—its materials, texture, and composition.

Objects in space are those elements such as sculpture, water features, and trees that provide accents or focal points and make the space memorable. Objects can be used to anchor the center

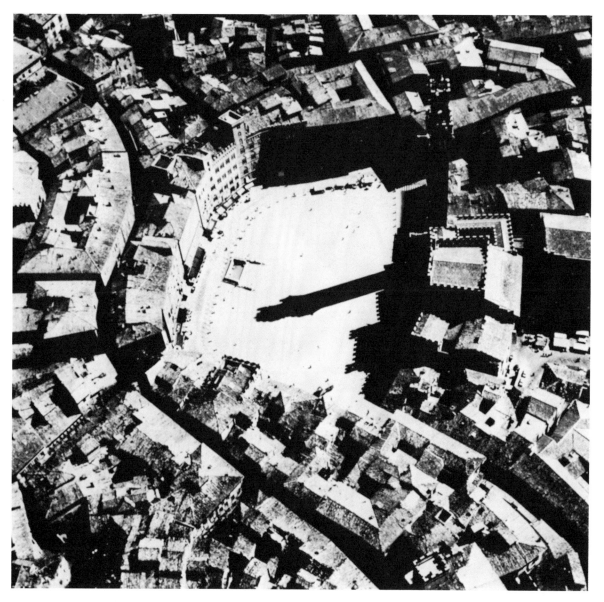

Figure 3-1. Piazza del Campo, Siena, Italy.
One of the most effective urban spaces in existence, the Piazza del Campo in Siena offers a number of important lessons to the urban designer. Much of its strength as a space stems from the contrast between the dense mass of surrounding buildings and the open piazza. The campanile of the Palazzo Publico serves as a vertical focal point. As early as 1262 a city ordinance governing the height and facades of buildings facing the square was effected in recognition of the role a consistent wall plays in defining the character of urban space. (From Benevolo, History of the City. *Courtesy: MIT Press)*

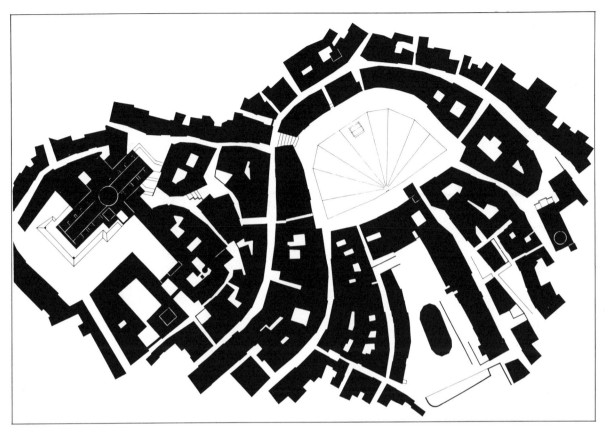

Figure 3-2. Piazza del Campo, Siena. Figure-ground Plan.
Not only does the piazza contrast with the surrounding density of the urban fabric, but the configuration of streets also reinforces the shape of the square itself. Urban space is the generator of urban form. (Drawing: Wayne Copper © 1967)

and to give vitality to spaces. The most vital elements of all are the human actors who use the space, giving it life.

The most successful urban-space precedents comprise a rich mixture of these three organizational concepts.

Historic Precedents: Squares

As suggested, the distinction between space and antispace has much to do with finite boundaries, a primary element of good urban space. The American Heritage Dictionary defines space (from the Latin *spatium*) as "a set of elements or points satisfying specified geometric conditions in a three-dimensional field of everyday experience; the distance between two points or the area of volume between specified boundaries."[40] For urban spatial design this can be interpreted as lateral enclosure.

In a milestone book written in 1889, Camillo Sitte wrote about the lack of artistic quality in exterior space and about the importance of urban spaces as enclosed entities.[41] His writings were of great importance at the turn of the century, in that for the first time in recent history the artistic principles of spatial design were made ex-

Figure 3-3. Le Corbusier. St. Dié Center. St. Dié, France. Figure-ground Plan. 1945.
The relationship of mass to void is the reverse of that found in Siena. There is, furthermore, no definition to the edges of the open spaces, and the composition is based on an arbitrary imposition of the orthogonal grid. In Siena there is a clear hierarchy of public space, while in St. Dié no apparent sequence or hierarchy exists. Freestanding buildings as icons are the determinants of urban form, and connected public space is lost. (Drawing: Wayne Copper © 1967)

plicit, and the designer's role in shaping space was given credence. Of Sitte's many principles, enclosure was the most significant. He argued convincingly for the beauty and positive visual and psychological effects of enclosed space in cities, for the importance of the spatial skin, and the careful placement of objects in space. In 1909 at Votive Plaza in Vienna's Ringstrasse (fig. 3-11), Sitte achieved enclosure by adding buildings and

arcades around the existing cathedral. This plan became one of the most influential precedents in modernday urban spatial design.

Dense edges reinforce the visual quality of enclosed space. Part of the success of the Piazza del Campo in Siena comes from its contrast to the tight, winding streets and dense mass of buildings surrounding its edges from which it seems to explode (see figs. 3-1 and 3-2). The Palazzo Pubblico

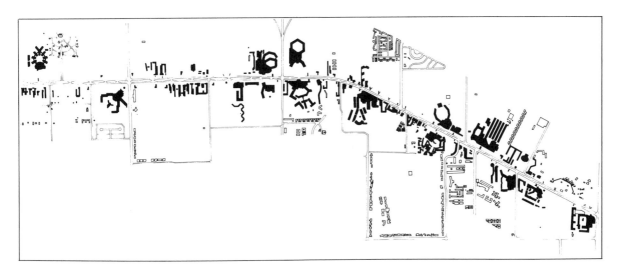

Figure 3-4. Las Vegas, Nevada. Figure-ground.
Along the Las Vegas strip, buildings are not registered in space and are randomly scattered. Open space lacks structure
and is simply the areas left vacant after construction. (Courtesy: Venturi, Rauch, and Scott Brown)

Figure 3-5. Michelangelo
Buonarotti. The Campidog-
lio. Rome. Begun 1544.
Aerial View.
Michelangelo's masterly
square on the Capitoline
Hill shows how a coherent
space can be created despite
diverse architecture, steep
topography, and an irregu-
larly shaped site. By altering
the facades and alignments
of existing buildings and
connecting new buildings to
them, the artist transformed
a derelict piece of land into
a composition at once pow-
erful and subtle. He took
advantage of the triangular
site to establish a "forced
perspective" while using an
elliptical paving pattern to
provide a stable center to
the piazza. (From Schulz,
Genius Loci. *Courtesy: Riz-*
zoli International Publica-
tions, Inc.)

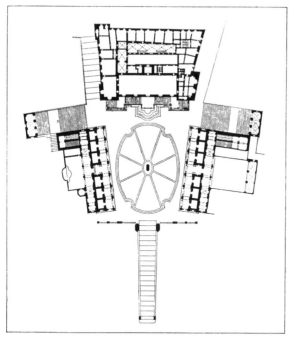

Figure 3-6. The Campidoglio Plan.
The oval paving pattern brings the piazza to rest, counteracting the directional pull established by the angles of the buildings. (Courtesy: Steen Eiler Rasmussen)

Figure 3-7. Piazza San Marco. Venice, Italy. Aerial View.
Like the Piazza del Campo in Siena, the Piazza San Marco is surrounded by a dense mass of building cut through by narrow streets and canals. Although the buildings at the edge are from diverse periods, they are relatively uniform in height. An arcade helps unify the space, while a dramatic paving pattern ties the two arms of the L-shaped square together. The campanile acts as a vertical focal point and as a "knuckle" between the two piazzas. (From Schulz, Genius Loci. *Courtesy: Rizzoli International Publications, Inc.)*

acts as the focal point in the design. Semitransparent enclosures are also effective. Bernini's extraordinary colonnade at San Pietro (see figs. 3-9 and 3-10) operates as a *datum* for design of the piazza, a frame for Carlo Maderna's facade of the basilica and semitransparent edge between internal and external space. Christian Norberg-Schulz makes the following connection between enclosure and place: "The distinctive quality of any man-made place is *enclosure* and its character and spatial properties are determined by how it is enclosed. Enclosure primarily means a distinct area which is separated from the surroundings by means of a built boundary." He continues, "the main urban elements are centers and paths. As such they are enclosures; their spatial density in fact depends upon the presence of relatively continuous lateral boundaries."[42]

Open space in the city provides for necessary relief from congestion, but need not be ill-defined and physically diffused. As Venturi observed, the contemporary city in fact contains more "open" space than it needs—space that is too open to be perceived as space and that is often located away from the pulse of urban life. The classic open urban spaces we all admire are really "closed" spaces. The Piazza San Marco in Venice is truly

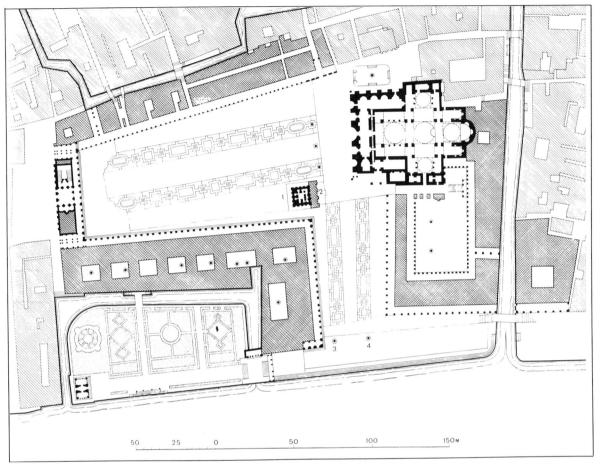

Figure 3-8. Piazza San Marco. Plan.
The plan of Piazza San Marco shows how a strong and coherent space can be carved out of irregularities in its physical configuration. Although nothing follows traditional precepts of plan design, the strength of the architectural edge holds the space together before it dramatically opens to the water. (From A. V. Bunin)

enclosed to the point of being segregated from the texture and block pattern of the city. The piazza functions as a physical focal point for community gatherings as well as a psychological extension of the open space of private dwellings in Venice. As the need to use urban land more efficiently increases, perhaps this will push us back to a more collective, concentrated style of urban life; maybe we can revive the social meaning and importance of enclosed urban space.

The traditional city was organized around a clearly defined network of interconnected streets and squares, where the space between buildings was at least as important as the buildings themselves. The square was probably the first organizing form of urban space and the street was an extension of the square once the periphery had been filled with houses. This traditional system of organization allowed for few, if any, loose ends or buildings that were not integrated into the pattern as a whole and consequently very little lost space. The organization established a clear vocabulary for integrating the component parts. As Moshe Safdie describes our current situation: "The problem is to find the *framework,* the common denominator which will enable several architects (and devel-

Figure 3-9. Gianlorenzo Bernini. Piazza San Pietro. Rome. Begun 1656. Aerial Photograph.
Bernini's piazza, which emerged over a period of 250 years, is a monumental forecourt to the seat of the Vatican.
The freestanding double colonnade provides dramatic definition to the wall of the parvis and a permeable demarcation
between inside and outside. An obelisk occupies the center, and the paving pattern reinforces the center's relationship
to the edges.

opers) each to work on a part of the city so that what each does is additive and contributes to the whole."[43]

In early Imperial Rome, the classic city room provided just that consistent vocabulary. In a flexible, additive, yet orderly system of design, the mixed-use buildings of the forums at Rome and Pompeii (fig. 3-12) in early Imperial times were

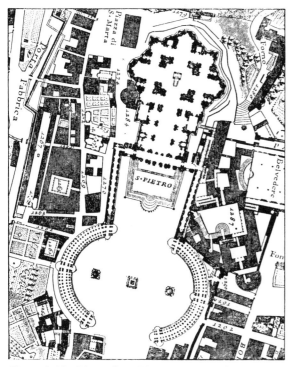

Figure 3-10. Piazza San Pietro. From Nolli's Map of Rome. 1748.
Within a surrounding fabric of dense but highly irregular buildings, Bernini created a unified, coherent space that effectively frames Bramante's church. The freestanding colonnade allows access from various directions and establishes a strong center.

grouped around a central plaza that took on greater significance than any individual building around its perimeter.

A loggia encircling the multipurpose public square helped reinforce the fusion of inside and outside space, connecting the functions at the edge to one another and to the center of the composition. The loggia as a major linkage device also acted as a gateway to the surrounding city streets—as the mediator between a legible centralized space and the looser structure of the outer area. The city room was clearly defined, transitional, and flowing. At Miletus during the Second Century A.D., central space became a collection of subspaces divided by an extended colonnade. Another example of the effective use of the colonnade is at Covent

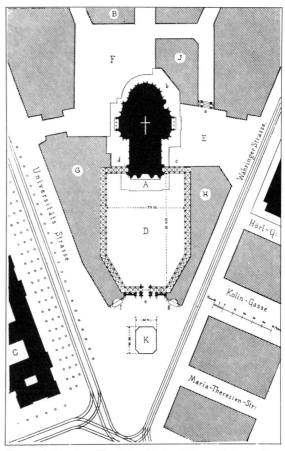

Figure 3-11. Camillo Sitte. Votive Plaza. Vienna, Austria. 1909.
Sitte was among the first theoreticians of urban space to look closely at historic precedents. Through this analysis he came to the conclusion that enclosure was the most significant component of successful urban space. In his plan for Votive Plaza he proposed extensive infill (elements G, H, J, and K) to enclose and define the forecourt to the church. (From Der Stadtebau, *1965.)*

Garden Square in London; here the loggia establishes an edge between the inner place and the external environment—both enclosing space and defining place.

Another component of successful squares is, as indicated, the two-dimensional pattern, which unifies the ground plane. In Siena, for example, the shape of the piazza is reinforced by a radiating pattern of stone strips. Michelangelo's elliptical

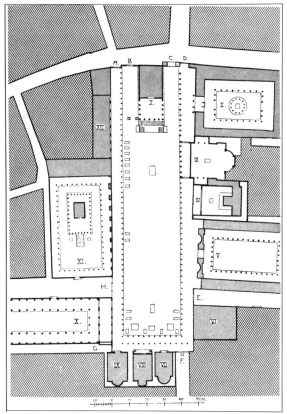

Figure 3-12. Pompeii. The Forum. Before 79 A.D.
In the classical city room, loggie developed as effective means of linking public and semipublic spaces of various functions. At the same time, they provided a unified framework to connect diverse alignments of individual buildings and open spaces. (From Der Stadtebau, *1965)*

with its impressive tower, are often found in traditional squares, providing a visual focus and giving social and cultural meaning to the space.

People, however, play the most important role in animating public squares. If the space can attract sufficient activity, it will almost certainly be perceived as successful in its design.

Historic Precedents: Streets

Successful street spaces, though linear in form, will also have the properties of three-dimensional frame, two-dimensional pattern, and objects to provide interest and focal points. Movement is the essence of streets, but they also serve broader functions, which have often been lost in the modern emphasis on rapid passage through the city. "Streets provide us with the essential freedom of movement on which city life depends. They make and reveal the city. But in the rush to connect, we have ignored their other functions. Should we not re-invent the street to reflect the reality of mixed uses?".[44] Streets can be organizers of the field (districts), linear centers, or links between entities. In a traditional street such as the main corridor leading through Isfahan, Iran (fig. 3-13), the street is conceived as positive exterior space of richly varied uses in which traffic of different types coexists and in which functional and social activities are gathered. The bazaar in Isfahan is an institution that takes place along the street and provides a connector into which mosques, schools, bath houses, and a whole hierarchy of public spaces, linear or contained, covered and open, can be integrated.

Effective street space can take on a variety of forms. The spatial elements of the street were established as early as Pompeii (fig. 3-14), where space was defined by building walls, curbs, gutters, and crosswalks in much the same manner as a street today. For the purpose of analysis, there are two main types of street space: inflected (curved) and uninflected (straight). A good example of an uninflected street is the Rossi Prospekt in Leningrad (fig. 3-15), where the width equals the height at 22 meters, and the length is

paving in the Campidoglio (see figs. 3-5 and 3-6), rising slightly toward the base of the Marcus Aurelius statue at its center, helps optically regularize this somewhat skewed piazza. The bold pattern of the Piazza San Marco (see figs. 3-7 and 3-8) similarly serves to unify and regularize the two parts of the square.

At the same time the placement of objects within the square can give the space animation and focus and can convey its social or cultural meaning. The statue of Marcus Aurelius in the Campidoglio, for example, holds the center and symbolically links renaissance to classical Rome. Important object buildings, such as the Palazzo Pubblico in Siena,

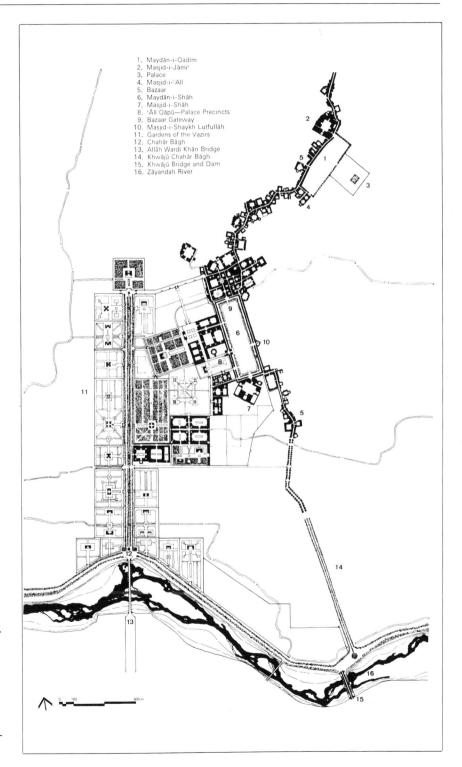

1. Maydān-i-Qadim
2. Masjid-i-Jāmiʿ
3. Palace
4. Masjid-i-ʿAlī
5. Bazaar
6. Maydān-i-Shāh
7. Masjid-i-Shāh
8. ʿAlī Qāpū—Palace Precincts
9. Bazaar Gateway
10. Masjid-i-Shaykh Lutfullāh
11. Gardens of the Vazirs
12. Chahār Bāgh
13. Allāh Wardi Khān Bridge
14. Khwājū Chahār Bāgh
15. Khwājū Bridge and Dam
16. Zāyandah River

Figure 3-13. Isfahan, Iran. At Isfahan the street forms a strong spine for the coexistence of varied activities, spaces, and types of traffic. Along this spine the bazaar provides continuous activity, whereas mosques, schools, bath houses, and an entire hierarchy of spaces—open and closed, linear and contained—are organically connected. (Drawing: Nadar Ardalan in The Sense of Unity *by Ardalan and Bakhtiar)*

Figure 3-14. Typical Street Scene in Pompeii Today. Street space in Pompeii was originally defined in much the same way as it is today: building walls, curbs, gutters, and crosswalks.

Figure 3-15. Below: *Rossi Prospekt. Leningrad, U.S.S.R.*
Rossi Prospekt is an example of an ''uninflected'' street. The Russian planners based its design on the ''golden proportion,'' a ratio in which the height of the buildings (22 meters) equals the width of the street, and the length is exactly ten times this measure.

Figure 3-16. Visby, Sweden. Main Street.
The main street of Visby is an "inflected" street. In contrast to Rossi Prospekt, it cannot be perceived in its entirety but unfolds gradually as the viewer walks through. Despite variations in building heights and facades, the "manners and rules" of the place establish a consistent vocabulary along its curved length.

exactly ten times it (220 meters). This distance became the so-called golden proportion of street design as defined by the Russian planners. In this example the entire street space is perceived at a glance. In contrast, the main street at Visby, Sweden (fig. 3-16), is an inflected street that gradually unfolds due to its curvature. Along with this, the facades are varied within a certain consistency of style, creating a richness and controlled diversity that seems to be absent in the Russian street. Vertical scale also differs greatly in the two examples—Rossi Prospekt displaying a monumental physical form and the Visby street much more in keeping with the human figure. Despite these con-

trasts, in both cases the design of the public spaces preceded the design and programming of individual buildings, establishing a relationship between the forms and activities on the site. Thus the designers prevent buildings from floating in space. The lesson we have to learn is that every building needs to be subordinate to the overall blueprint— that is, its scale and architectural vocabulary must harmonize with the existing system of public space. Urban space must not be destroyed but should be complemented by new buildings. If urban space is poorly defined, new buildings must create it. Buildings must, so to speak, tear no holes in the urban fabric, nor create any spatial vacuum.[45]

In an engraving of the mid-1500s, Sebastiano Serlio offered a cogent illustration of the street space as a rich and diverse microenvironment within a holistic framework (fig. 3-17). Using Pollio Vitruvius's account of the Roman theater, Serlio illustrated a broad, regular street in perspective, terminating on a monumental arch with an obelisk behind. Each facade is different and is in intentional contrast in scale and in its details of arched colonnades, architraves, pediments, and other types of articulation. The layers of pattern at the street wall are so rich that they define a human scale in a public space that is in itself devoid of detail, creating interesting contradictions by smashing together individual monuments whose architectural vocabulary suggests that they should be freestanding. If nothing else, Serlio's stage set attests to the potential of the street to act as a unifying urban framework.

The Asakusa Temple street in Tokyo, Japan (fig. 3-18), similarly unifies the diversity along a single street. The axial composition begins with an or-

nate Japanese arch, proceeding through six blocks of commercial use before arriving at the Temple Hall, placed symmetrically at the end of the corridor. Vendors lining the street create a bazaarlike atmosphere that contrasts with the religious function of the temple, expressing the dichotomy between contemporary Japanese society with its fascination with gadgetry and the traditional contemplativeness of its culture.

The Strada Nuova in Genoa, Italy, has been cited many times in design texts as a good example of street-space harmony, because the building facades belong both to the street and to the individual buildings themselves (figs. 3-19, 3-20). The buildings along the street are freestanding pavil-

Figure 3-18. Facing page: *The Asakusa Temple. Tokyo, Japan.*
On this Japanese street, commerce and religion coexist along the strong axis established by the gateway, the Temple, and the flanking pavilions. (Courtesy: © RE-TORIA/Y. Futagawa and Associated Photographers)

Figure 3-17. Sebastiano Serlio. Stage Design. Woodcut. 1545.
Based on Vitiuvius's account of the Roman theater, Serlio's stage design offers the student of urban space an illustration of how a strongly defined, simple framework of street space can accommodate great variations of scale and architectural style along its edges. (From Serlio's Architettura, *1545)*

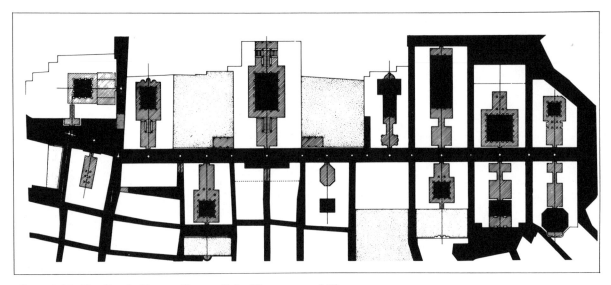

Figure 3-19. The Strada Nuova, Genoa, Italy. Figure-ground Plan.
Genoa's Strada Nuova is a remarkable example of a street defined by individual pavilions that nevertheless establish
a consistent wall. The facades belong both to the buildings and the street. (From Ghianda, Strada Nuova, *1967)*

ions, yet their volume is part of a much larger urban mass. This results in a high degree of street unity that is enhanced by connecting walls and horizontal bands defining the base of buildings and differentiating the lower and upper floors. On the Strada Nuova a consistent vocabulary of cornice details adds further to the unity of street space.

The memorable street design of Friedrich Weinbrenner's 1808 project for Langenstrasse in Karlsruhe, Germany, is also worthy of note (fig. 3-21). Here, as in the Rue de Rivoli in Paris, the arched colonnade unifies the exterior street space, masking the irregularities of high and low building frontages behind. Weinbrenner's proposal, however, was for a completely out-of-scale arcade, probably as a provocative gesture, behind which apparently anything could happen. His framework is hardly one that private businesses, seeking to display an individual image, would want to plug into!

An example of a successful streetscape is the grid-block organization of Savannah, Georgia (see figs. 2-11, 3-22). Generally speaking, complex, shifting spatial patterns are more interesting than regular, repetitive patterns, but Savannah is a well-known exception. Founded by James Oglethorpe in 1733, the famous plan is based on a systematic disposition of one basic unit, the square ward with internal streets and a shared open space at its center. Beyond the wards the entire community is ordered around a larger grid. Four of these wards were initially settled in Savannah, and subsequent growth over the next hundred years adhered strictly to the vocabulary. Each ward became a self-sufficient cellular unit containing forty housing plots and four lots for public buildings enclosing the central square. "The geometric order alone thus establishes one hierarchy which is internal to the ward and another which is external and evolves in the additive growth of the city."[46] The plan had no literal antecedents and is an inspired transformation of urban and garden types to establish squares as focal points for public and residential buildings.[47] Whereas most American cities were organized around the grid as a means of expediting investment, Savannah applied it as a tool for urban design to structure exterior space. The spatial discipline and rigidity of the plan are

Figure 3-20. Strada Nuova, Genoa. Perspective.
A formal vocabulary of consistent cornice lines, string courses, and garden walls creates a satisfying street space linking the individual pavilions. (From Gaetano Bonatti, *1864)*

embellished and varied by a lush landscape within the public space and numerous variations in the local architectural theme.

Modern urban and suburban streets in America are characterized by an ambiguity between the importance of blocks and buildings as pavilions in the landscape on the one hand, and the importance of the street space they form on the other. Scale is also a problem. In the urban core the vertical-to-horizontal proportion of street space is often 10 to 1, while in the suburban context the proportion is reversed—1 vertical to 10 horizontal (fig. 3-23). This indifference to the dimensional

proportion of street space is a major problem in urban design and should be addressed by applying the lessons learned from such examples as Strada Nuova and Visby. The street should be a spatial entity rather than what is left over after the buildings are built.

We have touched on the effectiveness of such traditional squares as the Piazza del Campo in Siena, and on the fact that it is the consistency and density of the wall that give character to the space. The modern American version of the square is the plaza, which proliferated during the 1960s as an urban symbol. Copley Square in Boston is an ex-

Figure 3-21. Friedrich Weinbrenner. Project for Langenstrasse, Karlsruhe. 1808.
As a means of unifying varied facades, Weinbrenner proposed an enormous, out-of-scale arcade. Irregularities in the buildings would be masked to provide a framework for public space.

ample of this type of city space, and a discussion of its success and failure will throw light on the problems contemporary designers have to face in creating viable public space.

Open versus Filled Space

The problem that confronted the firm of Sasaki, Dawson and DeMay Associates in designing Copley Square was how to unify buildings of conflicting architecture in a small space bounded on three sides by roadways. The square is directly adjacent to Henry Richardson's Trinity Church, one of the country's most important Romanesque Revival monuments. The plaza was to be a circulation zone, a space for events, but also a quiet place to sit. Prior to reconstruction the site was a classic example of lost space, with Huntington Avenue slicing a diagonal across the wasteland between Trinity Church and McKim, Mead, and White's Public Library. Historically, the area has had an important role in Boston's artistic, cultural, and institutional life; the name of the square honors

the great artist of late eighteenth-century Boston, John Singleton Copley. Over recent years, however, portions of this urban district have become increasingly "honky-tonk" in character.

Sasaki's plan (fig. 3-24) was to create a descending, gradually terraced square oriented asymmetrically to the church, with a pattern of lines to break up the large expanse of paving and allow for diagonal circulation. As a counterpoint to the church, the designers placed a fountain in the lowest part of the square.

Copley square was built well before the arrival of its new sixty-story neighbor, the Hancock Tower (see fig. 2-19). This tower was a true test of whether the square could indeed unify disparate elements of new and old. Fortunately for the square and Trinity Church, the attenuated rhomboid shape of Hancock, with its narrow side facing the square and its reflective glass, was intended to recede into the background. Somehow the radical juxtaposition of flat open plaza and huge Functionalist building works. Even though the plaza was successful in accepting the new tower

Figure 3-22. Oglethorpe Street, Savannah, Georgia.
The streets of Savannah, although rigid in plan (see fig. 2-11), are embellished in reality by a lush landscape and variations within the local architectural theme. (Photo: Stanford Anderson)

and the tower the plaza, one would still have to say that the plaza could fit into its surroundings more effectively—it could be more "contextual." The original idea of sinking the plaza below street level for protection against traffic has had some undesirable side effects. Hidden from public view, portions of the plaza have become havens for drug dealers, winos, and muggers. Separated by roads, the plaza lacks frontage and the adjacent buildings do not open out onto the public space. The modern geometry of the plaza itself was conceived as an abstract interpretation of the surroundings rather than a direct extension, and the forms that resulted appear somewhat alien to the Boston con-

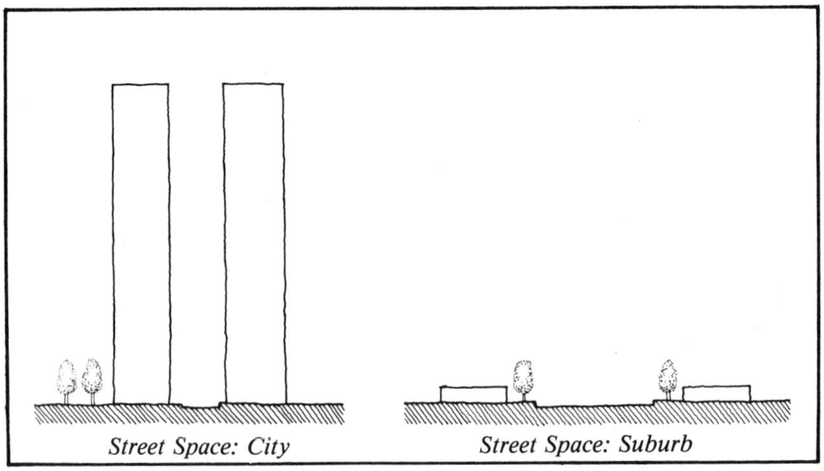

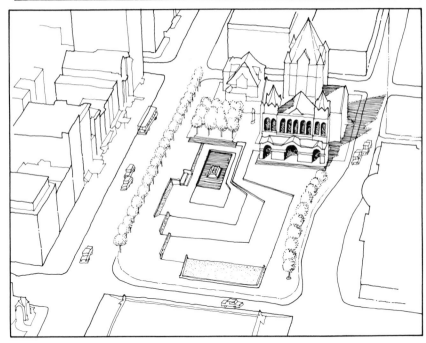

Figure 3-23. Diagram of Street Space Proportions: the City and the Suburb. In many modern cities the ratio between vertical building mass and street width is more than 10:1. On the outskirts of the city, however, the ratio is often reversed.

Street Space: City   Street Space: Suburb

Figure 3-24. Sasaki, Dawson, DeMay Associates. Copley Square, Boston, Massachusetts. 1969. The urban plaza is the modern American version of the European piazza. At Copley Square the Sasaki firm attempted to design an open space that would function as a European plaza, responding to its architectural surroundings and acting as a social gathering space. However, for a variety of reasons, including location, materials, and perhaps its abstract references to context, the design has failed to become an integral part of Boston.

text. Copley Square seems to have grown apart from rather than into its surroundings, and today it seems out of place. It also has a rundown, drab look about it because of the deteriorating low-quality materials the city chose to use when it was built some twenty years ago—concrete and asphalt paving instead of brick and granite, which are traditional to Boston.

Robert Venturi also submitted a scheme for the original Copley Square Design Competition in the sixties. He decided that the space was not enclosed enough by existing buildings to create a traditional piazza, and that Americans would not use it as such in any case. What he proposed was a "non-piazza," in which the entire area was filled with trees to define the space (fig. 3-25). A mosaic of

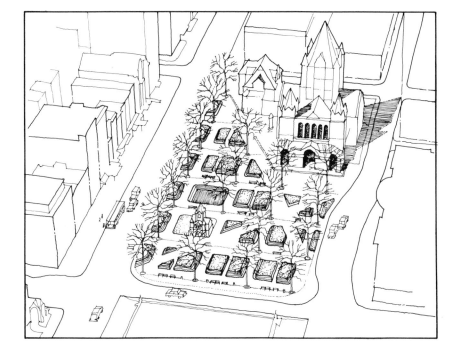

Figure 3-25. Robert Venturi. Competition Entry for Copley Square. Boston. 1969. Venturi submitted a scheme in marked contrast to the Sasaki design. His argument was that the buildings surrounding the site did not provide sufficient enclosure to create a European piazza, and that Americans did not, in any case, use open space in the same way. He proposed a "filled" square, heavily planted, that would symbolically represent the grid of the historic Back Bay.

trees would be planted in a grid of earth mounds mimicking, in miniature, the grid pattern of the historic Back Bay district around the square. Venturi also played with reversals of proportion by placing a scale model of Trinity Church as a piece of sculpture to show that "man can become supreme over monument"—a kind of polemic that has become the hallmark of Venturi's work. The Sasaki and Venturi comparison points out two different approaches—open versus filled space.

Currently, the city government and local business groups have decided to rebuild totally the square and have conducted a second national competition for new design plans. The winning competition scheme, chosen from among 309 entries, is by Dean Abbott of the New York firm of Clark and Rapuano. It represents a rediscovery of the traditional Boston park in contrast to the existing paved plaza. The redesign raises the sunken plaza to street level and suggests substantially more "green" with diagonal circulation paths cut through a parklike setting of grass and trees.

Smaller paved surfaces are designed to accommodate a variety of active urban uses (fig. 3-26). Forty percent of the plaza will be grassed over in the proposal. Unlike Sasaki or Venturi, the spatial design intends to reflect the visual character of the historic New England green and to provide nature as complement to surrounding urban districts, architectural monuments, and hard surfaces in the area.

Boston contains another contemporary square worthy of consideration in comparison to historic examples: the City Hall Plaza (fig. 3-27). Its open ground plane acts as a stage for circulation and major public events and as a forecourt to the civic monumentality of City Hall, as does the Piazza del Campo in Siena, Italy. Uncluttered space, an expanse of brick of at least one acre, was required to set off the monumental City Hall designed by Kallmann & McKinnell as a "rugged cliff, looming over the City in protest to the spindly thin forms of the International Style."[48] The red brick of the plaza is carried up the base of the building,

Figure 3-26. Clark and Rapuano. 1984 Winning Competition Entry for the Redesign of Copley Square.
Similar to Venturi in concept but different in form, Dean Abbott of Clark and Rapuano proposes substantially more
grass and trees, applying the visual character of the traditional New England Green to Copley Square. (Drawing:
Dean Abbott of Clarke and Rapuano, New York City)

tying the two together and calling attention to the concrete government offices above. At first, City Hall Plaza was seen as a disaster, but as the surrounding city fills in and density increases, the austere plane of brick devoid of fussy details seems more and more appropriate. The main point to be made about City Hall Plaza is that expansive uncluttered spaces at the base of monuments can be successful if there is sufficient density and public services to generate activity and if the perimeter is well defined. Our tendency is to overdesign and to fill up the space with unnecessary accoutrements.

Surface-articulated Space

All good urban design depends on the integration of architecure and landscape architecture. As already discussed, in Michelangelo's plan for the Campidoglio in Rome (ca. 1550), the three-sided, subtly triangular layout of the buildings is unified by an elaborate, elliptical paving pattern (figs. 3-5, 3-6). This paving pattern, a primary element in the plan, sets off the statue of Marcus Aurelius in its center and links the surrounding facades and stairs. The Campidoglio interacts with the spaces of the city, responding both to Ancient Rome and its newer Renaissance form. Michelangelo's understanding of the context of Rome is evident in the exquisite details that unite building form to exterior space.

The principle represented in Michelangelo's Campidoglio and inherent in Renaissance architectural thought is that the design of buildings and exterior spaces should be physically integrated. In

Figure 3-27. Facing page: *Kallman, McKinnell and Knowles. City Hall Plaza. Boston, Massachusetts. 1962–69.*
City Hall Plaza is another example of the open square. Serving as a platform for the new municipal government building, the space was also intended for civic gatherings. Perceived as a disaster when first constructed, this large open space is gaining increased acceptance as the surrounding density grows and new activity is generated. (Courtesy: Cervin Robinson, Photographer)

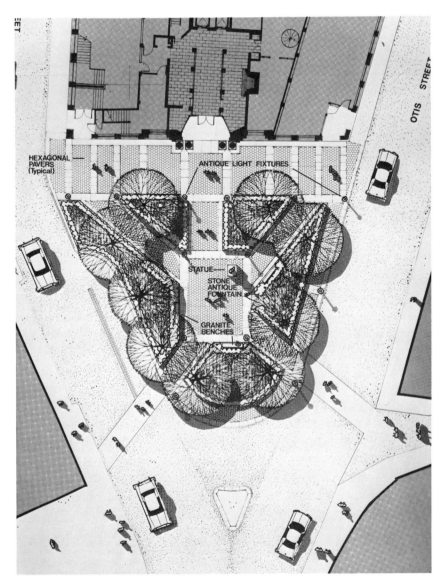

Figure 3-28. CBT Architects. One Winthrop Square, Boston, Massachusetts. 1974.
Many European piazzas are closely related in form and surface articulation to the surrounding architecture. In the design of a small triangular piazza in front of the nineteenth-century building at One Winthrop Square in Boston, the rhythm of columns on the building's facade were used as the generator for the paving pattern, tying the plaza to the building and giving it an aura of inevitability. (Courtesy: CBT Architects)

most modern cities they are separate. A modest exception is the recent design for One Winthrop Square in Boston (fig. 3-28), where the old building and the new landscape are successfully integrated in a small triangular piazza, and the rhythms of the columns on the facade of the building are mirrored in plan on the square by strips of granite that project in varied ways into the space to define entry, seating areas, and diagonal circulation. Because the plaza is an extension of its adjacent building, as articulated by the ground plane, it seems to fit naturally into its surrounding urban context and be a part of the total expression of architecture and landscape in Boston.

Monumental versus Intimate Space

Paley Park, a vest-pocket park in midtown Manhattan, is a commendable example of how small, leftover sites in the city can be transformed into viable public spaces. With a relatively small budget, this site was converted into a stage for public activity with white movable chairs and ta-

bles set on a simple but decorative paving amid a veil of green with a backdrop of cascading water (fig. 3-29). As one enters this oasis, city noise is largely masked by the sound of water, the air quality improves noticeably, and in summer months the

Figure 3-29. Zion and Breen. Paley Park. New York, New York. 1967. Paley Park initiated a new, and distinctly American, tradition of intimate "vest-pocket" parks in the city, demonstrating how small, leftover sites can be transformed into quiet retreats from the bustle of the street. (Courtesy: Zion and Breen Associates, Inc.)

vegetation and water cool the temperature. The park offers inexpensive food and functions as an important social space in the bustle of midtown Manhattan. The dimensions of the space and objects are in scale with the users. Paley Park is a well-liked public space.

On a completely different scale is the Christian Science Center in Boston (fig.3-30), a modern reconstruction completed in 1975.[49] This vast plaza features a gigantic reflecting pool in its center—a pool that serves as a mediator between existing and added architecture. The new architectural pieces are subordinate to the old church and defer to this historic structure as the centerpiece of the complex. Paley Park and the Christian Science Center are at opposite ends of the physical scale, but both fit well into their particular urban environments.

Communicative Space

We have looked at some samples of contemporary urban plazas in relation to the principles discussed in the historic precedents. We have also mentioned some of the problems of contemporary streets: the emphasis on rapid movement, the inappropriate scale, and the lack of a consistent, unifying framework. Another problem that affects urban space in general is the proliferation of signs in the modern city. All public spaces in cities communicate messages—functional, symbolic, or persuasive. These messages are conveyed in the manner in which buildings are grouped, in their facades, and especially on the commercial strip, in the signs they display. Objects in public space—lampposts, paving, planting—symbolically communicate the meaning of place. Often messages of the city are more cogently expressed by the complex fragments of the exterior environment than by the more massive architecture of individual buildings. The vocabulary of fragments dominates the view from the road or the sidewalk. In cities east and west, objects of communication often dominate our perception of urban space to the point where written messages or advertisements take over space, as if edge-defining buildings never existed

in the first place (fig. 3-31). What modern cities need is a clearer physical definition of the public domain that is less dependent on communication systems and the clutter of free enterprise. Space rather than signs should communicate the values of a culture.

SOFT SPACE

These comments offer a variety of ways of understanding the distinction between found and lost space in the urban environment. There are, however, other nonarchitectural types of space that should be considered by the designer. Although the architectural approach of a continuous void with hard walls is one approach to urban design, we must also explore natural, soft space in the central city for what it can offer as a contrast to the dense urban environment.

Human Space

As a means of understanding the nature of space and the physical and psychological dimensions of the exterior void, we must expand the discourse into areas beyond specific urban spaces to include the larger context within which they exist. In order to evaluate space in this broader context, two factors must be considered: (1) the meaning of a space based on its use and purpose as defined by the psychological and social needs of the individual; and (2) the relationship between a particular space or group of spaces and their regional characteristics, including history and local traditions.

The qualitative judgment of how well a space is

Figure 3-30. Facing page: I. M. Pei with Sasaki Associates. Christian Science Center. Boston, Massachusetts. 1975.
The plaza at Christian Science Center responds to the monumental scale of the surrounding architecture. Its primary function is to complete an impressive architectural composition and to link the old church with I. M. Pei's new additions. (Courtesy: First Church of Christ, Scientist)

Figure 3-31. Yokohama, Japan. Street Scene.
In modern cities architectural space is often obliterated by signs that actually define the space more than buildings define it.

designed comes from its functional meaning and from how well its physical shape accommodates social needs. Existing and proposed patterns of use can often be better accommodated in soft space containing the elements of nature and wilderness than in hard space expressed in architectonic forms. Eliciting the social criteria and translating them in the design process leads to the creation of a social space appropriate to the activities it contains. Ignoring human input leads to lost space.

Figure 3-32. Lofoten, Norway.
Rural space has qualities distinct from those of urban space. The value of each is enhanced by contrast, and boundaries should remain clear. In many contemporary environments, settlement has encroached on the natural landscape to the detriment of both "hard" and "soft" space.

Rural Space

Rural space fulfills a direct and meaningful purpose in providing wood, crops, and resources for human settlement. As extended, unbounded space, it interacts positively with manmade settlements, providing economic benefits and satisfying the human needs for open space and contact with nature. As a meaningful space with a distinct use and clear purpose, rural space, although architecturally unenclosed, is not lost space. Enclosure of rural space (fig. 3-32) is derived from natural features of topography and land form, water, vegetation in the form of hedgerows, forests, and plantations, as well as manmade enclosures of fences and stone walls. Therefore the natural landscape can also be defined as positive, structured space accommodating patterns of settlement and human activities.

It is important to distinguish clearly between rural and urban space. When the *limits* between townscape and rural space are unintentional, or ''blurred,'' the space usually loses its main purpose and results in undesirable urban sprawl. Maintaining town-country limits is critical for spatial management. The diffused configuration of the edge leads to scattered spaces as buildings in the landscape in what we have come to know as strip development and suburbs. In the Italian hilltown of Rivalto located in the Tuscan landscape, a clear, intentional limit separates rural and urban spaces (fig. 3-33). No urban fringe exists. On the outside, vast hills and plantations extend the unbounded spatial experience to the distant horizon; the contrasting interior space is made up of a compressed and tightly knit sequence of urban streets and squares. We should strive to attain this contrast and land-use control in modern urban design.

As an example of the confusion of urban and rural space, the later phases of Modernism developed an open-ended planning framework that was intended to provide for orderly growth and systematic urban development. Typical are the plans by George Candilis, Alexis Josic, and Shadrach Woods at Toulouse-le-Mirail, France, in 1961, which is a pure expression of the linkage theory of urban design (further elaborated in chapter 4). This composition of dendritic stems (like the branching pattern of a tree) rejects the limits between rural space and manmade urban space (fig. 3-34). The rural space becomes half-urban, the urban space half-rural. Both suffer. The contribution made at Toulouse is not to enclosed exterior space, but to a linear architectural system of open-ended pedestrian spines where activities and services are elevated and separated from the automobile traffic below. Toulouse is offered as an example, because its buildings are figural and continuous objects that dominate the landscape, and exterior space is of secondary importance in generating urban form.

Parklike Space

As suggested in our discussion of rural space, the distinction between space and lost space cannot be derived solely from attributes of containment, enclosure, hard versus soft, or architectural versus nonarchitectural elements. It is easy to assert that all spaces without clearly defined edges or walls, like those of the room of a house, are lost space. But is it possible to categorize the unenclosed urban parks of Frederick Law Olmsted, Capability Brown, and Jens Jensen as lost space because they are soft, nonarchitectural city rooms? Obviously not, since their designs are generated by the idea of nature in the city, and their energizing effect is derived from contrast to the city. To translate this concept of nature into right angles and enclosed space would be wrong. Let soft landscape remain soft. What makes these nonarchitectural rooms effective as city spaces is that they fill the void between buildings in a positive, useful way (fig. 3-35).

Beyond the American urban park, the hard/soft contrast is what gives characteristic atmosphere to the campus quadrangle, where soft landscaped space fills the hard square frame of buildings. At Harvard Yard, for example, the entire quadrangle is filled with ancient trees against a distinctive background of architecture, through which circulation routes establish the predominant pattern (figs. 3-36, 3-37). Similarly, the Lawn of the University of Virginia, designed by Thomas Jefferson, gains much of its majesty through the contrast between the natural interior and the architecturally unified colonnade at its edges (fig. 3-38).

One of the most meaningful spaces ever designed in America, the egalitarian Lawn expresses Jefferson's visions of an open society. Professors

Figure 3-33. Rivalto, Italy.
This Italian hill town is an admirable example of the coexistence of rural and urban space to the benefit of both. A compact urban environment makes a sweeping view to the horizon the more dramatic by contrast. The limits of settlement are clearly defined. There is no need for an urban fringe.

and students share views of the green from academic pavilions registered on both sides. The soft landscape space of contemporary parks and college campuses is a derivative of the English landscape-garden movement of the seventeenth and eighteenth centuries. This concept applied to the design of urban space idealizes nature in the city with the utmost regard for pictorial landscape composition. This kind of space is designed to cooperate with rather than coerce natural elements

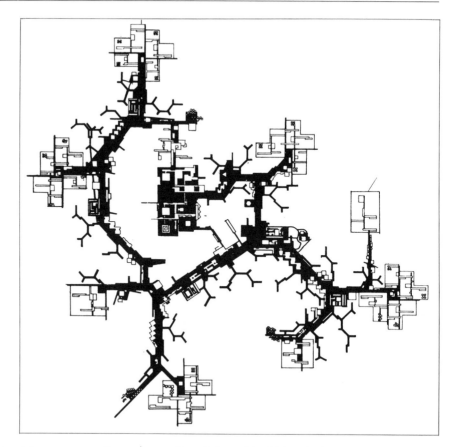

Figure 3-34. Candillis, Josic and Woods. Toulouse-le-Mirail, France. 1961.
In this example of "open-ended" planning from the later phases of Modernism, a branching megastructure reaches into the countryside blurring the distinction between rural and urban space. Toulouse-le-Mirail was a major contribution to the theory of linkage in urban design, but considers exterior space as secondary, a mere generator of form.

and to contrast the architectural form surrounding the space.

Symbolic Space: The Japanese Temple Garden

If the parks and quadrangles of America have generally been inspired by the English landscape tradition as a way of bringing nature into the city, a very different approach to spatial design is represented in the Japanese temple garden. The temple gardens of Japan, imbued with symbolic meanings and expressions, are highly structured and crafted spaces communicating the metaphysical aspirations of Japanese society. Natural materials—rock, sand, water, and plants—are composed as metaphoric representations of the philosophical relationships between man and his environment. The Japanese garden, which ac-

tually originated in China during the Han Dynasty (ca. 100 B.C.), provides the profoundly important place for meditative, self-contemplative withdrawal of the individual from his extremely dense, competitive environment. The connections between physical space and the Zen tradition of human values and intuition are well integrated throughout the garden, where the manmade and

Figure 3-35. Facing page: Frederick Law Olmsted, Sr. Jackson and Washington Park, Chicago, Illinois. 1871. In the many park systems Olmsted designed for American cities, the landscape architect wanted to bring nature into the urban environment to provide contrast, spiritual uplift, and places for physical recreation and social integration. Such "soft" spaces fill the voids between buildings in positive and purposeful ways and should not be classified as "lost" spaces simply because they are not architecturally defined. (Courtesy: Dumbarton Oaks, Trustees for Harvard University)

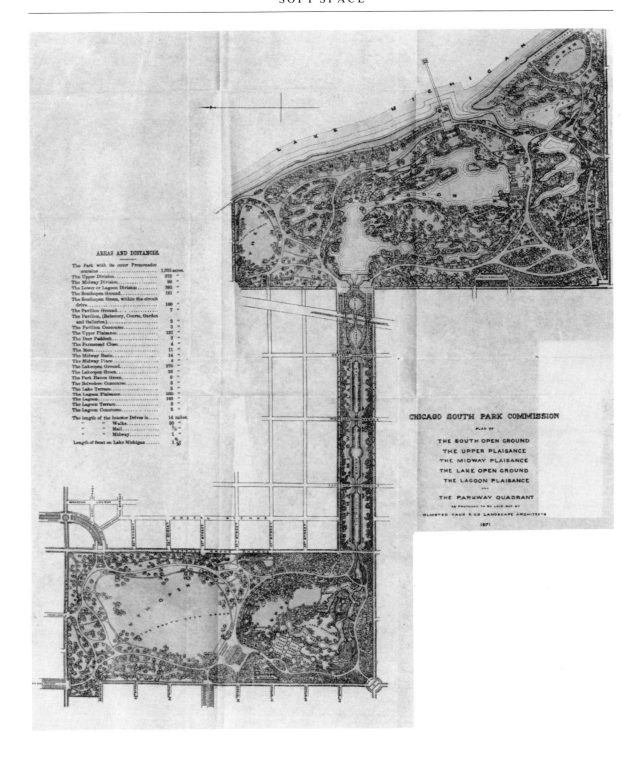

AREAS AND DISTANCES.

The Park with its outer Promenade
  contains .... 1,055 acres.
The Upper Division .... 372 "
The Midway Division .... 90 "
The Lower or Lagoon Division .... 593 "
The Southopen Ground .... 191 "
The Southopen Green, within the circuit
  drive .... 100 "
The Pavilion Ground .... 7 "
The Pavilion, (Refectory, Courts, Garden
  and Galleries,) .... 2 "
The Pavilion Concourse .... 2 "
The Upper Plaisance .... 137 "
The Deer Paddock .... 7 "
The Farmstead Close .... 4 "
The Mere .... 11 "
The Midway Basin .... 14 "
The Midway Place .... 4 "
The Lakeopen Ground .... 270 "
The Lakeopen Green .... 26 "
The Park Haven Green .... 9 "
The Belvedere Concourse .... 2 "
The Lake Terrace .... 3 "
The Lagoon Plaisance .... 230 "
The Lagoon .... 165 "
The Lagoon Terrace .... 2 "
The Lagoon Concourse .... 2 "

The length of the Interior Drives is ...... 14 miles.
    "   "   Walks .... 30 "
    "   "   Mall .... 7½ "
    "   "   Midway .... 1 "

Length of front on Lake Michigan .... 1 2/10 "

CHICAGO SOUTH PARK COMMISSION

PLAN OF

THE SOUTH OPEN GROUND
THE UPPER PLAISANCE
THE MIDWAY PLAISANCE
THE LAKE OPEN GROUND
THE LAGOON PLAISANCE
AND
THE PARKWAY QUADRANT

AS PROPOSED TO BE LAID OUT BY

OLMSTED VAUX & CO LANDSCAPE ARCHITECTS

1871

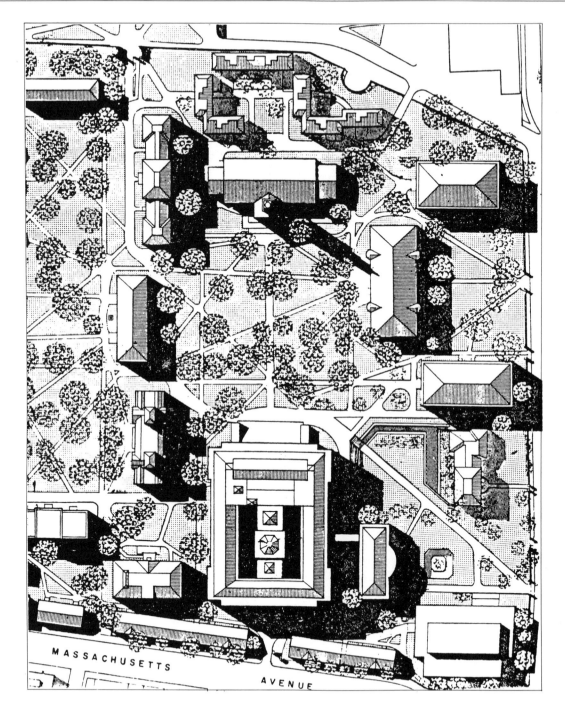

Figures 3-36, 3-37. Harvard Yard. Cambridge, Massachusetts. Plan and Eye-level View.
The distinctive atmosphere of the enclosed quadrangle of the English campus tradition is achieved by contrasting the "hard" architectural frame and the "soft" internal landscape of trees and grass.

Figure 3-37.

Figure 3-38. Thomas Jefferson. Campus Lawn, University of Virginia, Charlottesville, Virginia.
At the University of Virginia, architecture and landscape are integrated in an exceptionally sensitive manner. Designed
by Thomas Jefferson in 1817, a low Palladian colonnade frames the great Roman-revival Lawn, which in turn serves
to organize the academic pavillions around the edge. (Courtesy: University Archives, University of Virginia Library)

natural orders are brought together. As symbolic abstractions of nature, the great mountains, misty valleys, and placid lakes are represented in the Japanese garden by a few landscape elements; the rest of the picture is filled in by the imagination.

This symbolism is best expressed in the Ryoanji temple garden (fig. 3-39), where the raked sand represents clouds and the rocks are metaphors for mountain peaks penetrating the clouds. At Ryoanji there is a complete fusion of hard and soft space. Of the many principles of spatial design expressed in the Japanese garden, the concept of dynamic arrest is most significant to Western designers, because it addresses the suspension of time by resisting completion—by leaving some part of the design unfinished. This element of time, symbolic and real, is an important requirement for contem-porary spatial design, even in the Western World.

Conclusion

We have examined various precedents of urban space, both hard and soft. The designer should look at as many examples as possible to understand how the space is adapted to its surroundings and how it serves its function. For hard space the most important factors are the frame, the surface, and the focal points. Soft space has design requirements posed by nature as symbol and contrast. Both must fit their intended purpose.

In the following chapter we shall look at the three major theoretical approaches to the analysis of and spatial design in the city, showing how all three theories must be considered in order to find lost space.

Figure 3-39. Ryoanji Temple Garden, Kyoto, Japan.
The temple garden of Ryoanji is perhaps the finest example of symbolic space in the world, where natural and man-made materials metaphorically connect man to his total environment.

4

THREE THEORIES OF URBAN SPATIAL DESIGN

On the basis of research into the evolution of modern space and the analysis of historic precedents, three approaches to urban-design theory can be identified: (1) figure-ground theory; (2) linkage theory; and (3) place theory. These theories differ significantly from each other, but taken together can provide us with potential strategies for integrated urban design (fig. 4-1).

The *figure-ground theory* is founded on the study of the relative land coverage of buildings as solid mass (''figure'') to open voids (''ground''). Each urban environment has an existing pattern of solids and voids, and the figure-ground approach to spatial design is an attempt to manipulate these relationships by adding to, subtracting from, or changing the physical geometry of the pattern. The objective of these manipulations is to clarify the structure of urban spaces in a city or district by establishing a hierarchy of spaces of different sizes that are individually enclosed but ordered directionally in relation to each other. A predominant ''field'' of solids and voids creates this urban pattern, often called the fabric, and is punctuated by object buildings and spaces, such as major landmarks or open spaces that provide focal points and subcenters within the field. The figure-ground drawing is a graphic tool for illustrating mass-void relationships; a two-dimensional abstraction in plan view that clarifies the structure and order of urban spaces.

Unlike the figure-ground theory, which is based primarily on patterns of solids and voids, the *linkage theory* is derived from ''lines'' connecting one element to another. These lines are formed by streets, pedestrian ways, linear open spaces, or other linking elements that physically connect the parts of a city. The designer applying the linkage theory tries to organize a system of connections, or a network, that establishes a structure for ordering spaces. Emphasis is placed on the circulation diagram rather than the spatial diagram of the figure-ground theory. Movement systems and efficiency of the infrastructure take precedence over patterns of defined outdoor space.

The *place theory* goes one step beyond figure-ground and linkage theories in that it adds the components of human needs and cultural, historical, and natural contexts. Advocates of the place theory give physical space additional richness by incorporating unique forms and details indigenous to its setting. This response to context often includes history and the element of time and attempts to enhance the fit between new design and existing conditions. In place theory social and cul-

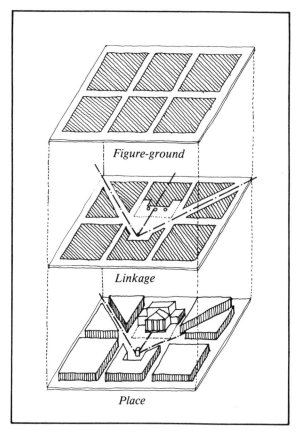

Figure-ground

Linkage

Place

Figure 4-1. Diagram of Urban Design Theories.
In recent years there have been three major approaches to urban design.

(1) Figure-ground theory: In this approach, the starting point for an understanding of urban form is the analysis of relationships between building mass and open space. Figure-ground analyses are powerful tools for identifying the textures and patterns of the urban fabric as well as problems in its spatial order, but can lead to a static and two-dimensional conception of space.

(2) Linkage theory: In this approach dynamics of circulation become the generators of urban form. The emphasis on connection and movement is a significant contribution, but the need for spatial definition is sometimes undervalued.

(3) Place theory: Designers have increasingly become aware of the importance of historic, cultural, and social values in urban open space. Contextualists have argued strongly against the tendency of the Functionalists to impose abstract designs from the outside.

Overlay: The integrated approach suggested in this text would incorporate figure-ground, linkage, and place theories, giving clear structure to solids and voids, organizing connections between the parts, and responding to the human needs and unique elements of the context.

tural values, visual perceptions, of users and an individual's control over the immediate public environment are as important as principles of lateral enclosure and linkage.

Each of these approaches has its own value, but the optimum is one that draws on all three, giving structure to the solids and voids, organizing the links between parts, and responding to the human needs and unique elements of the particular environment. The physical spatial structure of the urban landscape must be designed in response to these interrelated theories.

FIGURE-GROUND THEORY

The best illustration of the figure-ground theory of urban design is Giambattista Nolli's Map of Rome, drawn in 1748. The Nolli Map (fig. 4-2) reveals the city as a clearly defined system of solids and voids. The building coverage is denser than the exterior space, thereby giving shape to the public openings—in other words, creating positive voids, or "space-as-object." The open space in Rome is carved out of the building mass as a continuous flow linking interior and exterior spaces and activities. Without this critical land coverage, the spatial continuity would be impossible. In Nolli's map the outdoor civic space is a positive void and is more *figural* than the solids that define it. Space is conceived as a positive entity in an integrated relationship with the surrounding solids.[50] This is the opposite of the modern concept of space, where the buildings are figural, freestanding objects, and space is an uncontained void. In Nolli, the void is figural.

The figure-ground relationship in the Nolli Map is one of overall coherence, featuring a mesh between the block pattern and individual buildings. Object buildings are distinguished by their larger civic spaces in front and from the predominant field of tightly packed streets and squares registered within a continuous building mass or "pri-

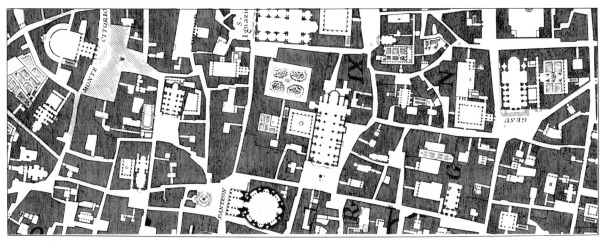

Figure 4-2. Giambattista Nolli. Map of Rome. 1748.
Nolli's map graphically illustrates the figure-ground relationship of a traditional city where public civic space is carved out of the private tissue. (See also fig. 3-2.) The predominant field is a dense continuous mass, allowing open space to become a figural void.

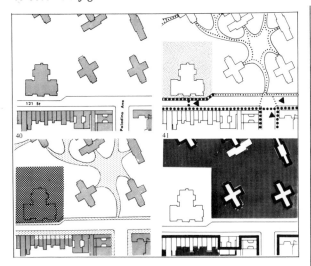

Figure 4-3. Robert F. Wagner, Sr. Houses. Upper East Side. New York, New York.
In contrast to Nolli's map, the predominant field is void in most modern cities. Buildings read as individual and isolated objects and the spaces between them are unformed. When buildings are principally vertical there is inadequate ground coverage and the intentional shaping of exterior space is virtually impossible. (Drawing: Victor Caliandro)

vate tissue.'' Thus, differentiating between *public* and *private* articulates the civic buildings (illustrated with ground floors exposed) from the "ur-ban poché'' surrounding them.

The term *poché* is often used in the figure-ground theory of urban design. It is a spatial field of solids, articulating the configuration of exterior voids. Poché is technically defined as the walls, columns, and other solids of buildings, indicated in black on architectural plans. On the exterior, however, *urban* poché is the supportive structure, which *registers* the spatial landscape, engaging the buildings to their adjacent voids, making a kind of continuous imprint on the plan. This results in spatial events that bring the design of the public realm together with that of the private object. Marketplace Center in Boston is a good contemporary example of the urban poché expressed in Nolli's figure-ground drawing.

The figure-ground theory further points out that when the urban form is predominantly vertical instead of horizontal—point-block towers, slabs, or skyscrapers common to the modern landscape—shaping coherent urban space is next to impossible (fig. 4-3). Most attempts to place vertical elements over a large ground plane result in vast open spaces seldom used or enjoyed. Vertical buildings strewn as objects on the landscape cannot give spatial structure to the environment because of inadequate ground coverage. When this occurs, the dominant reading, in contrast to the Nolli Map, is of the single building, and the connective block pattern is missing. In order to achieve form on the exterior, the perimeter of spaces and blocks must be well articulated to establish outdoor rooms containing corners, niches, pockets, and corridors. Alvar Aalto of Finland, one of the most influential architects of this century, often described the problem of spatial design as one of connecting the form of the building to the structure of the site, or of twisting and turning the building's facades to create positive exterior space.[51] This approach can be seen in almost all of Aalto's public buildings (prime examples include the Säynätsalo Town Hall and Riola Parochial Church), where an outdoor court or larger piazza forms the center and holds the composition together. Aalto's figure-ground concept for individual or small groups of buildings can be applied to urban design on a larger scale for the city.

The easiest way to achieve positive voids is to work with a horizontal building mass where the structures have more coverage than the surrounding field and where, conceptually, the space is carved out of the mass. In practice this figure-ground relationship is not always possible or even desirable, but it should always be kept in mind as a conceptual guiding principle in city design.

Certain definite types of positive voids should be created within the building mass of the city. Public spaces give symbolic content and meaning to the city by providing gathering places, paths, transitions between public and private domains, and arenas for discourse and interaction. As Susana Torre writes:

Urban voids are at once the vessel and symbol of human gathering, and represent the tension between the individual and the collective. Despite being physically endangered and politically fragile in the face of land speculation, squares and parks more often than not have survived while buildings around them were torn down and replaced. In America, squares and parks are expressions of civic pride. Important deeds are summoned to memory by such places as Independence Square, the Lexington Green and the Boston Commons. . . . However, the artistically

shaped urban void, a space of specific scale determined by the size of the gathering it can contain, and by the height, character and design of its boundaries, has been almost forgotten by modern planners.[52]

Space is the medium of the urban experience, providing the sequence between public, semi-public, and private domains. For these sequences to work, circulation barriers and gaps in continuity must be minimized or eliminated. Spatial orientation is defined by the configuration of urban blocks that collectively form districts and neighborhoods. It is the articulation and differentiation of solids and voids that make up the fabric of the city and establish the physical sequences and visual orientation between places. Figure-ground analyses (fig. 4-4) are especially useful in revealing such relationships. The nature of the urban void depends on the disposition of solids at its perimeter (buildings, groups of buildings, and/or urban blocks), on the scale of these elements, and on the horizontal dimension of the opening or ground surface between vertical components. Larger composite patterns of street space form districts, where the ensemble of spaces creates an urban character that dominates and unites individual, isolated spaces. Figure-ground studies re-

Figure 4-4. Typical Figure-ground Plan of a Portion of the City. Figure-ground studies are useful not only in revealing the composite patterns of street space but also in indicating the distinctive characteristics of districts. (Refer also to figure-ground studies for Boston and Göteborg, figs. 5-18 and 5-60.)

Figure 4-5. Six Typological Patterns of Solids and Voids.
The solid-void relationships formed by the shape and location of buildings, the design of site elements (plantings, walls), and the channeling of movement result in six typological patterns: grid, angular, curvilinear, radial/concentric, axial, and organic.

Grid Angular Curvilinear

Radial Concentric Axial Organic

veal the collective urban form as a combination of patterns of solids and voids (fig. 4-5) that can take on many configurations, such as the orthogonal/diagonal overlay (the modified grid), the random organic (generated by terrain and natural features), and the nodal concentric (linear and wraparound forms with activity centers), to name just three. Most cities are built from combinations and permutations of these patterns as well as through the juxtaposition of larger and smaller patterns. The organic shifting patterns of Imperial Rome and the regular grid of midtown Manhattan are the particular organizing structures of those cities. The shifting relationships of streets and blocks throughout an urban district give it its aggregate form.

Beyond revealing the character and aggregate urban form, figure-ground drawings help articulate the differences between urban solids and voids and provide us with a tool for classifying them by type. As we have indicated, distinct types of solids and voids contribute to the design and perception of public space (figs. 4-6, 4-7).

Urban-solid types include public monuments or dominant institutional buildings, the field of urban blocks, and directional or edge-defining buildings; urban-void types include entry foyers, inner-block voids, networks of streets and squares, parks and gardens, and linear open-space systems.

Urban Solids

The first important type of urban solid can be characterized as public monuments or institutions, which serve as centerpieces in the city fabric. These object buildings, often visual foci, need to sit prominently in open space to announce their presence and express their social and political significance. They are often freestanding—like the typical American city hall—or welded to blocks of more ordinary buildings, as frequently occurred with Gothic or Baroque churches in the traditional European city (see the Pantheon in Rome, fig. 4-8). The forecourts to public monuments and institutions, with their grand entrance stairs and the open spaces surrounding them, are often as important as the monuments themselves, as in the Campo in Siena or the Campidoglio in Rome. "On the European continent the cathedral is preceded by an urban space which serves to unite the symbolic interior of the building with the town as a whole. . . . A splendid answer to the problem of urban gathering is also offered by St. Mark's Square (and monumental cathedral) in Venice,

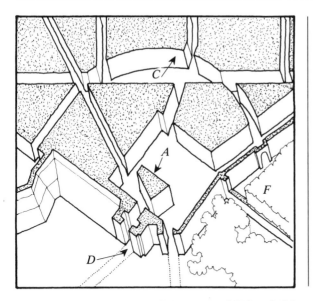

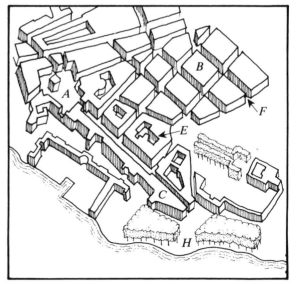

Figures 4-6, 4-7. Diagram of the Types of Urban Solids and Voids.
In the traditional city three principal types of urban solids have evolved: public monuments and institutions (A); the predominant field of urban blocks (B); and edge-defining buildings (C). There are five main types of urban void that perform various functions in the exterior space of the city: entry foyers (D) act as passageways between private and public space; inner block voids (E) are semiprivate transition zones; the network of streets and squares (F) corresponds to the predominant field of blocks and contains the active public life of the city; parks and gardens (G) are nodes that contrast with architectural urban forms, while linear open space systems (H), usually associated with natural features such as riverways, waterfronts, and wetlands, cut through urban districts to establish edges and create larger-scale connections.

Figure 4-8. The Pantheon, Rome. Detail from the Nolli Map of Rome.
A type of urban solid found in all cities is the public monument or institution. In many cases this monument needs to be set off by an important public space, which may well be as significant as the architecture it frames. At the Pantheon in Rome, a piazza links the interior space to the outdoor structure of the wider city. Public monuments or institutions serve as focal points or centerpieces in the city. (See also Richardson's Trinity Church at Copley Square, fig. 2-19, and Boston City Hall, fig. 3-27.)

where the large piazza forms a meaningful transition between the dense labyrinth of the city and the glittering expanse of the sea."[53]

A second major type of urban solid can be defined as the predominant field of urban blocks. According to Leon Krier, the size, pattern, and orientation of the urban block is the most important element in the composition of public spaces.

The *field* is organized by a repetition of preshaped parcels forming a pattern determined by use, such as residential, office, retail, or industrial, with appropriate spacing, bulk, and vertical dimension. The *field* of blocks sometimes forms a carpet pattern of recognizable, coherent textures that define a center. They might also be formed by neighborhoods or districts of a consistent group form.

Another category of solids in the city is formed by directional or edge-defining buildings that are generally nonrepetitive, specialized forms, often linear in configuration. These could be buildings that are intentionally designed to violate the predominant field and adjusted to face a boulevard, circle, or square, or to establish the edge of a district. They can also serve to surround and set off a monument, to define axial lines of sight, and to frame important places. Amsterdam South, the landmark Dutch housing district designed by H. P. Berlage in 1915, reveals a masterly treatment of the directional, edge-defining solid (fig. 4-9). Berlage's perimeter blocks form figural street space and squares that establish a continuous urban fabric, setting up a vocabulary that governs building volumes and facade styles as well as the treatment of landscape.

These three types of urban solids should be interconnected through design in such a way as to make the voids emerge as a figural network of linked spaces, as in Nolli's Map of Rome.

Urban Voids

As in the case of urban solids, there are certain definable urban voids. These need to be carved out of and pushed into the solids to provide functional and visual continuities, thereby creating an integrated, humane city in which architecture and exterior space are inextricably fused.

Five types of urban voids (with different degrees of openness and enclosure) play a part in the exterior city. The first is the entry foyer space that establishes the important transition, or passage, from personal domain to common territory. Security—the "eyes on the street" surveillance by a doorman at the porte-cochère or neighbors peering out their windows—is a significant design and social consideration of the entry foyer. Oscar Newman in his work, *Defensible Space,*[54] stresses the importance of the semipublic entry foyer in crime prevention. The entry space is a private gateway visible to a select few and announcing the arrival of individuals to their living or work spaces. In form it can be forecourt, mews, niche, lobby, or front yard. In scale it is intimate, a place where one can be both public and private.

The second type is the inner block void—the enclosed "hole in the doughnut"—a semiprivate residential space for leisure or utility or a midblock shopping oasis for circulation or rest. Paley Park in Manhattan (see fig. 3-29) and the many courtyards and cloister gardens of Copenhagen fall into this category (fig. 4-10).

A third type of void is the primary network of streets and squares (fig. 4-11), a category that corresponds to the predominant field of blocks and that contains the active public life of the city. Historically, the streets and squares were the unifying structures of the city; in modern times (as we have previously discussed), they have lost much of their social function and physical quality. As extensions of the home and places for discourse among neighbors, urban streets and squares traditionally formed a systematic hierarchy of order from locally controlled space to citywide routes for communication. Streets and squares were places to be—to spend time in—as well as corridors through which to move. Throughout most of urban history the network of streets and squares functioned as the principal structure for civic design and spatial organization. Too often today they do not serve this role, as the mixed-use street has been replaced by shopping centers.

Public parks and gardens (fig. 4-12) are the fourth type of larger voids that contrast with architectural urban forms. Acting as nodes for the preservation of nature in the city, they are incorporated into the urban grid to simulate rural settings, to provide both relief from the hard urban environment and accessible recreation. Urban

Figure 4-9. H. P. Berlage. Amsterdam South. The Netherlands. 1915.
Berlage's linear blocks represent a masterly use of the edge-defining directional solid. Berlage's perimeter blocks form
figural street space and squares that establish a continuity of urban fabric, setting up a vocabulary governing building
volume, facade styles, and landscape treatment. (Photo: KLM Aerocarto)

Figure 4-10. Typical Entry Foyer and Inner-block Courtyard, Copenhagen, Denmark.
The entry foyer establishes the important transition, or passage, between personal domain and public territory. It is intimate in scale, visible to a small group, and provides a vital buffer of security between private and communal zones. The inner-block void is also an important transition zone between semiprivate and fully public space, whether as a residential space for leisure or utility or as a midblock oasis or urban park. (Refer also to Paley Park, fig. 3-29.)

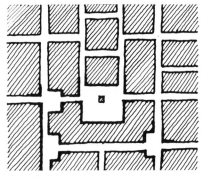

Figure 4-11. Plan Diagram of Streets and Squares.
As urban voids, the network of streets and squares corresponds to the predominant field of solid urban blocks. Extensions of the home and places of neighborhood interaction, streets and blocks traditionally provided a systematic hierarchy from locally controlled territory to citywide communication routes. Places to move through, they were also places to spend time in.

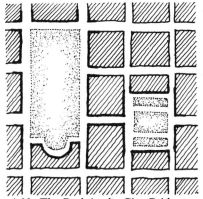

Figure 4-12. The Park in the City Grid.
Parks and open gardens are urban spaces that provide contrast to the hard urban environment and opportunities for relaxation and recreation.

parks and gardens shape adjoining sites by enhancing property values at their edges, but they are independent landscape compositions internally. One of the most formidable natural commons in any city is Olmsted's Central Park in New York City.

The final type of urban void is the linear open-space system (fig. 4-13), commonly related to major water features such as rivers, waterfronts, and wetland zones. These formal and informal greenways slice through districts, create edges, and link

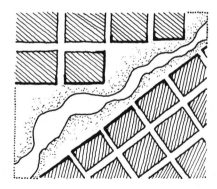

Figure 4-13. Linear Open Space Systems within the City. Often related to watercourses, linear open spaces slice through districts, establish edges, and link places. The landscape treatment may be formal or informal, but linear open spaces generally offer continuous greenery in contrast to the regular grid of urban streets.

places. The organic Riverway in San Antonio, Texas, and Olmsted's ''Emerald Necklace'' of greenways in Boston are linear systems that give richness to the city form by contrasting with the urban grid and providing a pervasive presence to the landscape. In Edmonton, a modern boomtown of close to one million people in northwest Alberta, Canada, the city grid, derived from the larger grid of the prairie, is superimposed over a natural system of linear ravines at a dramatically lower elevation. This juxtaposition forces the grid to change direction and allows for recreation in an untouched natural setting at a separate topographical elevation. In Edmonton's open-space amenity one is totally unaware of the active city above. Similar spatial structures are present in several of the new towns of Scandinavia, notably in areas of Tapiola, Finland, and Vallingly on the outskirts of Stockholm (see figs. 2-35, 2-36).

In conclusion, the crux of the figure-ground theory lies in the manipulation and organization of urban solids and voids. When the dialogue between the urban solids and voids is complete and perceivable, the spatial network tends to operate successfully. Fragments are incorporated into the framework and take on the character of the district. If the relationship of solids to voids is poorly balanced, fragments become disjointed, falling outside the framework; the result is lost space. In order to reclaim our lost space, there must be a willingness to reconsider the object and evaluate the ground rather than worship the figure. Design of the object must be considered in conjunction with structuring the void, so that building and space can effectively coexist.

LINKAGE THEORY

As previously outlined, the linkage theory involves the organization of lines that connect the parts of the city and the design of a spatial *datum* from these lines relate buildings to spaces. The concept of datum in spatial design is analogous to the staff in music, upon which notes are composed in an infinite number of ways. The musical staff is a constant datum, providing the composer with continuous lines of reference. In urban spatial design, the determinant lines of force on a site provide a similar kind of datum from which a design is created. A spatial datum can be a site line, directional flow of movement, an organizational axis, or a building edge. Together they indicate a constant system of linkages that are to be considered when proposing additions to or changes in the spatial environment.

In his landmark treatise, *Investigations into Collective Form,* Fumihiko Maki discusses several factors that go into the creation of a framework of spatial linkages. Maki addresses linkage as the most important characteristic of urban exterior space, stating that:

> Linkage is simply the glue of the city. It is the act by which we unite all the layers of activity and resulting physical form in the city. . . . urban design is concerned with the question of making comprehensible links between discrete things. As a corollary, it is concerned with making an extremely large entity comprehensible by articulating its parts.[55]

From this emphasis on the linkage theory, Maki

defines three different formal types of urban space: compositional form, megaform, and group form (fig. 4-14). Compositional form, he says, consists of individually tailored buildings in abstract patterns that are composed in a two-dimensional plan. Linkage is implied rather than overt, and reciprocal tension is a product of the positioning and shapes of freestanding objects. Linkage elements are static and formal in nature. Maki cites as examples of compositional form Chandigarh Government Center (see fig. 2-9) and the new city of Brasília. In compositional form, perimeter edges to open space are not considered as important as the object buildings themselves.

The second formal type in Maki's linkage theory is the megastructure, in which individual components are integrated into a larger framework in an hierarchical, open-ended, and interconnected system. In megaform, linkage is physically imposed to make a structure. In describing megaform, Maki points out several administrative and engineering advantages, principally the advantage of efficiency in ordering varied functions and investment within a simple infrastructure. The works of Kenzo Tange and Noriaki Kurokawa are given as models, with particular reference to a new community designed at the Massachusetts Institute of Technology in the 1960s (fig. 4-15).

The tight structure of megaform encloses the internally covered space and the perimeter is formally defined, but the structure is indifferent to exterior space. It tends to turn its back on the physical context and creates its own milieu by embracing a very large room without specific reference to human scale. In such examples the form generator is often the high-speed road network.

Maki calls his third formal type of linkage space "group form." This is the result of incremental accumulation of elements in space along an armature and is particularly typical of the spatial organization of many historic towns. In group form linkage is neither implied nor imposed but is naturally evolved as an integral part of the organic, generative structure. Group form is further char-

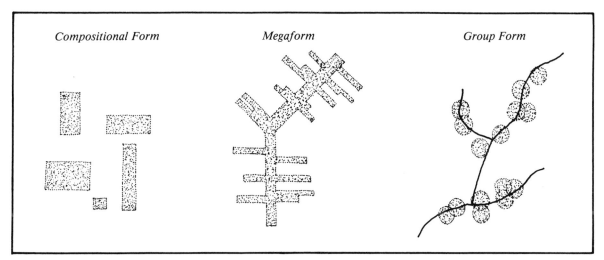

Compositional Form   *Megaform*   *Group Form*

Figure 4-14. Fumihiko Maki. Three Types of Spatial Linkage.
(1) Compositional form: individual buildings are composed on a two-dimensional plane. In this type of urban form, spatial linkage is implied rather than overt and is typical of Functionalist planning methods. (See chapter 2.)
(2) Mega form: structures are connected to a linear framework in a hierarchical, open-ended system where linkage is physically imposed. Experiments in megaform were especially popular in the 1950s and 1960s.
(3) Group form: group form results from an incremental accumulation of structures along an armature of communal open space, and linkage is naturally and organically evolved. Historic towns and villages have tended to develop in this pattern.

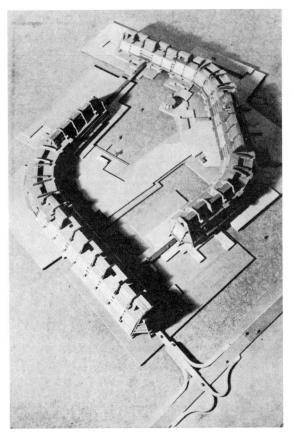

Figure 4-15. Kenzo Tange and Noriaki Kurokawa. Plan for a New Community. Cambridge, Massachusetts. M.I.T. 1960s.
Tange and other architects of the 1960s attempted to redress the problems of the modern city by looking at the possibilities offered by megastructures. Although important as studies in the potential of linear structures to create efficient linkages, these experiments generally lacked a concern for well-shaped, useful exterior open space. (From Maki, Investigations in Collective Form. *Courtesy: School of Architecture, Washington University, St. Louis, Missouri)*

acterized by a consistency of materials, a wise, often dramatic response to topography, deference to human scale, and by sequences of spaces defined by buildings, walls, gateways, and spires. Maki illustrates group form with images of the Greek village and the linear Japanese agrarian village (fig. 4-16), where the two-story streetfront forms a tight, continuous village facade that links

the individual house to the larger fabric of houses and connects private family life to the public life of the community. In this type of organization the house generates village form, the village generates house form, and individual buildings can be added or subtracted without changing the basic structure. In group form urban spaces are derived from the interior, and the rural space outside imposes limitations and conditions that define the place of the community within the landscape. The structure of the settlement responds to a necessary quid pro quo between factors of the internal and external site.

In all three formal types, Maki stresses linkage as the controlling idea for ordering buildings and spaces in design. From Maki we learn that there are several methods of organizing coherent spatial relationships under the linkage theory of urban design. What emerges from his important work is that the composition of public space is established as a totality before either individual spaces or buildings are planned.

Linkage theory was highly popular in the design thinking of the 1960s. A leading figure in exploration of structures generated by linkage was Kenzo Tange. His New Community, designed at MIT (see fig. 4-15), and his plan for Expo '70 are studies in futuristic forms connected by circulation systems. At Expo '70 (fig. 4-17) networks of pathways linked experimental structures at various levels. The scheme for horizontal linkages between high-rise elements, developed by the Regional Plan Association and published in *Urban Design Manhattan*, is another example of this theory and is a fascinating concept, but points out the problem of containing exterior space (fig. 4-18). The work of Candilis, Josic, and Woods at Toulouse-le-Mirail (see fig. 3-34) is also designed around branching circulation patterns, at the ex-

Figure 4-16. Facing page: *Japanese Village Street.*
In the group form of the traditional agrarian village, street is the armature that unifies the community. Individual buildings can be added or subtracted without injury to the basic organization. (Courtesy: © RETORIA/Y. Futagawa and Associated Photographers)

Figure 4-17. Kenzo Tange. Expo 70. Osaka, Japan. 1970.
At Expo '70 Tange created a complex of linked, futuristic structures connected at various levels by an extensive circulation system.

pense of exterior and interior space. A further illustration of the highly experimental and conceptual aspect of linkage theory is Peter Cook's Plug-in City of 1964 (fig. 4-19). A latticelike framework of intersecting tubes for service, supply systems, and escalators provides an interconnected structure. Prefabricated units could be plugged into the structure interchangeably, while horizontal traffic systems ran through the community at various levels. In all these projects linkage forms a nonspatial configuration organized around horizontal and vertical circulation.

Such proposals stress utopian ideals for community regeneration but do not address the need for traditional urban spaces formed by solids and voids. In these experiments, proposing linked megastructures, the environment becomes a diagram of movement systems. A fascination with the machine aesthetic and high technology dominates the search for spatial opportunities.

The study of circulation and connection, however, is extremely important to the understanding of urban structure. One of the best-known applications of this type of linkage theory to the large-scale environment was Ed Bacon's guidance of the revival of Philadelphia (fig. 4-20). The attempt was to use citywide connections as a tool for restoring urban coherence and guiding new development in desired directions. Such planning can also be a powerful means of stimulating new investment.

*Figure 4-18. Regional Plan
Association. The Three-
dimensional Grid. 1969.
Linkage dominated planning
theory during the 1960s. In
this scheme horizontal connections between vertical
structures are effectively created, but there is no system
of contained exterior space.
(Courtesy: Regional Plan
Association, Inc.)*

*Figure 4-19. Peter Cook.
Scheme for the "Plug-in"
City. 1964.
Peter Cook's fascination
with the idea of the city of
interchangeable parts linked
by transportation systems
was the ultimate expression
of megastructure theory. His
proposal for an infinitely
extendable city based on a
vertical latticelike framework of escalators, supply
systems, and service tubes
connected by transportation
corridors at various levels is
an important investigation
of the three-dimensional
grid. On the other hand,
such futuristic concepts denied the traditional social
function of urban space as
well as the importance of
the exterior landscape.
(Courtesy: © Peter Cook)*

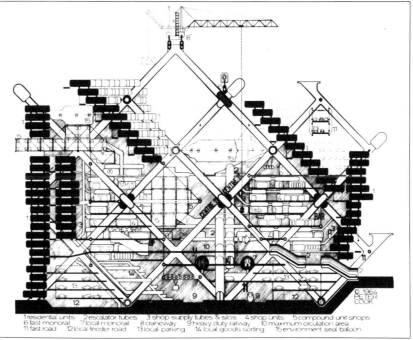

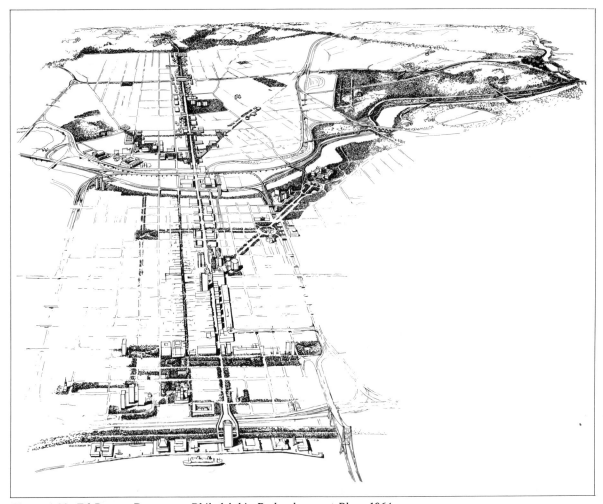

Figure 4-20. Ed Bacon. Downtown Philadelphia Redevelopment Plan. 1964.
One of the major contributions of the linkage theory has been in the area of large-scale urban planning. Ed Bacon, planner in charge of the redevelopment of Philadelphia for over twenty years, emphasized the need for strong spatial corridors to connect important buildings and public spaces. Such systems for connection should be incorporated into urban design in order to clarify the total structure. (From Bacon, Design of Cities. *Drawing: Irving Wasserman)*

The case studies of Boston, Washington, Göteborg, and Byker in chapter 5 will show how important large-scale linkage systems are in creating a comprehensible urban form.

PLACE THEORY

Place theory represents the third category of ur-

ban-design theories. The essence of place theory in spatial design lies in understanding the cultural and human characteristics of physical space. If in abstract, physical terms, *space* is a bounded or purposeful void with the potential of physically linking things, it only becomes *place* when it is given a contextual meaning derived from cultural or regional content.

While types of space can be defined by cate-

Figure 4-21. John Wood the Younger. The Circus and Royal Crescent in Bath, England. 1764 and 1769. Plan.
The effectiveness of the curved crescents of Bath does not stem merely from geometric clarity. As special "places" they gain meaning as responses to the environment they evolved within, encompass, and have helped form. The primary spatial design moves include the Circus (enclosed circle at the center of the plan), the Royal Crescent (open elliptical arc to the left), and the Landsdowne Crescent (serpentine wall at the upper left).

gories or typologies based on physical properties, each place is unique, taking on the character or *Stimmung* of its surroundings. This character consists both of "concrete things having material substance, shape, texture and color"[56] and of more intangible cultural associations, a certain patina given by human use over time. The curved wall of the Circus and Royal Crescent in Bath, for example, is not merely a physical object in space but also has a unique presence expressing the environ-ment it grew out of, encompasses, and exists within (fig. 4-21).

People require a relatively stable system of places in which to develop themselves, their social lives, and their culture. These needs give manmade space an emotional content—a presence that is more than physical. The boundary, or definite edge, is important to this presence. As Martin Hei-degger says, "a boundary is not that at which something stops, but as the Greeks recognized, the boundary is that from which something begins its presencing.''[57]

Architecture and landscape architecture must respond to and, if possible, enhance environmental identity and the sense of place. The essence of Norberg-Schulz's influential *Genius Loci* is contained in the following statement:

A place is a space which has a distinct character. Since ancient times the genius loci, or spirit of place, has been recognized as the concrete reality man has to face and come to terms with in his daily life. Architecture means to visualize the genius loci and the task of the architect is to create meaningful places where he helps man to dwell.[58]

The role of the urban designer, then, is not merely to manipulate form to make space but to create place through a synthesis of the components of the total environment, including the social. The goal should be to discover the best fit between the physical and cultural context and the needs and aspirations of contemporary users. Often the most successful design of places stems from minimal interference in the social and physical setting instead of radical transformation. This ''ecological approach'' to design (a term popularized by Ian McHarg in *Design With Nature*) aims at discovering and working with the intrinsic qualities of a given locale and is diametrically opposed to the internationalism advocated in the early Modern Movement.

Later offshoots of Modernism (as discussed in chapter 2) began to move toward a more contextual approach, at least in concept. In the 1950s, Team 10 promoted the idea of ''the house as a particular house in a particular place, part of an existing community that should try to extend the laws and disciplines of that community.''[59] During this period, Team 10 was preoccupied with the definition of urban place, a goal that they attempted to achieve in such forms as perimeter walls, pedestrian nets, and cluster blocks, as in the scheme of the English architectural couple Peter and Alison Smithson for the Haupstadt in Berlin (fig.

4-22). The intention was right, but the physical expression is questionable as a contextual response to existing urban conditions and the need for diversity at street level. The Berlin scheme, like some other Team 10 proposals, does not, in fact, fulfill Dutch architect Aldo Van Eyck's manifesto for the group: ''Whatever space and time mean, place and occasion mean more. For space in the image of man is place; articulate the in-between . . . . Space experience, I repeat, is the reward of place experience.''[60]

For designers to create truly unique contextual places, they must more than superficially explore the local history, the feelings and needs of the populace, the traditions of craftsmanship and indigenous materials, and the political and economic realities of the community. All designers are fallible, but to the best of their ability they should first determine what the configuration ''wants to be'' (Kahn)[61] within the existing setting and in deference to human requirements. The Dutch architect Herman Herzberger, one of Europe's leading ''contextual'' designers, puts it this way: ''Designing is nothing more than finding out what the person and object want to be: form then makes itself. There is really no need for invention—you must just listen carefully.''[62]

Clearly, with these ideas in mind, most recent city development, new towns, and suburbs are environments that have failed to create a concept of place that responds to the social, cultural, or physical environment. Symbols and fragments of the past are missing; the continuity of time, with successive layers intact, is lacking. In new developments of the 1960s even basic constraints of site were often ignored. Real-estate economics and technological experiments became driving forces of urban and suburban development.

One of the problems, both in urban renewal and new-town development, is that designers have felt compelled to complete every detail of a project, without leaving loose ends for transformation either by the individual or to accommodate needs that change with time. Especially in new towns this has been a major dilemma, as they have often been completed absolutes that do not allow user manipulation. Inhabitants have not had the opportunity to bring along their old patterns and styles of living or to modify their new homes in ways that allow them to feel the comfort of familiarity and continuity with their previous lives. Individuals must exercise some control over their environments. There was too much planning, too much zoning, and not enough humane inquiry into the regional and social context. Peter Smithson, the English architect and member of Team 10, writes:

> Let no one pretend that quality of place will arise from zoning or master planning by themselves. Part of the presence of any good place is the feeling we have of it embodying and being surrounded by a field of its own sort of space with its special limits and potentials. It is this field that we have previously said is only interesting today if it implies connection: roads with buildings, buildings with buildings, with trees, with the seasons, with decorations, with events, with other people in other times.[63]

Kevin Lynch, planner and author of several significant books on place theory, further develops this idea:

> Just as each locality should seem continuous with the recent past, so it should seem continuous with the near future. Every place should be made to be seen as developing, charged with predictions and intentions. The concepts of space and time appear and develop together in childhood, and the two ideas have many analogies in their formation and character. . . . space and time, however conceived, are the great framework within which we order our experience. We live in time places.[64]

The crucial question becomes: How do we as designers respond to time and place, when overdesigning and too much planning are almost as dangerous as allowing the marketplace to shape cities in a random, ad hoc fashion? We have dis-

Figure 4-22. Peter and Alison Smithson. Scheme for the Haupstadt. Berlin. West Germany.
In recognition of the importance of the sense of place, members of Team 10 experimented with edge-defining perimeter walls and concepts of the "pedestrian net over the street net." Although the intention in this project was well meant, it is doubtful that the physical expression was an appropriate response to the existing context or the need for diversity at street level. (Courtesy: Alison and Peter Smithson. Drawing by P. Sigmund)

cussed the dangers of underdesign, of what happens in the modern city when all is left to individual developers. At the same time we have discussed the issue of overdesigning—too much zoning, too much planning—which denies historic continuity and inhibits future change. Our cities must of necessity be historically and physically fluid and mobile; we cannot lose that flexibility as we impose our designs. The critical issue of this book, even beyond that of dealing with our contemporary urban space, is how designers, architects, and landscape architects should perceive their roles. Perhaps the most destructive aspect of the Modern Movement and of recent trends in planning has been the self-aggrandisement of designers and a tendency to make simplistic assumptions about human needs. The humility to look at the historical context, to respond to the self-perceived desires of the community, and the flexibility to allow the community, present and future, to alter its own environment, are perhaps what contemporary design needs most pressingly.

By way of illustration, the examples to follow are of recent urban designs that have attempted to respond to historic context, human needs, and the essential qualities of place. Naturally, the questions of spatial definition; of establishing or maintaining nodes, paths, landmarks, edges; of connecting and defining districts, monuments, and the primary elements that give imageability to a city are crucial physical tools. However, in the instances that follow, successful spatial design has been achieved without creating buildings in isolation, but by taking into consideration how new and old buildings and spaces fit together into the established urban context.

If place theorists tend to agree on the values they are trying to express, their approaches have been remarkably varied. Ralph Erskine represents an attempt to respond to vernacular, organic systems; the new classicists look at formal devices to connect the new to the existing. French contextualists create nostalgic collages to emulate the evolution of the city. Kevin Lynch has studied the mental mapping process of individuals in the city, while Stanford Anderson has studied the ecology of the street. Gordon Cullen explores the experience of sequence through space, whereas Lucien Kroll allows clients to create their own designs. These represent some of the major approaches to place theory.

Erskine has perhaps become one of the best-known and most respected of the contextualists. His work has gained widespread fame in Europe for its response to local place—human and physical. He has probably built more projects than any other contextualist, designing housing communities, shopping complexes, and workplaces that stress, in their physical form, the human meaning of place and the history of the site. His designs blend proposed and existing structures in an informal organic arrangement that seems to grow out of the local and regional vernacular. His strong, villagelike spaces immediately assume an aura of inevitability, as if they had always been there (Västervik, fig. 4-23). Chapter 5 contains a detailed case study of his community at Byker, Newcastle, perhaps the most outstanding example of Erskine's contextual urban design.

In contrast to Erskine's concern for organic order, one of the responses to the issue of contextual design has been a revival of classical compositional devices that include the use of symmetry, perspective, and other formal interventions. The drawings for Helsingborg's Konserthus Square by Sven Markelius in 1926 (fig. 4-24) and Francesco di Giorgio's image of an ideal piazza of the 1500s (fig. 4-25) illustrate the idea of using classical principles to organize disparate elements around an idealized exterior space. In contrast to the design of space by Erskine, which is entirely circumstantial, these examples illustrate the power of *idealized* urban space.

Similarly, the recent work of Leon Krier shows that an urban design of idealized public spaces will mediate between radically different styles of architecture if there is sufficient strength and clarity of layout. Krier's new classicism is not only inclusive and multivalent but also highly ordered (and often symmetrical), providing coherence and unity to the variables he intends to structure. He makes the sharp distinction between the values inherent in what he terms the "classical society" versus those inherent to the industrialized society. To the classical, Krier assigns the values of permanence and structure, wherein describing the industrialized world he derisively points to the evolving qualities of the trivial and abstract. "Classical," Krier says, "means the best of its kind. Not of any specific period, but simply the best possible, most perfect, most beautiful form of any given structure."[65] Krier's mission is to reconstruct the traditional urban block as the definer of streets and squares. In two of Krier's reconstruction schemes, one at Echternach (see fig. 2-14), the other in Lux-

Figure 4-23. Ralph Erskine. Västervik, Sweden. Sketch for the Revitalization of the City Core. 1971.
Erskine has become one of the most widely respected of contextual designers. His proposal for the revitalization of this Swedish town on the Baltic Sea reveals a sensitivity to vernacular architecture, organic spatial structure, and the natural setting. (Courtesy: Ralph Erskine)

Figure 4-24. Sven Markelius. Konserthus Square. Helsingborg, Sweden. 1926.
One of the responses to the issue of contextual design has been the revival of classical compositional devices, including the use of symmetry, perspective, and axes. As in Markelius's fine example of Nordic classicism in Helsingborg, an "idealized" structure is created to give coherence to diverse elements at its edges. (Courtesy: Chalmers School of Architecture)

embourg (fig. 4-26), he attempts to give cohesiveness to the city through a formal, multidirectional, horizontal pattern of spaces. Public space becomes a positive entity relating new and old, high and low, stone and glass, black and white.

The complex linking [of urban spaces] provides an accommodation of the conflicting public and private domains, offering a place for the unpredictable and a location for intermediate transitions. . . . an architecture advocating the city of contextualism.[66]

Figure 4-25. Francesco di Giorgio. Image of an Ideal Piazza. 1500s.
Di Giorgio's ideal piazza is composed of several classical elements: four freestanding columns, a small ornamental
fountain, and an arch that reinforces the central axis. The symmetrical design of these elements along with a very
simple retaining wall and clear paving pattern are powerful enough to unify the diversity of the buildings around it.
(Courtesy: Walters Art Gallery, Baltimore)

Another European movement that has reacted against the anticontextual approach of the Functionalists is the French contextualism of the Laboratory of Urban Form in Paris, (TAU Group, fig. 4-27), established by, among others, Antoine Grumbach, Alain Demangeon, Bruno Fortier, Dominique Deshouliéres, and Hubert Jeanneau. Their work reflects a disenchantment with the modern large-scale development of France. They express a nostalgia for the traditional city, refusing to accept the antiurban ideology of recent years and seek to revive traces of the lost city. Preoccupied with developing and transforming the neoclassical image, their search is for a more meaningful urban continuity by exploring monumentality as an armature to reconnect the parts of the city. Their approach to contextual design is not to look at specific typologies of buildings but at typologies of open space that make up environmental form. Within the urban fabric, they deliberately introduce contrasting elements—angular buildings and spaces that penetrate the existing spatial geometry. The result is a stratified and sedimentary collage of urban form in which proposed elements seem to have an accidental relationship to existing ones. In this way, place is established by simulating urban growth over time.

Looking at the city in parts, the French contextualists see it as a complex system of confrontations between forms and spaces that are juxtaposed—confrontations that enrich the meanings of each constituent district.[67] These French urban designers talk a lot about the city as a theater of memory, with the idea of nostalgia and accumulation as the sources for the perfect design. Consequently, their drawings show an incredible depth in superimposing disparate geometries and resolving contradictory spatial patterns. The points of juncture between geometries serve as "shock absorbers" between dissimilar adjacent patterns that add to the richness of their designs. Their image of the city, as fragmentary and evolutionary, is a critique of the fixed rationality of large French developments of the Modern Movement.

Kevin Lynch, like the French contextualists, also looked at the city in parts in an attempt to define a theory of place. In his work *Image of the City,* which was instrumental in redirecting urban de-

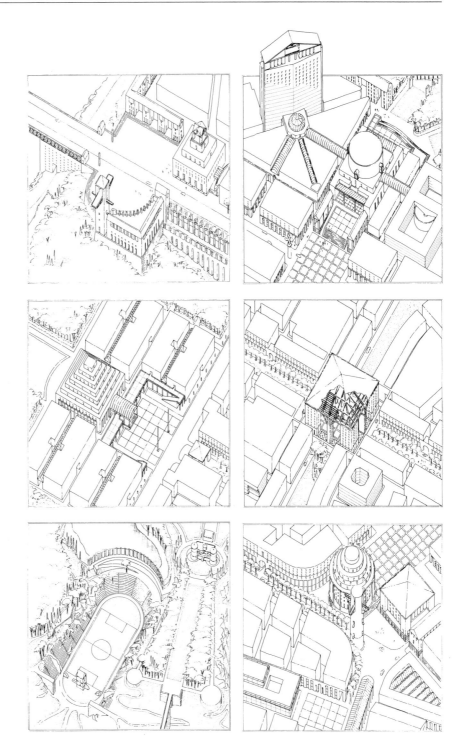

*Figure 4-26. Leon Krier.
Proposals for the Recon-
struction of Luxembourg.
1978.*
*A leading exponent of con-
textual design, Leon Krier
has looked intently at classical spatial structures to de-
rive principles for linking
old and new, high and low,
and diverse materials,
colors, and textures. His
plans are based on values of
permanence and frequently
incorporate strongly defined
geometric spaces as ordering
devices. (Courtesy: Leon
Krier)*

Figure 4-27. TAU Group. Rochefort, France. Plan. 1977.
In contrast to the rationalism of such New Classicists as Krier, the French Contextualists look with nostalgia at the organic disorder of the evolved city. They see the city as a "theater of memory"—fragmentary and evolutionary in nature—and attempt to recreate the apparently accidental confrontations of conflicting geometries in their plans. (Drawing: TAU Group)

sign theory in the early sixties, Lynch presents his principal rules for designing city spaces: (1) *legibility:* the mental picture of the city held by the users on the street; (2) *structure and identity:* the recognizable, coherent pattern of urban blocks, buildings, and spaces; (3) *imageability:* user perception in motion and how people experience the spaces of the city. Lynch said that successful urban spaces were those that met these requirements, and that the parts of the city, which he termed "elements of urban form," should be designed around these requirements. His five elements of city form were paths, edges, districts, nodes, and landmarks (fig. 4-28). According to Lynch, every city can be broken down into these five parts and its spatial structure analyzed and used as a basis for design.

Hans Hollein's drawings for the Municipal Museum in Mönchengladbach (1972–80) are yet another illustration of the power exterior space can have in conceptually welding new and old architecture and creating a sense of place (fig. 4-29). By representing the broader relationship in his design—adjacent neighborhoods, open space, and roads—Hollein graphically illustrates the hierarchy of existing conditions to which his design responds. The emphasis he places on contextual elements is the driving force for the form of this project, which succeeds in being both modern and sensitive to the historic fabric it restructures. This approach gives him the opportunity to create a contemporary interior for a museum without leaving a spatial vacuum in the public realm as a byproduct. Hollein believes that urban architecture should be understood at various levels, from "small shops and coffeepots" to the "whole city where illusion and reality come into play."[68] In other words, a design should work for the man on the street as well as for those who wish to penetrate its deeper meaning.

Contextual space as sequentially complex and villagelike is effectively illustrated by townscape artist Gordon Cullen, who used drawings to capture the sensation of movement through space. In addition to the perception of place and the image of space, he implicitly addresses the psychic content of the exterior city, the relationship between

Figure 4-28. Kevin Lynch. Diagrams of the Spatial Elements of the City.
Lynch looked at the city as a system that contains a set of organizing structures of psychological significance to its inhabitants. He recognized that each individual forms a "mental map" of his or her environment, in which paths, edges, districts, nodes, and landmarks provide the important reminders of physical and psychological orientation. (Drawings based on diagrams by Kevin Lynch)

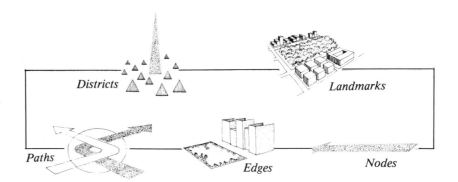

Figure 4-29. Hans Hollein. Municipal Museum. Monchengladbach, Germany. 1972–1980.
Hollein's Municipal Museum is at once modern and responsive to the historic and physical context it restructures. (Drawing: Hans Hollein)

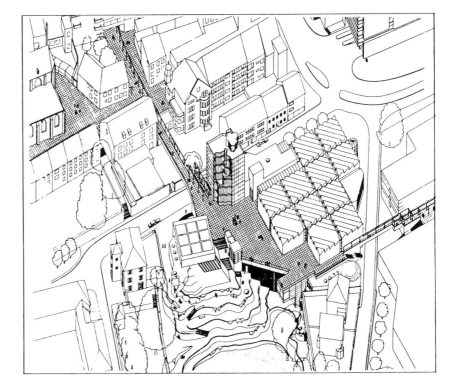

object and movement, as well as the event of arriving at or leaving city rooms. His drawings (fig. 4-30) explore the fluidity of sequence through space with an artistic flair for the picturesque. Cullen brings two-dimensional plans to life—"like nudging a man who is going to sleep in church"[69]— by sketching perspective sequences that illuminate contrasts and transitions, emphasizing the powerful effect of the third dimension. At eye level, even the slightest deviation, projec-tion, or setback in the alignment of the plan is expressed. Cullen's images of rural and urban environments strive to define place and context as well as to provide commentary and analysis of design.

Another approach to the understanding of context is the work of Donald Appleyard in the residential streets of San Francisco. In *Liveable Streets Project*[70] he explores the physical and social complexities of street space and developed an ecology

Figure 4-30. Gordon Cullen. Perspective Sequence of Townscapes.
Gordon Cullen's graphic illustrations of the experience of moving through urban spaces capture the unique sense of place from street level. His works are a powerful demonstration of the need to understand and graphically analyze the individual character and sequence of public spaces in the built environment.
(Drawings: Gordon Cullen from Townscape. *Courtesy Van Nostrand Reinhold Company)*

of street life that assesses the impact of traffic on indoor life and on activity relationships within the household (fig. 4-31). He further documented how people modify their environment as a defense against traffic and their efforts to control traffic itself. Appleyard's studies are critical to our understanding of the street in context as a spatial entity for mixed use and social discourse, beyond its function for vehicular movement and storage. Street frontage is the delicate foil between the interlocked public and private lives of urban space.

What has to emerge from the current wave of contextualism is a form of city space that combats the inhospitality of the no-man's land by providing people with an environmental structure rich enough to accommodate everyone. In restructuring lost space we must, in the words of Dutch architect Herman Hertzberger,

> contribute to an environment which gives people more chances to impress it with their own individual characteristics . . . enabling it to be taken over by each person as an essentially familiar place. . . . In this way, form and user interpret and adapt to each other, each enhancing the other in a process of mutual submission.[71]

Hertzberger applied his critique of self-contained single-purpose environments to the design of several important European building projects (such as the Centraal Beheer in Apeldoorn and the Theater for the Arts in Delft), which are commentaries on the city as a whole and accommodate diverse social patterns in overlapping and interpenetrating spaces—spaces that he intentionally left unfinished in order to invite occupants to fit the environment to themselves.

Lucien Kroll takes the commitment to social architecture one step further in his student housing complex at the Catholic University of Louvain Medical School in Brusssels in 1970, where occupants take an even more active role in structuring space according to how they want to live. Working directly with the architect, the user-clients manipulated a "kit-of-parts" inside the building and on the exterior (fig. 4-32) and combined materials—bricks, cement blocks, asbestos tiles—as an ad hoc expression of the history of the city and the complexities of its residents. What Kroll says about this building is applicable to urban design in general:

> Fortunately we wanted to see these spaces turned neither into a work of art nor an intellectual achievement, but a living process, an open-ended dynamic activity in which each genera-

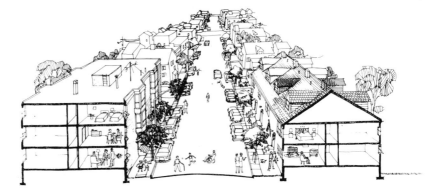

Figure 4-31. Donald Appleyard. The Ecology of the Liveable Street. Berkeley, California. 1981.
From a social-behavioral point of view, Appleyard analyzes the street as an ecological system. His studies have made an important contribution to the understanding of the street as an environment for social and personal existence as well as for vehicular movement and storage. (Drawing: Donald Appleyard)

BEFORE TRAFFIC IMPACTS

Pleasant, Quiet Rooms
Adjacent to Street
Adequate Parking
Sidewalks Safe for Play
Emission-free Air

No Noise, Vibrations
Safe Environment for the Elderly, Handicapped
Clean Streets
Many Outdoor Activities Like Gardening
Conversation with Neighbors

tion adds a new meaning and enriches it with its contradictions.[72]

We have seen that contextual space is inclusive and multivalent, incorporating fragments of past artifacts, associations, and events in a rich, layered blend. Cultural symbols, replicated or reflected in modern forms, are important in making these urban spaces fit into context, as are the physical connections to the surrounding site or buildings. We have also suggested that an evolved, indigenous urban form is more satisfying than complete order imposed from outside. The former generally suggests a more fluid, villagelike space (Maki's group form) in which disparate elements are connected and into which new pieces can be fit as the place changes over time. Classical formalism, however, is not precluded as a frame for the changeable parts and can provide an armature for various hierarchies of idealized public and private space as well as for the redesign of lost space. We have also seen that regionalism and contextualism have a lot to do with livability—with the resident's sense of identification with and control of personal space. In approaching design contextually, we find that we already have an enormous re-

source upon which to base a new kind of pluralistic design for the Postmodern city. These kinds of approaches are necessary if we are to restore and revive context and place as design considerations.

In conclusion, we have examined three theories of urban spatial design: the figure-ground theory, the linkage theory, and the place theory. A common problem has been that designers have become obsessed with one of these theories, setting aside the other two in their urban-design pursuits. This is an inadequate approach, as the living city consists of a layering of elements in each theory. For instance, if an urban complex is designed around the linkage theory alone, it falls short because the product becomes nonspatial and therefore nonexperiential. If the place theory is applied without regard to linkage and figure-ground, important connections outside the design area and new spatial opportunities within may be lost. Conversely, if the figure-ground theory is exclusively used, the results often become totally spatial and possibly unrealistic in terms of user needs and implementation. The key, therefore, is to apply these theories appropriately and collectively to each urban-design project.

Figure 4-32. Lucien Kroll. Catholic University of Louvain, Medical School. Belgium.
Yet another response to the awareness that designers must address issues of place and user needs is reflected in the work of Lucien Kroll. At the Catholic University of Louvain, the architect acted as a structural advisor to the student-clients, who manipulated a "kit of parts" to create individual spaces within the building and an eclectic collage of forms and materials on the exterior. (Courtesy: Lucien Kroll)

CHAPTER

5

CASE STUDIES

INTRODUCTION

We will now turn our attention to four urban case studies as laboratories for illustrating the spatial-design theories outlined in the preceding chapters. We have chosen two American prototypes: Boston, Massachusetts, and Washington, D.C.; and two European: Göteborg, Sweden, and Byker, Newcastle, England. These four case studies were selected to elaborate on the application of urban-design theories at various scales. For instance, the figure-ground theory is best illustrated in the Boston and Göteborg examples because of their tight building-to-space patterns, whereas the linkage theory is best illustrated in Washington, D.C., with its many axial relationships. Byker represents the best example of the place theory of design with a successful process for reconstructing an urban district for existing residents while maintaining valued neighborhood traditions. There are also significant similarities and differences between the growth and evolution of these urban plans throughout the city and in districts and individual spaces within districts. Comparisons among the case studies of the designer's role in shaping the urban landscape can also be readily observed. In all of them, however, figure-ground, linkage, and

place theories need to be applied together to support the structure and respond to the unique historic context.

Three of the four examples are comparable in size, containing 500,000–800,000 people; however, the fourth example, Byker, represents a slightly different case study of a self-contained district of 10,000 people within a larger urban area.

In the case studies we can explore several types of urban geometries: the regularized grid forming rectangular blocks and streets at right angles; the sweeping diagonal boulevards radiating from centralized nodes; and the irregular organic pattern of streets and buildings that are arranged according to local site conditions. In Washington (fig. 5-1) the grid of local streets is overlaid by a system of broad diagonal thoroughfares that were intended, in Pierre L'Enfant's historic plan, visually and functionally to connect monuments or high points of the planned city. These straight thoroughfares were meant for grand governmental processions through the city, defining a very different type of urban space than the narrow, crooked carriageways of Boston. Washington, in contrast to Boston and Göteborg, was designed as a holistic master plan conceived in its entirety by one man at one point in history. Although the present form

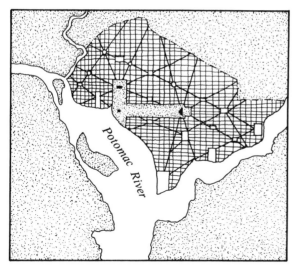

Figure 5-1. Washington, D.C. Sketch Plan.
The layout of Washington was based on a grand master plan linking strategically placed monuments on high points. The current problems in its urban form often result from a lack of density and consistency along the street, especially at the intersections between the regular grid of streets and the diagonal boulevards.

Figure 5-2. Boston, Massachusetts. Sketch Plan.
There was never a master plan for Boston, which developed incrementally in response to landfill and waves of ethnic immigration. The form is organic, with strongly defined neighborhoods. Problems of linkage between these districts and to the waterfront are the major design issues.

of Washington developed over a hundred years, its skeleton was laid out at once with a stroke of L'Enfant's pen. L'Enfant never thought in terms of districts but of the city as a whole.

In Boston, however, the city grew incrementally as a series of separate districts without ever having a grand master plan to guide its evolution. Boston's city form (fig. 5-2) followed the filling and dredging of the numerous coastal islands, peninsulas, and marshlands, creating the ground upon which the city now sits. Consequently its form is organic, the crooked street alignments determined by geologic and topographic landscape conditions.

In Göteborg we witness a combination of incremental growth by accretion and the one-shot master-plan approach. Here, according to King Gustav's specification, the engineers built the infrastructure of the central core and surrounding fortifications, but the city's pattern of outward growth beyond the walls (fig. 5-3) resulted from several design-competition plans. The engineer's rational grid of streets and canals on the lowland

site for the city center was modified, as the city grew, by the addition of formal boulevards and informal curvilinear streets following the contours of the more hilly terrain. In a matter of 300 years Göteborg was transformed from a closed, walled-in city to an open metropolis, whereas Washington was open-ended from the very beginning. Considering the process of urban growth, Boston is different from both Göteborg and Washington, as it was always a city comprised of separate physical neighborhoods that emerged one by one as each new group of immigrants set foot on North American soil. The physical composition of these urban enclaves can be clearly seen by looking at a current road map of Boston.

Having developed an understanding of the differences in city plans of our prototypes, we can explore various means of redesigning urban spaces within them to achieve enclosure, continuity, place, and linkage. For instance, the urban spaces in Washington do not support the very strong pat-

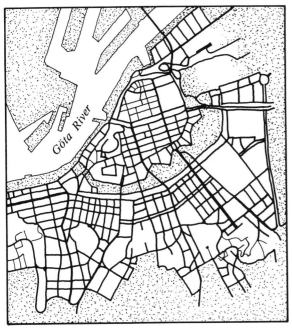

Figure 5-3. Göteborg, Sweden. Sketch Plan.
The core of Göteborg is a planned city, but districts have evolved around this center. Major problems occur at the junctions between the outlying districts and the core, as well as along the waterfront.

tern of streets designed by L'Enfant. Gaps are readily apparent, especially at points where the grid of local streets meets the broad diagonal thoroughfares. Here large amorphous zones of lost space cause breaks in the continuity of city form. These areas are visually confusing and unpleasant for pedestrians, and there is no sense of spatial enclosure or identity. The system of grand parks, formal circles, and boulevards needs reclarification through rules describing how new buildings should be sited to fill in these amorphous zones and how the open space system should be restored as an important urban amenity.

In Boston and Göteborg the urban spaces within districts are consistent, but linkage problems exist between them. This problem is more severe in Göteborg than in Boston, as the ring road forms a continuous surface barrier surrounding the core and blocking important pedestrian entry and destination points. These critical points (five in all) need restructuring in order to weave back together

the spatial form of Göteborg. In Boston the central artery severs the waterfront but is elevated, allowing pedestrians to flow underneath. They still have to cross surface streets, however, and the visual and auditory experience is far from desirable. Within the older urban districts of Göteborg, urban spaces are well defined and continuous, punctuated by many important historic buildings and landmarks. Site coverage is great and the pattern of spaces and buildings compact.

As in Washington, D.C., the building heights in Göteborg are consistently 80 to 100 feet. But in Boston the high-rise has intruded and has had a major negative impact. On the verge of completely losing its historic form, Boston's streetscape is the recipient of a new kind of tall building that promises to change the character of the city. The point-block tower does not treat the edge of its site with due respect to neighboring buildings, nor does it define positive urban space. Along Boston's waterfront, individual buildings are placed, with wide spaces in between, without establishing frontage to define open space. Important connections to and along the harborfront are not made and the whole spatial structure of the area falls apart.

Important distinctions of use and theme also occur between the case-study prototypes. As we have seen, use and theme have a direct bearing on the redesign of urban space. The Washington Plan of 1791 was always intended to symbolically unite the monumental city of federal government and the localized city of everyday life. Although this fusion has never quite been successfully achieved, it points the direction for future design intervention. Because of the extensive governmental bureaucracy, L'Enfant's Washington is a city "implemented by committee." Decision-making and planning in Washington, D.C., unlike Göteborg or Boston, often occur in a committee format. Strong ideas are sometimes compromised for reasons unrelated to design—the results of extended processes of design review. This is evident in most contemporary projects, such as the Pennsylvania Avenue debacles involving Western Plaza and Market Square, discussed later in this chapter.

While Washington's use and theme have not changed over time, Boston's have quite dramatically, from a major port tied to shipping and boat-building to a cosmopolitan city of universities, research-and-development industries, and big business. Boston's decision-making tactics have also changed from the public forum, reflective of the New England tradition of open debate, to one internalized—within the mayor's office. During the previous mayor's tenure of sixteen years, Boston's public-planning and urban-design function was all but eliminated. Decisions on future growth were made by the mayor himself, largely independent of professional input, making for a most difficult and complex process subject to private negotiating and subversion. The current administration, which has been functioning now for two years, is trying to open up the process once again. In contrast, urban design in Göteborg is easier, because the socialized Swedish bureaucracy stresses public expenditure, maintenance, and improvement for the good of all. Strict controls on private development are a regular part of daily professional practice.

In Byker the designer, Ralph Erskine, had the freedom to redesign totally an entire urban district for working-class people in Newcastle-Upon-Tyne (fig. 5-4). Instead of imposing a plan from the outside, the Byker plan grew incrementally from the inside, involving the local residents who were to be rehoused in the new neighborhood. In the process the designers retained important physical artifacts of the old environment—important streets, place names, landmarks, and social institutions, such as churches, schools, and pubs. By designing new spaces around these community cornerstones, a strong sense of place and historic continuity was achieved.

With this brief introduction, we can now proceed with a more detailed discussion of the urban-space question in each case study.

CASE STUDY 1: BOSTON, MASSACHUSETTS

Boston is probably America's most "European"

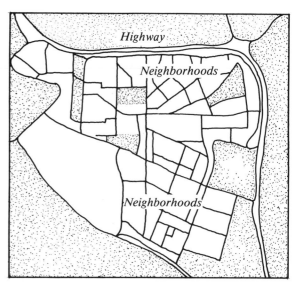

Figure 5-4. Byker, Newcastle, England. Sketch Plan. *At Byker issues of maintaining community identity and the sense of place were paramount. Erskine retained important fragments of the past and encouraged strong community participation in the development of the design.*

city. Certainly it has one of the longest histories of any in the country, dating back to the early 1600s. The image of Boston, or at least of "Old Boston," is one of crooked narrow streets and well-defined neighborhoods formed by an irregular arrangement of densely packed brick buildings (fig.5-5). Most North American cities founded in the late eighteenth century or early nineteenth century lack this tightly knit European character. Furthermore, Boston's street pattern predates the orthogonal grid that dominates so many American cities, which allowed them to succumb easily to automobile access, the skyscraper, the unarticulated plaza, and the surface parking lot.

Close to the sea, Boston has a setting of great physical and economic importance to its region. Much of the character it has acquired over the past 350 years has resulted from its role as a major port city of the East Coast. Within this maritime community the New England tradition of civic democracy and public debate governed growth and change. However, public participation in decisions about development has declined significantly over

Figure 5-5. Salem Street. North End, Boston. 1901.
Narrow, winding streets and compact, low-rise buildings give Boston a distinctively "European" character. Although many historic areas have been destroyed by urban-renewal and highway programs, in some well-defined neighborhoods this physical character has survived. In North End, the first American neighborhood for many European immigrants, the social fabric is changing as gentrification spreads through the area. (Photo: Copyright © 1978 Dennis Michael Brearley)

the last decade. The increased power of private interests has led to the imposition of the vertical city of corporate image on the traditional horizontal harbor city. As we have discussed, verticality in the form of skyscrapers without a transitional layer at street level tends to create large areas of lost space. In Boston this relatively recent development, predicted as a disaster some fifteen years ago by Lewis Mumford, one of America's leading urbanologists,[73] is especially destructive, clashing violently with the long, low profiles of so many of the great historic buildings such as the Quincy Markets, Mercantile Wharf, and the entire Back Bay. The traditional urban fabric has been further undermined by the widening and straightening of streets under urban renewal (fig.5-6). Straight boulevards with "streamlined-sixties" globe lighting emphasized traffic flow at the expense of the pedestrian.

Perhaps more than any other city in the country, Boston is a living museum of American urban history. It passed through every phase of the national tradition and has retained physical remnants of this tradition. There are grand historic pieces of

nineteenth-century urban space: the Public Garden, Beacon Hill, and Commonwealth Avenue. At the same time, smaller, more intimate areas evoke their own memories of the past.

The Lack of Connection between Districts

Although the richness of Boston owes much to its unplanned, incremental evolution, this has also created areas of confusion and neglect. Boston is a city of neighborhoods. The areas between these strongly defined districts are frequently confusing and chaotic, isolating one district from another. In many cases there are huge areas of underused land between neighborhoods. A figure-ground diagram (see fig. 5-18) shows strong patterns of urban space within the districts but weak links between them. The reinforcement of the links, however, must respect the tight, evolved form of historic neighborhoods and their unique sense of place.

As we have indicated, Boston's evolution differs significantly from the grandiose master plans that L'Enfant devised for Washington or Corbusier for Chandigarh. Because Boston grew incre-

Figure 5-6. Atlantic Avenue. Boston.
Under urban renewal, many traditional narrow streets (see fig. 5-5) were demolished to make way for wide roadways to provide for smoother traffic flow. Streamlined globe lighting and concrete sidewalks replaced the richer materials of Boston's traditional street furnishings.

mentally in response to environmental conditions (fig. 5-7), no one in 1640 knew what the land area or shape of the city would become. The result is a city of historic textures and well-defined neighborhoods but lacking a cohesive framework to tie its districts together. In particular, incremental growth has left Boston with areas of very dissimilar geometries—geometries that support successful enclaves but often do not interact well together. This can be seen as Boston's special attraction as well as its spatial dilemma.

On Boston's original Shawmut Peninsula, the focus of our study, the disparity of geometries and the separation between neighborhoods are a major problem. The most striking and significant of these is the separation between the downtown core and its principal resource and public amenity, the harborfront. The design problems of how to reconnect the core and the waterfront are the focus of this case study and are discussed later in this chapter.

Urban Renewal

Another factor influencing Boston's current situation has been the urban-renewal plans from the early sixties. Although the city's redevelopment projects were among the most impressive in the country, unusually farsighted in their quality of architectural design, they often ignored the vital factors of the shape of public squares and streets. A notable exception might be City Hall Plaza (see fig. 3-27). In general, however, as happened so often at the tail end of the Modern Movement, emphasis was on the detached building or complex of buildings. Because the form of the spaces around these projects was not given prior attention, they tend to be isolated in reconstructed but residual space. Boston has reason to be proud of the architectural quality of its new developments, but public space has often become a viewing platform for the new architecture.[74] This is especially true of the harborfront, where each addition

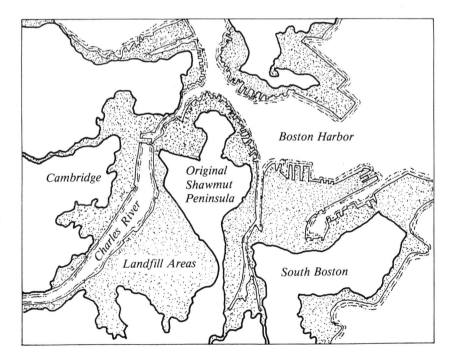

Figure 5-7. Diagram of Boston's Land-fill Sequences. Boston developed gradually through a series of extensive landfill operations. This has given richness to the neighborhoods, which have identifiable character and form, but has also created confusions in the areas between districts and the lack of an overall clarity to the urban plan.

Figure 5-8. Urban Renewal of Boston Harborfront. 1982.
The historic open space context of Boston has been severely changed by renewal projects. Although buildings themselves were often of high quality, they rarely responded in their overall form and configuration to the existing spatial context or to one another, as this view of the harborfront reveals. (Photo: Linda J. Cook)

stands in isolation and a coherent context of open space is lacking (fig. 5-8). The designer's task is to undo the destruction to the finely textured, closely knit Old Boston, to try to recapture the positive aspects of a tradition that came close to being lost under urban renewal.

Figure 5-9. The Central Artery Under Construction. One of the greatest disasters for Boston's downtown core was the construction of the central artery and necessary feeder streets in the 1950s. Numerous buildings, both commercial and residential, were torn down to make way for an elevated highway that acts as an almost insurmountable barrier between the core and the harborfront. (From Benevolo, History of Modern Architecture. *Courtesy MIT Press)*

The Highway

Even before urban renewal, the elevated central artery had sounded the death knell to continuity between the city core and its harborfront. Sweeping close to the water, this wide expressway created a "Chinese Wall" of lost space, a linear barrier between downtown and the waterfront along its entire length. Bostonians still recall in disbelief the demolition of substantial buildings, businesses, and homes in the early 1950s to clear a path for what has come to be known as the Green Monster (no apparent reference to the left-field fence at Boston Red Sox Fenway Park, which has affectionately received the same label) (fig. 5-9). To make things worse, the highway does not even function efficiently: constantly congested,

inexpressibly repugnant, it is among the most unsafe roadways in the country. One of the major constraints in restructuring contemporary Boston is this wide barrier that fractures the physical connection between downtown and its harborfront.

Architectural Diversity

Another difficulty in designing for New Boston stems from the diversity of its architectural styles. Like the neighborhoods, architectural diversity is a mixed blessing. It contributes to the visual wealth of the city, reflecting the variety of its social groups and the length of its historic evolution. But it is also part of the problem, creating a staccato disjointedness (fig. 5-10), especially in the core as the city struggles to retain its historic fabric while encouraging new development. Since most current projects are to occur within the relatively limited area of the Central Business District, their impact on its skyline and streetscape will be enormous. Decisions about building height and mass, site coverage, material, style of facade, and programmed activities on the streets and promenades will have a profound effect on the future of the city. Without a policy for unified public space, Boston will almost inevitably emerge as a Postmodern hodge-podge of styles and forms, each the individual expression of the architect or client. Unwittingly, the development will create discontinuous space and important opportunities for making connections will be lost. However, if the rules of public space can be established before individual buildings are erected, a sensible level of architectural diversity can contribute to the historic setting.

Unplanned Development

One of the major obstacles to the creation of a coherent set of rules for public spaces is that very little, if any, predevelopment planning has taken place in Boston since the Edward Logue era, discussed later. Apparently no one is concerned with an overview of the city core as a complete organism. The last formal master plan was prepared in 1965—twenty years ago! Consequently the city government has operated by ad hoc decisions, without reference to a unified plan or set of guidelines. Criteria for judging new proposals are limited to local "packaging" considerations, instead of the broader concern for how a particular development might affect the collective experience of the entire city. What Boston needs is a general policy for public space that can govern new development in the streets, squares, and parks of downtown. Perhaps the administration that took office in 1984 can promote a more urban-design-oriented approach under its public themes of "Downtown By Design" and "Harborpark" (see fig. 5-26). One can be certain that an overall plan is needed.

Figure 5-10. Recent Construction in the Central Business District.
Boston is already emerging as an architectural hodge-podge of various styles, periods, materials, and heights packed closely together. Without a policy for public space, this will become the pattern in the future. (Courtesy: Boston Society of Architects. Photo by Nanette Sexton)

The Harborfront

As suggested, Boston's major resource has historically been its harborfront, the important edge to its central core and the psychological and economic link to the outside world. Some of the most dramatic spaces of the city have been shaped by projecting waterfront piers, reinforced by such linear warehouses as Long, Commercial, Lewis, and Sargent wharves (fig. 5-11). The potential of these spaces has not been fully realized or ex-

Figure 5-11. Aerial View of the Boston Harborfront.
The essence of Boston has been its relationship to the sea, a relationship that has determined its historic importance, ruled its economic growth, and given it dramatic urban spaces along the waterfront piers. The opportunity to make full use of the harborfront has not yet been fully realized. (Courtesy: Boston Redevelopment Authority)

ploited. Unlike Washington, where L'Enfant's city was intended to nestle in the landscape of the fertile Potomac Valley, the essence of Boston has been its relationship to the ocean. Its urban form has developed as a response to its closeness to the water. From the days of clipper ships and the China trade to modern container shipping, the link to the sea has been vital to economic and industrial growth.

Harbor Evolution and the Deterioration of Downtown

It is worthwhile to look at the historic transformation of Boston's waterfront, since it illustrates the evolution experienced by many port cities of comparable size. The transition has typically been from shipping to industry to railway yards or highways, culminating recently in residential and recreational uses.

Over the past 350 years the evolution of Boston's harbor has been marked by an impressive land reclamation through fill and dredging (see fig. 5-7). Beginning in 1625 with one causeway be-tween Shawmut Peninsula and the mainland at Roxbury Neck, the massive land creation eventually gained 3,000 acres for the city. The history of this reclamation is still evident in the layout of the city. High-rise buildings, with the exception of the Hancock and Prudential towers, have been concentrated on the firm soils of old Shawmut Peninsula. The street layout of the peninsula continues to reflect the configurations seen in Samuel Clough's map of 1640 (fig. 5-12) as an organic system organized around the contours of the land but focused on the sea. This map shows that Great Cove had already been formed as a port facility, with High Street, now Washington Street, as the major crosstown connection.

By 1720, major piers were reaching out to world trade. Long Wharf, the principal pier, assumed political and economic dominance as a focus for maritime exchange and as the place where Americans said farewell to the British. With the North End on one side and the financial district on the other, the city began to wrap around the emerging port in the late 1700s and the Inner Harbor took

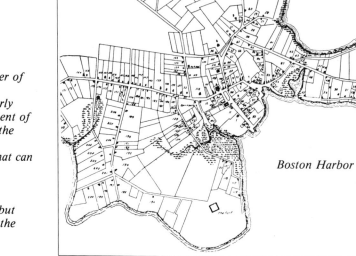

Figure 5-12. The Center of Boston in the 1640s. This map shows an early phase in the development of the street patterns on the original Shawmut Peninsula—patterns that can still be traced in contemporary Boston. Streets followed the contours of the land, but were closely linked to the sea. (Map by Samuel Clough)

Boston Harbor

on even greater importance as the determinant of public space (fig. 5-13). Virtually all streets and squares in the core had a vital, positive relationship to the harbor. The spaces created by the jutting piers and their connections to the land became major centers of public life. King Street, now State Street, provided an axis that pulled activities at Long Wharf up into the core.

By the end of the eighteenth century the harborfront as an urban edge was functionally and formally tied to the central core. The clarity and definition of public space were a fitting background to intensive human use and the shipping industry.

As international maritime trade grew, so did Boston. During the early to mid-1800s the city became a prosperous port of over forty wharves and twelve major shipyards. Along the harbor important urban spaces and fine architectural complexes

developed in response to the edge of the city (fig. 5-14). However, as the piers were extended into the harbor and the density of the mainland increased, two different forms of urban fabric began to emerge—the linear repetition of the wharves along the urban edge and an unrelated matrix of blocks in the core. By 1840, as historic maps reveal, a distinction between the form of the city and the form of the harbor buildings was appearing. In Bonner's map of 1722 the city form spilled out onto the piers; in Boynton's map of 1844 a ring road, Commercial Street, intercepts the city before it reaches the piers. The urban port experience of this era was apparently still intensive and continued to reflect its maritime origins.

Over subsequent years further construction occurred, including the completion of the landfill that forms the current base of the city, together with related improvements in transportation. Of

Figure 5-13. Boston in 1722. As Boston assumed increasing importance in maritime trade in the 1720s, major piers were extended into Great Cove. The most significant of these, Long Wharf, assumed political and economic dominance and was important in structuring the physical form of the harborfront. (Map by Captain John Bonner)

Figure 5-14. Boston Harbor. 1854.
During the early 1800s, Boston became a prosperous port of over forty wharves and twelve major shipyards. The fine architecture of the harborfront closely reflected the form of the wharves, creating a homogenous linear fabric along the water's edge. (Courtesy: The Bostonian Society Old State House)

all the roads constructed, Atlantic Avenue (fig. 5-15) has probably been most significant to the form of contemporary Boston. Bridging over sev-

eral piers, it establishes the current edge to the downtown district.

Other forces of change were at work during the

Figure 5-15. Atlantic Avenue Bridging over Great Cove. 1840.
By the 1840s, the wharves were no longer extensions of the city streets, but became separated from the core by collector streets such as Commercial Street. The close relationship of waterfront to the city was further cut off by the construction of Atlantic Avenue, which bridged over several piers and, after additional land filling, established the present edge of the downtown district. Two types of urban form began to emerge: the linear repetition of the piers and an unrelated matrix of blocks in the core. (Courtesy: Boston Redevelopment Authority)

tury, and areas such as the Back Bay are Victorian interpretations of traditional architectural styles in new materials.

At the turn of the century, furthermore, Boston experienced the same reaction to its dirt, density, and deterioration that affected other American and European cities. Suburbanization led to an exodus from the center, and expansion into the hinterlands in search of clean air and open space. The invention of the streetcar fostered this outward migration, and, in the 1940s and 1950s, the automobile escalated population dispersion at a geometric progression.

As the population spread outward, so did industry and jobs. An expansion of the highway system followed. The most disastrous manifestation of the road-building program was the previously mentioned elevated central artery of the 1950s, which separates the core from the harbor. As the population moved away from the center, Boston turned its back on the waterfront. The vital focus was gone. The area became a derelict wasteland of underused property. What had been the greatest port in the nation rotted into a crumbling ruin on the tip of Boston's peninsula. And with this loss of connection to the harbor, the central district of the city lost its sense of identity; if it had been ordered around the grid it could as well have been a Midwestern downtown.

At this point efforts to revitalize the core began. The Boston Redevelopment Authority was created and was given enormous funding, administrative responsibilities, and legal clout under the Federal Urban Renewal Program. The agency gathered a brilliant staff in acknowledgment of the enormous task ahead.

The Boston Redevelopment Authority

Prior to the election of Mayor John F. Collins in 1959, Boston's efforts at planning were weak and ineffective, isolated from the decisions made through collaboration between government agencies and private enterprise. As long as planning remained dormant, the city had continued on the

late nineteenth century, some the result of physical accident, others of social forces. In 1871, fire swept through a major portion of downtown Boston. The city began a major program of reconstruction, outlawing wooden buildings in reaction to the traumatic devastation of its center. Brick now seems the essence of Old Boston. In fact its pervasive use dates back only slightly over a cen-

physical and economic downslide characteristic of its post-World War II period.

In an effort to revise the trend toward decay and the dispersion of both business and population, the new mayor set out on a policy of major redevelopment and capital improvement. The mechanism was to be urban renewal. To coordinate and evolve the ambitious plan he sought out Edward J. Logue, then head of New Haven's extensive and well-publicized renewal program. As a consultant to the city, Logue proposed in 1960 a $90-million redevelopment package and a radical change in the administrative structure and function of planning in Boston. In 1961, Collins appointed Logue Development Administrator to the Boston Redevelopment Authority (BRA), giving him enormous authority and responsibility. These included proposing and administering renewal plans, developing comprehensive redevelopment guidelines, and evolving capital improvement programs for municipal departments. Planning and implementation were thus united under one agency and under one powerful and dynamic administrator. In Logue's words:

> Our program is comprehensive. In its way it is probably the most comprehensive of any city in the United States. It's a program rather than a collection of projects. It involves a quarter of the land area and a third of the population. In both high- and low-priority areas we are trying to make some reality out of that old adage of Burnham's, "Make no little plans." The reason is that, with all the progress that has been made in the last three years in Washington in the Housing and Home Finance Agency and the Urban Renewal Administration, it's still just as easy to process 600 acres as six. So we do it wholesale, and you get support in a community when you do it wholesale. We also have found that by taking this overall look and by giving people an awareness that the City of Boston is going to be concerned about their areas, not with a bulldozer but in a preservative kind of way, then we see as a result a regeneration, an increase in home ownership, an increase in value of homes which before seemed almost to be

given away. The South End is a striking example. We don't claim to have accomplished all this; we report it, but we certainly think that urban renewal gets some credit.[76]

Logue's Urban Renewal Program for Boston divided the city into discrete districts for purposes of planning, administration, and funding. The harborfront, the central business district, government center, and some ten to fifteen other areas were designated as separate districts. A problem with organizing Boston into clearly prescribed, easily administered boundaries was that the physical districts, as well as the professional units charged with planning them, became separate entities with their own internal energy. It seems that by dividing the city in this manner connections between districts were given little thought. More attention could have been placed on the linkage theory of urban design, as in Ed Bacon's Philadelphia. Hence government center, the central business district, the financial district, and the harborfront have been treated as independent entities and the links between them remain undesigned to this day. Problems created by the central artery are especially significant since the expressway was peripheral to any of the district plans. As we have seen, master plans and zoning laws tend to separate a city into isolated districts for administrative convenience. Apparently innocuous and functional, the first decisions about administrative responsibility have unforeseen consequences on the city form of the future.

In 1959, prior to the involvement of the BRA, the chamber of commerce had begun active promotion and funding of redevelopment of the waterfront. Their team included MIT's Professor Kevin Lynch (who had just completed his seminal book, *Image of the City*), a close colleague, Jack Myer, and a local architect, Sy Mintz. When the BRA took over responsibility, Logue incorporated this project into a special waterfront section of his department. Concurrently, under the direction of Charles Hilgenhurst, chief of the downtown administration under Logue, and David Crane, head of the urban-design group brought in from Philadelphia, the waterfront redevelopment project proceeded. Simultaneously, Victor Gruen's plans for the central business district were on the drawing boards.

The strategies developed through these urban-renewal efforts included removal of older buildings, improvements in automobile access and parking, and the segregation of automobile from pedestrian circulation. To give new economic strength to downtown, the planners proposed large developments—a departure from the traditionally small-scale patterns of solids and voids in the old city. Superblock planning resulted in street closings and the channeling of traffic onto fewer larger roads, which greatly changed the urban texture. Congested areas that inhibited new development were opened up to create wide plazas and broad streets. The slogans of the day were "Beauty in the City," "City of Ideas," "Better Neighborhoods"—slogans that were translated into bricks and mortar with amazing energy and foresight.

For the harborfront specifically, the BRA put forth ten design objectives: (1) to mitigate the effect of the elevated expressway and the surface roadway beneath as a physical and psychological barrier to effective connections and linkages between the downtown and the waterfront; (2) to establish an active urban character for the area by the intensive utilization of land and by the mixing of compatible land uses; (3) to provide maximum opportunity for pedestrian access to the water's edge; (4) to establish an orderly sequence and hierarchy of open spaces and views for both the pedestrian and the motorist; (5) to establish a relationship between buildings, open spaces, and public ways that provides maximum protection to the pedestrian during unfavorable weather conditions; (6) to achieve a proper integration of buildings and spaces by retaining a careful relationship of scale and materials in new development to architecturally and historically significant buildings; (7) to establish a continuity of scale between the existing North End residential community and the new development to take place adjacent to the North End and along the water's

edge north of Commercial wharf; (8) to maintain the fingerlike outline of the wharves; (9) to create an unobstructed visual channel from the Old State House at Washington and State streets down to Long Wharf and the harbor beyond; and (10) to establish at the foot of State Street a vehicular-free focal point of converging pedestrian ways and down-harbor views.

Conceptual Milestones in Design: 1959–1980

Between 1959 and 1980, the BRA supervised an impressive amount of urban redevelopment governed by these ten design objectives. One of the concepts it came up with early on was "development synergy," in which public and private activity were brought together to create sufficient force to transform the urban district. Also called the "Captial Web" (a coinage of David Crane), this strategy funneled investment into different parts of the city to give districts independent identity. In the waterfront area, there were energetic proposals for superhighways and towers on the wharves (fig. 5-16)—holdovers from the Modern Movement. Although many of the grand designs were never built, they served to raise popular confidence and excitement about Boston after its post–World War II decline.

Considered as designs, however, the plans suffered from the weaknesses of their time, still reflecting many of the problems associated with Modern Movement architecture. Towers were dotted over the harborfront, and linear parkways and an aggrandized New Atlantic Avenue gave an inordinate amount of space over to the automobile. Numerous large office buildings were proposed for the area between the avenue and the water. Over the last twenty years the interaction of professional design and community participation have produced continual variations in the models—variations that summarize changing attitudes toward design over the two decades.

Along with the idea of combining public and private investment, the BRA developed certain design attitudes for critical growth corridors in the

Figure 5-16. BRA. Harborfront Redevelopment Model. Early 1960s.
The redevelopment schemes of the BRA were often highly ambitious, large-scale projects such as this proposal for the harborfront. The planners believed that extensive construction, including high-rise towers and superhighways, was necessary to stimulate the transformation of blighted urban districts. Although most schemes were never fully executed, they generated public excitement and optimism in the possibility of saving Boston from its post–World War II decline. As such, they continue some of the major design philosophies of Functionalism, such as isolated towers and an open ground-plane. (Courtesy: Boston Redevelopment Authority)

harborfront area. One of these was to promote a "State Street Spine," a high-density corridor of buildings along this important thoroughfare that would generate a link between development downtown and at Long Wharf. This spine was intended to open up maximum down-harbor views. The focus of this proposal, however, was on parcels of development and a vertical massing of new construction instead of a coherent pedestrian link at street level. An emphasis on the pedestrian experience soon followed in the recommendations for

the "Walk to the Sea" and "Great Cove." This emphasis was eventually fully realized in the Quincy Markets redevelopment. However, the importance of State Street itself, as the axis between the urban center and the harbor edge, has never been given complete recognition in the New Boston.

Great Cove, in the past a point of direct contact between shipping and land, is the area occupied by presentday Waterfront Park. Over the years there have been numerous proposals to dredge this area, allowing the water back to old bulkhead lines and to recreate the historic harbor context of this urban space. While the economic and practical viability of these proposals can be challenged, the underlying principle of enhancing the relationship of city to water deserves more than cursory dismissal as romantic fantasy. The Walk to the Sea, which was to end at Great Cove, provides a visual and functional link from city hall through the markets to the waterfront and is probably the most important spatial and visual sequence in Boston (see fig. 2-25; fig. 5-17).

A consistent problem in this sequence, however, has been the barrier of the central artery. Possibly an evaluation of ways to penetrate this barrier might result in alternatives to the ideal solution of depressing the artery below grade, which will probably never happen. The importance of the link between the center and the harbor at Quincy Markets is too great for it to depend on long-range, unfundable ideas. Short of the optimum, we need an interim achievable solution.

The present form of the harborfront has emerged from the partial realization of these policies adopted under the BRA. But there have also been other influences. One is the influence of the historic-preservation movement. The arrival of new residents adjacent to established neighborhoods sparked debate over issues of architectural preservation. This debate also stirred up opposition to large roads and high-rise buildings. The most visible result in the harbor is the preservation of old commercial warehouses and their adapta-

Key:
A. *City Hall Plaza*
B. *Walk to the Sea*
C. *Proposed Congress Street Bridge*
D. *Central Artery Barrier (re: Marketplace Center, fig. 5–20 A, B)*
E. *Waterfront Park*
F. *Financial District*
G. *North End*

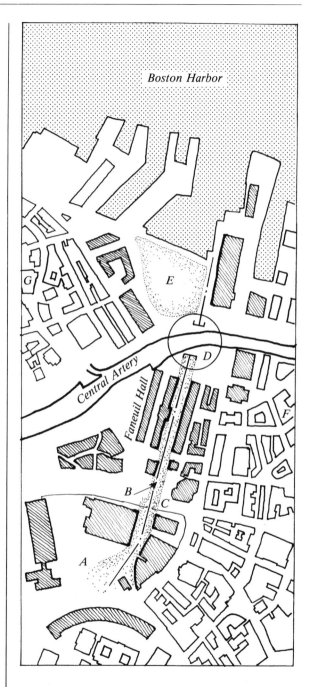

Figure 5-17. Walk to the Sea, Boston.
Currently the redevelopment of the Quincy Markets is the most important link—the "walk to the sea"—between the center and historic harborfront. However, the central artery interferes with the coherence of the se-

quence and some solution must be found, even if the optimum one of depressing the roadway below grade proves unfeasible and unfundable (see also figs. 5-21, 5-22).

tion to residential and commercial uses. However, the issue of preservation runs deeper than details of design, popular taste, or even the historic artifacts themselves. The public demand for preservation indicates an awareness of the need to retain the sense of place in the environment and should influence profoundly the way designers operate—as an expression of real, as opposed to perceived, human interests.

In summary, recent development of the Inner Harbor is beginning to shape this area as a new city room, a place for industry, commerce, transportation, housing, and recreation. Buffered from the open ocean by a six-mile archipelago, the Inner Harbor is a lifeline to the economic revitalization of the entire waterfront. The area has proved highly attractive to developers. Hotels, offices, and condominiums vie for a piece of the view and closeness to the sea. On the water itself a new world is opening up to pleasure boating, commuter transportation, and recreational use of the harbor islands. This energetic redevelopment has given birth to a new awareness of the waterfront as an amenity of major significance to the city and as an important determinant of land values in the core. With all this as fact, it would behoove Bos-

ton to improve those key linkages between the core and harborfront.

Improving Linkages between the Core and Harborfront

As one moves away from the harbor, one passes through a number of subareas in the downtown core. These areas differentiate themselves by varying patterns of streets and blocks, building mass, and the configurations of space between buildings (fig. 5-18). A major subarea is the financial district, bounded on the waterfront side by the central artery, on the city side by government center. The form of this district roughly corresponds to the outline and contour of the original Shawmut Peninsula. At first glance the streets seem randomly ordered in an organic pattern determined by the horse and buggy. However, as one studies the figure-ground plan more closely, an overlay of concentric ring streets emerges—a system that probably followed the original topography of the peninsula. Radiating from the concentric streets are a series of "finger" streets reaching out from State Street and terminating at the artery.

Figure 5-18. Figure-ground Study of the Central Business District.
Following the severance of the waterfront from the city core, each developed independently. The street plan of the financial district (lower right) seems randomly ordered, but on closer inspection a pattern of concentric ring streets emerges parallel to the water and cut through by radial finger streets. (Courtesy: Harvard Urban Design Program)

The results of this concentric/radiating system are urban blocks that offer considerably greater variety than the normal orthogonal grid (fig. 5-19). On the other hand, there are major problems of orientation, since the angles of the grid shift constantly. Moving through this area one loses reference to the compass points. The four major concentric streets that arc through the area are Water, Milk, Franklin, and High. Nine finger streets (India, Broad, Batterymarch, Oliver, Pearl, Congress, Federal, Devonshire, and Washington) intersect these ring streets in various ways. Part of the problem of orientation stems from the number and inconsistency of types of intersections and the lack of a spatial hierarchy or obvious differentiation of the ring from the concentric streets.

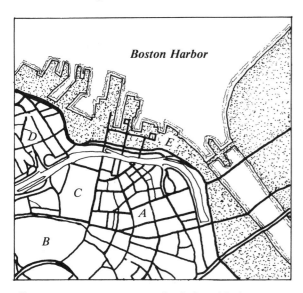

Boston Harbor

Key:
A. Financial District   *C. Quincy Markets*
B. City Hall   *D. North End*
                           E. Waterfront District

Figure 5-19. Diagram of the Street System of Boston's Core and Harborfront District.
The concentric streets of the financial district probably developed in response to the contours of the peninsula, with the radial finger streets connecting them to the water edge. Although this radial-concentric pattern gives character to the district, it also creates problems of orientation.

On the other hand, this very confusion contributes to the special charm of Boston, reminding us of the layers of history that underlie the irrational, sedimentary evolution of the city. The branching finger streets form points of cleavage where triangular squares emerge as important small-scale urban spaces such as Customs' House, Liberty, Post Office, and Winthrop squares (see fig. 3-28). Instead of being residual holes, as the triangular intersections of the grid and diagonal often are in Washington, Boston's more compact, dense fabric gives form and purpose to these junctions. If properly designed, these, in turn, can act as important points of reference in clarifying the sometimes confusing sequences of public spaces in the financial district. State Street itself is something of a gathering edge for the finger streets and establishes a demarcation zone between the financial district, government center and Quincy Markets. It should be developed as such.

In general the buildings in the financial district respond to the concentric grid, with sheer bulk as their principal characteristic. Since buildings vary considerably in height, mass, and architectural detail, the street level will have to provide the unifying form. This is especially true if current trends toward a dense concentration of vertical office towers continue. The more high-rise development occurs, the more pressing the need for intervention from the public realm will become. Images of Houston, Texas, and Sixth Avenue in Manhattan come to mind—canyons of towers without a transition to street level could easily obliterate the historic texture of Boston's original site. As in almost every other city, Boston's center needs a clarification of solids and voids.

Beyond State Street, in the city hall-Quincy Markets area, one enters another distinct subdistrict. The character of the buildings and the quality of space change. Individual buildings sit like pavilions, unrelated to the field of streets and blocks. Some places such as City Hall Plaza and the Quincy Markets are relatively well defined, but in general, open spaces have specialized relationships to specific buildings and do not contribute to a continuous, connected sequence.

Perhaps the worst problem in this area is, once again, the central artery, and the band of lost space that results along the waterfront (fig. 5-20). The challenge to designers is to infill this area creatively and shift the boundary of the city core back to where it once was at the water's edge with the artery intact.

We have identified some of the problems and opportunities in central Boston. The goal of all efforts to intervene in restructuring its urban space must be toward creating a framework of continuous, well-defined streets, squares, and blocks strengthening the figure-ground relationships. This framework must preserve the historic geometries and make them more comprehensible. An overriding concern should be, as indicated, the connection of the city core to the harborfront—a concern that requires modifications to the street system of the central core.

A way to lessen the impact of the barrier between downtown and the waterfront would be to remove the west lanes of Atlantic Avenue to create sites along the highway wide enough for redevelopment. The existing east lanes of this enormous boulevard could accommodate two-way traffic and provide approximately the same width as the newest section of the road at Waterfront Park. If enough room for development were created, structures could be built to mask the avenue and the artery, and to provide spatial links under the artery. The goal of creating spatial links under the artery is especially important at such sites as parcel D-10, which encompasses the area behind Quincy Markets (see text that follows) as well as India, Milk, and Broad streets.

The streets under the artery would also have to be reexamined. Extending the finger streets from the urban core to the waterfront could create pedestrian links and view corridors. These would require a layer of low-rise infill buildings to make a compact fabric of streets and squares around and between the telephone building, the aquarium, the

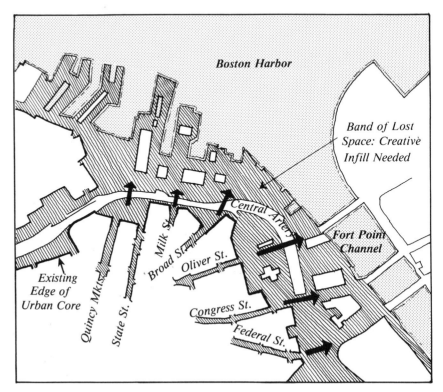

Figure 5-20. Lost Space Diagram.
A band of lost space flanks both sides of the central artery. The diagram identifies key points (black arrows) where linkages need to be established between finger streets and the waterfront.

harbor towers, and the garage. This fabric could be extended laterally along the waterfront to embrace Rowe's Wharf, the Congress Street Bridge, and Fort Point Channel. A good beginning is the Marketplace Center design for parcel D-10, located between the Faneuil Hall Markets and the central artery (see fig. 5-17; fig. 5-21). Marketplace Center, under construction as of this writing, is the product of a successful design review process and the consideration of public and private entities. It is comprised of a three-story commercial base and a sixteen-story office tower along

Figure 5-21. Marketplace Center, Figure-ground Plan. Boston. 1984.
Marketplace Center is an urban infill project whose form is influenced in no small way by the surrounding spatial context. Covering most of its oddly shaped site, this "poché" building successfully shields the elevated expressway, continues important street edges, and forms a semicircular piazza and gateway for the walk to the sea. (Drawing: WZMH Architects)

State Street. The oddly shaped parcel required a specialized poché building form (see chapter 4) to create a cohesive pedestrian structure in the area. The complex conforms to preexisting geometries and fills nearly the entire site in order to shield the view and noise of the elevated expressway. The figure-ground relationship is modulated to form a semicircular plaza to receive pedestrian flows at the juncture of Market Street and Commercial Street. This "exedra" space carved out of the mass (fig. 5-22) shapes an outdoor vestibule for the continuation of the Walk to the Sea. The glass-covered canopy, designed as a gateway, provides shelter for major shop entrances. As an urban infill piece, Marketplace Center is strongly influenced by its surrounding spatial context. The

Figure 5-22. Marketplace Center Model, Boston. 1984.
View along the walk to the sea toward the harborfront with the "exedra" of Marketplace Center establishing a new gateway. (Design: WZMH Architects, Photo. © Peter Vanderwarker Photographs)

driving force is public space rather than the private building as object.

If this kind of tightly knit fabric were broadly established as public space design policy in downtown Boston, a real sense of waterfront edge and the vital connection between the city and the harbor could be recaptured. The damage caused by the central artery and destruction of buildings under urban renewal could be repaired. Walks along as well as to the waterfront could become connected experiences (figs. 5-23, 5-24, 5-25). Above all, the restructured space must guide new development in such a way that the people of Boston would never again lose their access to and identification with the sea (fig. 5-26).

Opening up access to the water would enhance the meaning of both the city core and the harbor. By strengthening the concentric ring streets that distribute activity to the finger streets, the sequences between the harbor and the core could be

greatly improved. The artery has to be accepted as a reality, but changes of grade, dredged channels of water, market facilities, and other construction could bridge, mask, and penetrate this formidable barrier. It is still possible for Boston to regain its harbor frontage.

Conclusion

In Boston, then, figure-ground analysis reveals a pattern of compact neighborhoods with strong internal structure but with problems of linkage between them and, most importantly, to the harborfront. At the same time, the unique character and historic districts must be respected to maintain the sense of place. Although well-intentioned and imaginative, urban-renewal projects often ignored these issues. What the city needs is a new planning policy that will take them into account.

CASE STUDY 2: WASHINGTON, D.C.

In contrast to Boston, *linkage* was the overriding consideration in the development of Washington. Major Pierre L'Enfant's 1791 plan (fig. 5-27) was meant to express the symbolic role of the capital as the heart of a great new nation. Toward this end, L'Enfant created a plan of sweeping diagonal boulevards cutting across a grid of secondary streets. Grand vistas linked monumental public buildings. Systems of open space, planned with the meticulous geometry of a designer schooled in the traditions of the late French Baroque, ran through the city, giving form and meaning to the entire fabric.

If Boston suffers from lack of connection, Washington suffers today from a lack of density and land coverage. The linkages, supported by adequate density and coverage of building mass as well as landscape, require substantial strengthening to clarify the original plan. In all redevelopment plans for the city, furthermore, its primary character of monumentality must be respected.

Figure 5-23. Sketch of Possible Infill Development. Low-rise infill is one possibility for reconnnecting the downtown to the waterfront. This kind of infill could reinforce the linear form of the piers while creating viable public spaces and opportunities for private development. (Drawing: Rocco Maragna, Harvard Urban Design Program)

Figure 5-24. Axon of Possible Redevelopment Along the Central Artery.
This proposal suggests methods of repairing the damage caused by the central artery through infill to reinforce building edges, reconstruction of the road to grade, and strengthening of pedestrian connections. Walks to as well as along the waterfront would be established. The increased density of development would make the roadway less obtrusive. (Drawing: Bill McGee, Harvard Urban Design Program)

Key:
A. 40'0" min. easement.
B. Building bulk to center of site.
C. Entertainment arcade along waterfront edge.
D. Possible development parcels with reconstructed Central Artery.
E. Infill development subject to design review.
F. Parking.
G. Focal Point.
H. Historic Preservation.
I. Pedestrian Easement.

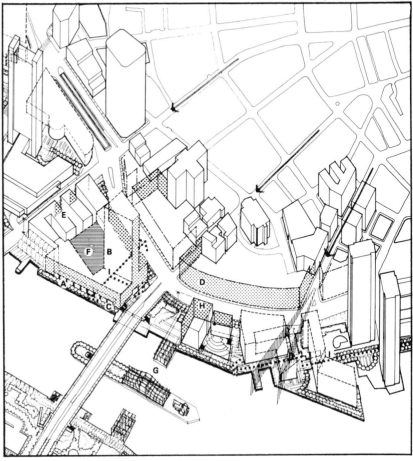

As has happened so often, the grand design for Washington was never realized. Even here, at the center of federal decision-making, where one might think that a model for public urban space might be created, laissez-faire incrementalism has governed the development of the city. The ideals of a coherent, historically derived plan have been pushed aside, forgotten in the pressure of private development. The continuous space of L'Enfant's plan has been eaten away by the automobile and by shabby, uncontrolled commercial enterprise. What should be—what was intended to be—the pride of the nation is on the verge of being a national disgrace. Again and again the city has thrown away opportunities to become a true icon for the country.

Most of L'Enfant's urban squares were never built or have been obliterated by later construction. Although a two-dimensional plan reveals the historic structure of spaces, from eye level the streetscape of contemporary Washington is fragmented, the clarity of its organization disrupted by lost space to the point of being unrecognizable. One sees an attractive, horizontal city of pavilions sitting in green space, but without the drama and legibility inherent in its original design. Both the clarity of the linkages and the spatial structure of its figure-ground need strong reinforcement.

In addition to drama and monumental symbolism, L'Enfant's plan called for a close relationship between government and urban life. There was no separation of functions. Each important building

Figure 5-25. Aerial perspective of Rowes Wharf redevelopment. 1985.
Continuous public access to the water's edge is a crucial urban design principle in Boston's redevelopment process.
The Rowes wharf project is exemplary, with 10,000 square feet of public space, ground floor retail, and a water taxi
terminal on the piers. (Courtesy: The Beacon Companies)

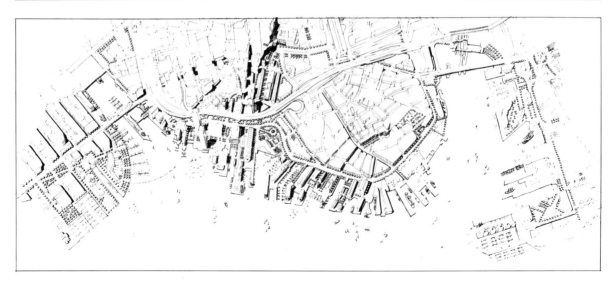

Figure 5-26. Axon: Harborpark. Waterfront Planning Framework, BRA. 1985.
The many bits and pieces of waterfront redevelopment must now be interconnected into a comprehensive pattern of
public pedestrian spaces along the water's edge. (Courtesy: Boston Redevelopment Authority. Drawing by Herb Ka-
shian)

was to have had its district of background squares, streets, and buildings, logic being that people could live and work conveniently nearby. Symbolically, too, with the dispersal of federal buildings around the L'Enfant Plan, the government was not to be zoned away from the people.[77] Over the years, however, the activities of urban life in Washington have been segregated into clearly defined zones for government, work, shopping, and living.

Since 1901 serious efforts have been made to revive the clarity of the L'Enfant plan; some progress has in fact been achieved. But if the city is ever to fulfill the noble objectives of the original concept, it must return to the fundamental structuring principles of shaping monumental, symbolic exterior space—principles of the bounded, extended void, in which space is the continuous, connective fabric of public life. To revive the organization of the Baroque plan the spatial edges must be redefined, given new coherence and continuity. Washington has evolved into a modern city of islands in formless green space instead of a city of positive voids (fig. 5-28). It would be appropriate to transform it into a city of continuous

geometries responding to the axes, the urban blocks, and framed monuments of L'Enfant's ideals. Formal landscaping can provide at least part of the grammar for establishing this clear, geometric order.

L'Enfant's Preconceptions

When Major Pierre Charles L'Enfant, under the direction of President Washington, set out to design the new capital for a new nation, he had in mind numerous preconceptions based on his European experience. The primary influence, as suggested, was the late French Baroque, with its tradition of broad axial relationships, symmetrical balance, and superimposed order on a grand scale (fig. 5-29). L'Enfant applied these theories carte blanche to his scheme for Washington. What emerged was a plan not unlike its predecessors in Paris, Vaux-le-Vicomte, or Versailles, incorporating at the same time elements of great squares from other points in Europe. Judiciously, L'Enfant placed important, monumental buildings on high points of land, superimposed a functional grid of

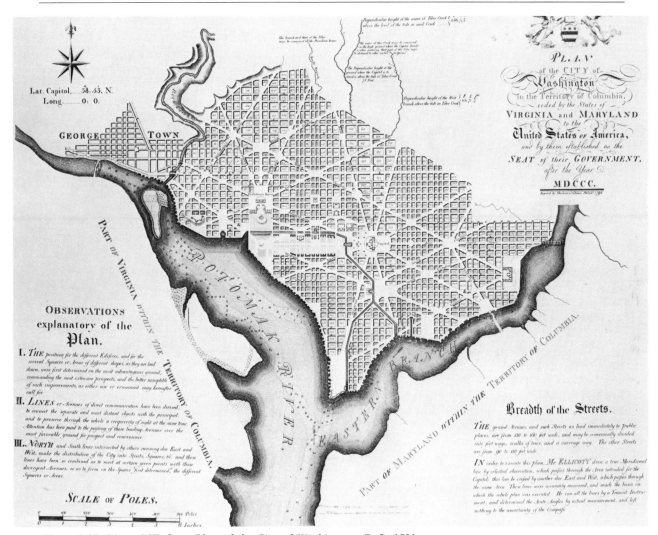

Figure 5-27. Pierre L'Enfant. Plan of the City of Washington, D.C. 1791.
Washington was laid out with a monumental master plan intended to symbolize its role as the heart of the new nation.
Sweeping diagonal boulevards cut across a grid of secondary streets, creating grand vistas and linking public mon-
uments. (Courtesy: Pennsylvania Avenue Development Corporation-PADC)

streets over the site, and then carved out straight, diagonal boulevards to connect the monuments. The result was a series of triangular districts with layers of order defined by minor orthogonal streets and major diagonal boulevards. This grand plan was not without its problems at the microlevel, particularly at the intersections where the grid meets the diagonal, points where residual gaps occur in both the grid and the diagonal systems.

These two ordering structures of space created a holistic framework that left numerous unresolved connections at specific sites. The extended stretched-out space of Washington, in which the noble vista predominates (fig. 5-30), is the opposite of Boston's compressed, evolved space in which monuments are discovered by accident as you wind through the narrow corridors of streets. The sweeping scale of its plan needs much more

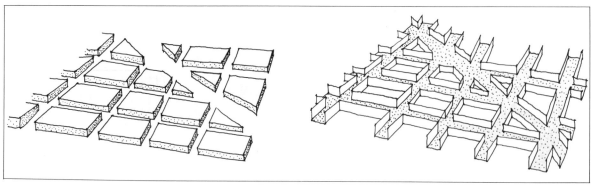

Figure 5-28. Diagrams of the Grid Cut through by Diagonals.
The monumentality of Washington D.C. was never realized. Especially problematic, as seen in these diagrams, have been the intersections of the grid and the diagonal. At these critical points, the edges of the streets must be redefined to revive the clarity of the original Baroque layout. (Courtesy: Joseph Passonneau)

Figure 5-29. Versailles. André Le Nôtre.
L'Enfant was profoundly influenced by the traditions of the French Baroque, particularly by the strong axes, long vistas, and symmetrical balance of such designs as Vaux-le-Vicomte and Versailles. His intention was to create a series of strong formal linkages using similar principles on an equally grand scale.

Figure 5-30. Diagram of the Major Vistas.
The entire structure of Washington was governed by a series of vistas established along major boulevards connecting important places. However, these are often achieved at the expense of the smaller-scale environment. Strengthening micro-scale open spaces will also strengthen the extended vistas and axes themselves.

Key:
A. White House
B. U.S. Capitol
C. Washington Monument
-----L'Enfant's Planned Vistas and Axes
• L'Enfant's Sites for Important Public Monuments

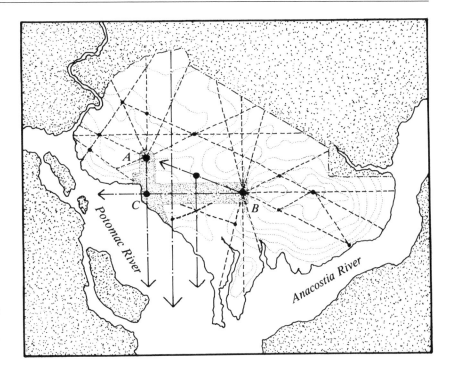

building, or formal landscape, to make it comprehensible. Furthermore, the spatial gaps along the avenues are difficult to recreate as enclosed entities for pedestrian use. The whole is a magnificent work of art, a great concept, but the parts suffer from a lack of form and identity. Washington's grand vistas are achieved at the expense of the small-scale public function.

Although L'Enfant's reputation in the United States is as an architect and engineer, he was in fact trained as a landscape painter. His education, therefore, was in the creation of optical illusion through perspective, depth of field, color, plant materials, topography, and the limits of visual comprehension—the point where the average eye no longer perceives true color, scale, or detail.[78] As a follower of André Le Nôtre, L'Enfant applied the principles of spatial illusionism to the urban-design plan for Washington. The city is a city of illusion, but without sufficient depth in reality today to successfully carry it through.

Washington as a Formal Landscape: Strengthening the Linkages

In almost every American city the center has a peculiar disparity between extremely vertical and varied buildings and the ground plane (or city of towers previously discussed). In Washington, however, where zoning height restrictions have been religiously adhered to, the disparity is a horizontal one, especially evident at the intersection of the two geometries (fig. 5-31). Massive rectangular structures of consistent height leave broad, amorphous spaces when they meet the diagonal. The *patte d'oie,* or intersection of multiple angles formed by converging or radiating axes, requires that buildings reflect the angular geometry—something along the lines of the Flatiron Building in Manhattan, the structures that enclose Trafalgar Square in London, or the Piazza del Popolo in Rome (fig. 5-32).

In the great French gardens of the Baroque, the

Figure 5-31. View of Pennsylvania Avenue toward the Capitol.
One of the problems in Washington stems from the disparity between horizontal and vertical. Streets are exceptionally wide, while restrictions of building height have been religiously observed. This has lead to vast street intersections, with ragged, poorly defined building edges along L'Enfant's Avenues. (Courtesy: PADC)

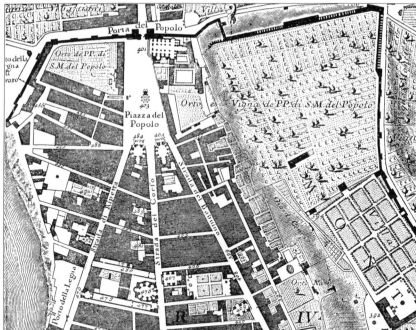

Figure 5-32. Piazza del Popolo. Nolli. Map of Rome. 1748.
In the Piazza del Popolo, the configuration of the buildings reinforces the structure of the open space, resolving irregularities in the geometries and clearly defining the edges.

radiating intersection was resolved by an elaborate system of parterres, broderies, and walkways, as at Paris's Tuilleries or Versailles's Parterre du Sud. If there is no geometric regularization of these odd spaces, they bleed into chaos. L'Enfant's plan called for a formal structure to these points of intersection, structures that were only partially constructed. One of the more successful intersections in the L'Enfant plan can be found at Dupont Circle (fig. 5-33).

The challenge in restructuring these unfinished but very important spaces is to capitalize on the contradictory geometries by inserting new development and formal landscaping to enclose the intersections. This would at once repair the broken areas and crossaxes, reinforcing both the grid and the diagonals. The issue is that both systems need to be strengthened by creating infill that maintains the street walls at the intersection and reinforces the view corridors in the plan.

A main feature of L'Enfant's original plan, the reciprocity of view from monument to monument, from one topographic feature to the next, can be recreated by the formal allée, a linking device in which a dense planting of street trees carries the visual experience through linear space. As a landscaping means of filling in lost space, pleached and pollarded trees in allées can effectively create spatial enclosure, vista, and sequence (figs. 5-34, 5-35). A proposal by the Pennsylvania Avenue Development Corporation, one of the major development planning offices in Washington, is to plant a triple allée of willow oaks along the length of Pennsylvania Avenue, Washington's important processional boulevard, to strengthen and unify the linearity and perspective of the space (fig. 5-36).

Another landscaping form appropriate to Washington is the bosk, or dense grid of trees.

Borrowed from the formal gardens of France and Italy, the bosk is a highly architectonic use of natural elements that can achieve dramatic spatial effects, as in Le Nôtre's palace gardens or Dan Kiley's 1970 Jefferson Memorial Park in St. Louis (fig. 5-37). Kiley, who has been called the "lone classicist," is one of the few contemporary American landscape architects to have consistently made creative use of these formal, historic elements of landscape design. For instance, his bosk at Independence Mall in Philadelphia is conceived on a grand scale, containing over nine hundred honey locusts.

Monumentality and Enclosure: Urban Solids and Voids

In the urban design of Washington, it is desirable and even necessary to maintain the open spaciousness and strong linkages of L'Enfant's monumentality and at the same time provide enclosed, well formed spaces for human activity (such as in the U.S. Capitol Master Plan, fig. 5-38; see fig. 5-52). This contradiction has to be resolved with appropriately scaled landscape elements and carefully placed building frontages. Outdoor space in Washington must be contingent or at once open and closed to address simultaneously the contradictions of large- and small-scale design concerns.

Figure 5-33. Dupont Circle, Washington.
L'Enfant's plan called for a formal treatment of intersections where the diagonals converge such as at Dupont Circle. Most of these urban structures were only partially built. The challenge is to capitalize on the divergent geometries by inserting new development and formal landscaping. (Photo: Joseph Passonneau)

Figure 5-34. *Pennsylvania Avenue Development Corp. Model for the Redevelopment of the Mall and the Avenue. 1969.*
This proposal shows how reinforcement of the edges through infill and formal landscaping could clarify the linkages and create a hierarchy of urban space. (Courtesy: PADC)

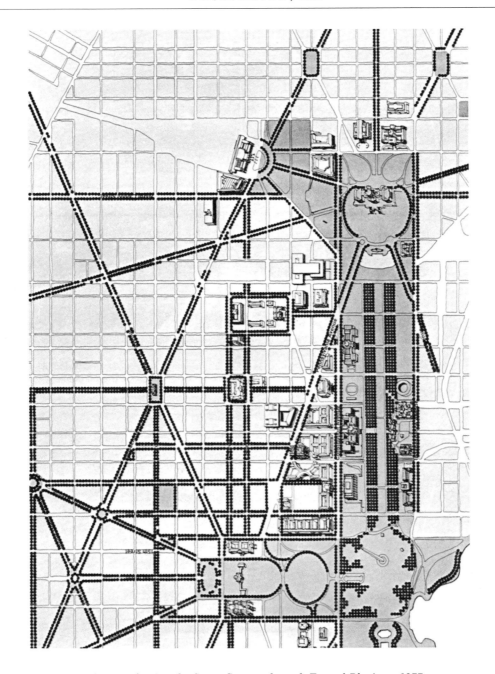

Figure 5-35. Suggestions for Reinforcing the Street System through Formal Planings. 1977.
Passonneau's plan shows how strong formal plantings along major corridors could strengthen the unity and overall structure of Washington's street system. Lack of continuity at intersections could be overcome by regular allées of trees, to the benefit of both the grid and the diagonal. (Courtesy: Joseph Passonneau)

Figure 3-36. Rendering of Proposed Allées along Pennsylvania Avenue. A current proposal for Pennsylvania Avenue is to plant a triple allée of willow oaks along its length. This would both reinforce the visual axis between the White House and the Capitol and correct disparities in the alignment and style of buildings. (Courtesy: PADC)

Washington's stretched-out spatial system with its straight axes is directional, in contrast to the inflected or bent alignments of the medieval city (see ''Street Space'' in figs. 3-15, 3-16) and creates a reciprocal tension between monuments that must be respected. In the historic plan, these street alignments were designed to relate buildings at the scale of specific sites but also to extend the city's formal relationship to the wilderness beyond. The sweeping perspective along these distant axes provides a frame of reference for the surfaces along the sides, an axial sweep that depends on continuous street walls. Without this discipline, the angular spaces along the avenue merge with traffic corridors and become incomprehensible to pedestrians. The axis itself almost becomes lost. For example, along Pennsylvania Avenue it becomes

Figure 5-37. St. Louis Arch. Eero Saarinen and Associates and Office of Dan Kiley.

Another type of formal planting appropriate to Washington is the bosk. One of the few contemporary landscape architects to make creative use of formal plantings, Dan Kiley demonstrates how the bosk can convey a sense of monumentality and grandeur. This kind of treatment would be highly suitable to L'Enfant's intentions for the city. (Courtesy: Dan Kiley)

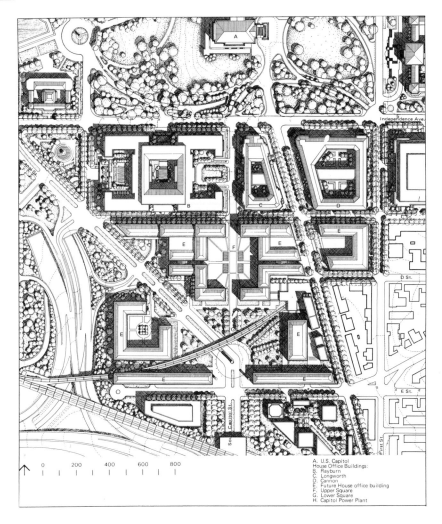

Figure 5-38. Capitol Master Plan. 1982.
If the linkages need to be strengthened in Washington, so does the structure of urban solids and voids at the smaller scale. The new Capitol Master Plan shows how a hierarchy of enclosed public spaces can be linked to the primary spatial order to fulfill the need for more intimate urban spaces. (Courtesy: Office of the Architect of the Capitol)

essential that the buildings actually face the avenue. If they are oriented to the grid instead of the diagonal, they consequently disrupt the frame of visual perspective. The question of whether new development in these critical corner sites should line up with the diagonal or the grid is under vigorous debate.[79] In fact, they should line up with both systems.

The potential for a close relationship between buildings and exterior space, a necessity of good urban landscape design, is illustrated by Joseph Passonneau's 1979 "Nolli Map of Washington" (fig. 5-39). Passonneau's map illustrates the tran-

sition from the public street to the semipublic inner-block courtyards and squares where urban space is allowed to flow through arcades and gateways. Sequences become part of a structured progression. Spaces within space define a hierarchy and relationship between the formal large-scale parks and boulevards and the small-scale street landscape that frames blocks and freestanding monuments, giving Washington its unique urban character. Within the urban block the definition of place occurs as the classical city room and outside as formally landscaped public avenues and grid streets. In Passonneau's map one sees how ur-

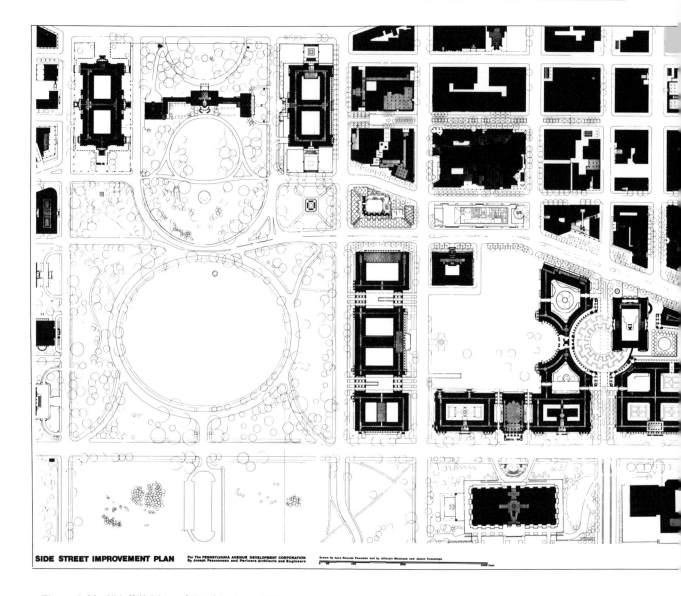

SIDE STREET IMPROVEMENT PLAN   For The PENNSYLVANIA AVENUE DEVELOPMENT CORPORATION By Joseph Passonneau and Partners Architects and Engineers   Drawn by Jane Rhonda Passman and by Allistair McIntosh and James Cummings

Figure 5-39. "Nolli" Map of Washington. 1979.
Through closely integrated buildings and well-defined exterior spaces, Passonneau illustrates a hierarchy linking inner block areas to the monumental scale of the larger system. (Courtesy: Joseph Passonneau. Drawing by Jane Rhonda Passman et al.)

ban space and nature can potentially reinforce one another (see The Crescents at Bath, fig. 4-2l). These qualities must be preserved in contemporary design.

Monumentality as Place

As mentioned above, L'Enfant's plan called for a close interaction of the natural and manmade environments. It also called for a link between the

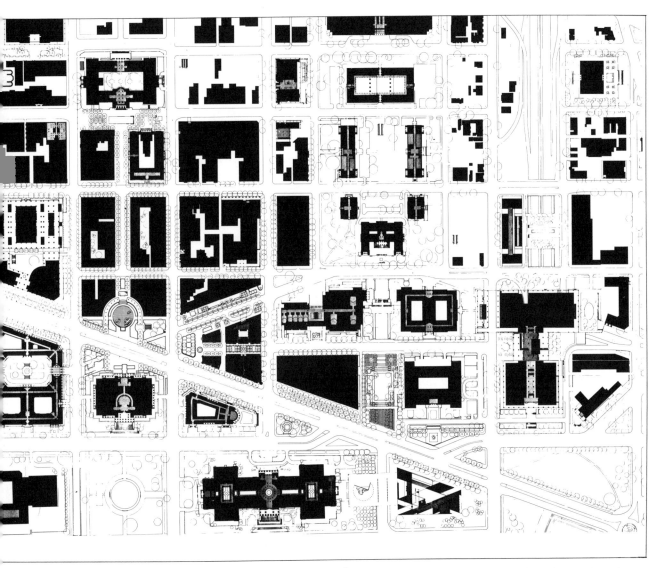

city of government and the city of private life. Residential and commercial districts were to co-exist with the national life of the capital. The symbolic, ceremonial function of public space is expressed in monumental formality, giving a contextual frame to which all segments of the fabric are tied. Monumentality, by definition, transcends period styles, giving a timelessness, an enduring historical framework to form and space. The idea of monumentality is an abstraction expressed

through size, symbolism, and setting rather than through an explicit formal vocabulary. All cities have some monumental components, but in Washington it is the theme of the entire city. It is this overriding characteristic that should guide the restoration of Washington's plan.

During the years following L'Enfant, the tradition of monumentality through landscape was interpreted in Washington by distinguished designers such as Andrew Jackson Downing (1850–51:

various open spaces) and Frederick Law Olmsted (1874: Capitol Grounds; 1899–1902: Mall), who were both commissioned on separate occasions to restore the plan. Yet much of their work was never realized, and severe deterioration has resulted from the impact of parking lots and freeways.

Pennsylvania Avenue Corridor

In 1937, Elbert Peets commented on Pennsylvania Avenue's fate:

> Poor old Pennsylvania Avenue. . . . A vast open space, largely to remain open, weakens its eastern end; Constitution Avenue crashes across it; the plaza at Eighth Street is maimed; vast walls of stone weigh down one side of the Avenue, while parking lots cut gaps in the other. . . . finally, the plaza between Thirteenth and Fourteenth Streets has been ruined by an open space yawning wide toward the west.[80]

Efforts to reconstruct Pennsylvania Avenue, a showpiece of L'Enfant's plan, began in 1964 when President Kennedy, appalled by its dilapidation, appointed an Advisory Council on Pennsylvania Avenue with Nathaniel Owings as chairman. This council published a plan to illustrate a pattern of development, define major public improvements, and arouse public and governmental enthusiasm for the project. The plan had several objectives: to reconnect the avenue to its adjoining areas, to give a special character to the nation's ceremonial promenade honoring its function as a link between the White House and the Capitol Building, and to reclaim and develop it as a unified urban space for pedestrians and vehicles. In 1972 the Advisory Council was superseded by the Pennsylvania Avenue Development Corporation (PADC), which is currently responsible for the planning and development of the Avenue.

L'Enfant envisioned Pennsylvania Avenue as the center of civic activity, a place where the residential city would meet the federal city. He saw the avenue lined with noble residences and major government buildings, the executive-department

buildings, a playhouse, and the market exchange. Instead, Pennsylvania Avenue developed into the main commercial and business street of the city during the nineteenth century, a street of boardinghouses, hotels, saloons, and shops. In 1901 a commission of notables that included Charles McKim, Daniel Burnham, and Frederick Law Olmsted was formed by Senator James McMillan to reverse this trend along the avenue and to reinstitute the official Washington urban core as a city of buildings within parks.

The so-called McMillan Plan (fig. 5-40) placed new emphasis on the Mall as a focus for government and promoted the idea of a Federal Triangle located on Pennsylvania Avenue (subsequently built in the 1920s and 1930s) as a unified complex giving a boundary to the governmental city. This was an important decision since it effectively divided government from the rest of the city. Pennsylvania Avenue became a barrier street, separating the massive institutional buildings on the south from the downtown area on the north. The avenue therefore emerged as a backdoor to two districts, losing its meaningful form and purpose. Eventually this took its toll on the physical and social structure of the avenue, leading to the 1964 Advisory Council decision to rebuild (fig. 5-41).

Restructuring the Monumental Core

Pennsylvania Avenue and the Mall are the two great armatures that give structure and coherence to the monumental core of Washington (fig. 5-42). Any strategy for urban design has to build upon these two corridors and redefine the hierarchies of public space within the axial organization. The extensive landscaping of the Mall gives a pervasive greenness and horizontal spaciousness to the Capitol area. As an entity in the urban landscape, the Mall functions both as a formal link between monuments and an informal park in the heart of the city. This dual function should be expanded and given more importance in regenerating the larger urban core. Rather than conceptually confine the Mall to a rectangular strip between Con-

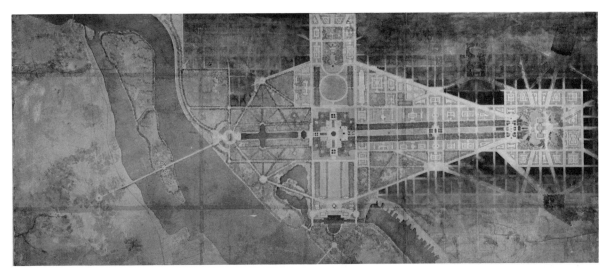

Figure 5-40. The McMillan Plan. 1901.
There have been several attempts to restore the monumentality of L'Enfant's scheme. The most influential was the 1901 McMillan Plan. This placed new emphasis on the Mall and promoted the idea of a federal triangle along Pennsylvania Avenue. However, Pennsylvania Avenue itself became an edge between the federal city and the downtown to the north, losing much of its intended function and form. In following years it became severely dilapidated and has been the focus of many efforts at revitalization. (Courtesy: PADC)

Figure 5-41. Advisory Council on Pennsylvania Avenue. Master Plan. 1964.
In 1962 President Kennedy appointed an Advisory Council to develop a scheme for rehabilitating Pennsylvania Avenue. This plan had three goals: to define Pennsylvania Avenue as an integral part of its adjoining area, to provide it with a special character as the nation's ceremonial way, and to make the avenue a fitting connection between the Capitol and White House. (Courtesy: PADC)

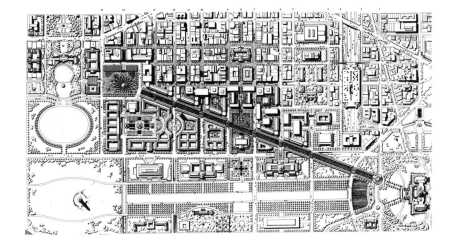

stitution and Independence avenues, the continuous armature of green should reach into the city to the north, encompassing important public buildings and urban blocks and integrating the two types of cities in Washington. Pennsylvania Avenue and the Mall could begin to interact and the new cross-axes could serve as pedestrian links that extend the formal landscape of the Mall into the city at key infill sites.

Secondary cross-axes over Pennsylvania Avenue

Figure 5-42. Central Washington Redevelopment Model.
Together with Pennsylvania Avenue, the Mall provides the great structuring armature for the core of Washington.
It functions both as a formal link between monuments and an informal park within the city. Continuous green links
should be extended to the north in order to integrate the planting of the Mall with the surrounding city. (Courtesy:
PADC)

between the Mall and the city would serve to identify nodes that give the avenue meaning as a junction rather than a barrier without destroying the integrity of its axis. Along the Pennsylvania Avenue axis itself the nodes would become small public squares for social interaction. The linearity of

the avenue would be strengthened by increasing continuous building and plantings along its edges to define the space within existing height restrictions. The lesser density that the horizontal background buildings give to Washington should be compensated for by increasing land coverage (the reverse of Raymond Hood's tower experiment of the 1920s; see figs. 2-16, 2-17) — a means of infilling gaps and mending connections.

Square of the Grand Fountains

The energetic redevelopment efforts of PADC include the reconstruction of five important squares along the avenue. Opposite the National Archives on Pennsylvania Avenue, Market Square is an important example of disruptive, residual spaces that result from the intersection of the diagonal and the grid (fig. 5-43). The square has a dominant position between the President's House at one end of the avenue and the Capitol Building at the other. Its Baroque form results from the juncture of three axes: Pennsylvania Avenue, Eighth Street (originally planned as a through street to the Mall but now blocked by the archives), and Indiana Avenue from City Hall to the Washington Monument (interrupted by the Justice Department Building). The geometry of the site, framed by Seventh and Ninth Streets as well as C Street, is given monumentality by the classical facade of the archives to the south. The area of the public square itself is very large, occupying three to four acres pending the final location of the new building line to the north

L'Enfant originally planned this space as a market enclosed by four narrow structures with a fountain in the center of a large, open intersection, permitting views back and forth along the three axes. The 1901 commission revised the plan to block the Eighth Street axis, and the more recent Federal Triangle obliterated the diagonal to the Washington Obelisk. Currently the Archives Building sited on the grid geometry squares up the plaza to the south. L'Enfant envisioned the plaza as a ''Square of Grand Fountains'' (fig. 5-44), no doubt as a smaller-scale version of the Place de la Concorde in Paris, complete with an elaborate water feature.

The current proposal for the square is to make it the site for the new United States Navy Memorial. If the plans are approved, it will contain a band shell and support facilities for moderate-sized

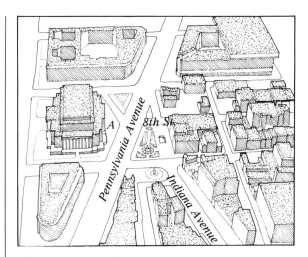

Figure 5-43. The Market Square Site.
Market Square is one of several key sites along Pennsylvania Avenue that has become a major focal point for redevelopment. Opposite the National Archives Building (A), the square is formed by the juncture of three axes. The area is fragmented into several pieces of ''lost'' space at this junction, establishing a need for stronger spatial enclosure and definition. These residual pieces should be united by conceptually extending the square outward across adjoining streets to buildings defining its perimeters.

Figure 5-44. Elbert Peets. Reconstruction of L'Enfant's Intention for the Square of Grand Fountains.
L'Enfant apparently intended this site as a monumental ''Square of Grand Fountains,'' part of a series of major public spaces that were never realized. The current proposal is to use this area for the new United States Navy Memorial. (From Spreiregen, On the Art of Designing Cities, *Courtesy: MIT Press)*

performances. The surrounding buildings are a mixture of offices and retail establishments, and a new residential community of 750 units is planned on the adjacent site to the north. Close to the Mall, the square will become an active tourist crossroad between downtown destinations. Its importance as a circulation node is increased by the new Metro Station, the only subway access to Pennsylvania Avenue. The intention is to capitalize on its location by establishing active cafes, restaurants, and shops at the ground level.

The specific design problem is that of resolving the conflicts between the grid and the diagonal, of restructuring the residual, triangular islands of lost space left by streets slicing through the site. In order to resolve these conflicts it is necessary to explore the possibilities for creating a singular identity to the square.

Inherent in the site is a contradiction between the enclosed, self-contained square, and the open, citywide plan of which it is a part. Visually and physically the seven or eight pieces of lost space at this intersection should be united by extending the spatial boundaries of the square outward to the buildings defining its perimeter. Intervening roadways that cut up the space should be closed, limited, or transformed by streetscaping, superimposing a unified, identifiable geometry. The vertical definition should be confined to the perimeter, and the inner square should not be chopped up into smaller enclosures but remain open in deference to its prominent position on the avenue. Human scale could be defined by landscaping and movable seating, which may or may not be associated with cafes and the theater.

This important space provides an opportunity to apply several design principles (fig. 5-45). First, the square can reach out to encompass the Archives Building, pulling it into the composition and providing a visual bridge over Pennsylvania Avenue. This could be achieved with dense allée plantings along Seventh and Ninth streets that, in addition to their function as borders, will form new visual extensions to the Mall. The archives would then sit in the plaza rather than alongside it.

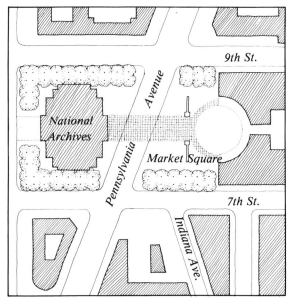

Figure 5-45. Diagram of Design Principles for Market Square.
The square could reach out to encompass the Archives Building across Pennsylvania Avenue, thereby pulling it into the composition and providing a visual bridge over the avenue. Strong plantings could define important connections to both the avenue and the Mall. A series of transitional spaces could link the square to the Eighth Street axis, creating a connection to the residential neighborhoods to the north. Gateways could emphasize points of arrival and changes between districts.

A second opportunity is to form a series of transitional spaces to the north, leading from the open square to the Eighth Street connector and the neighborhood. This could be done by manipulating the forms of the residential block planned for this site. The transition from public to private space could be reinforced by a gateway on Eighth Street, emphasizing arrival and changes between districts. A gate could also give definition and scale to the dominant perspective toward the National Archives.

Another opportunity is to reinforce the multiple sight lines through the plaza by judiciously placing objects to support views across adjacent space. With a unified pavement, the square becomes a stage for sculptural objects, strengthening the crossvistas and tying together the various outdoor anterooms as a whole. Water in placid bands or as gushing fountains could reinforce these views and would recall L'Enfant's original idea.

Several design firms have been engaged by PADC to redesign Market Square along these spatial principles. One of the more interesting preliminary designs by Conklin-Rossant called for an "Arc de Triomphe" placed along the grid at the foot of the Eighth Street corridor (figs. 5-46, 5-47). The arch, of monumental proportions at 112 feet, would house the Navy Memorial, and acoustical panels could be lowered within it to form the backdrop for band concerts. The attic, ten stories above the street, would contain the Navy exhibition. Apart from marking the significance of the square's location at midpoint along the avenue, the visually prominent arch helps define an urban room. In the center, the designers created a wedge-shaped Palladian-style plaza formed by arcaded buildings intended to be seen in forced perspective from the avenue side. The designers also used a decorative paving pattern to provide a carpet for this space and further enhanced the space with formal tree plantings and a central water feature.

In the scheme the arch becomes a mediator between the grid and diagonal geometries of the site by overpowering the conflict through its object presence. The urban-design proposal establishes a monumental relationship between the archives and the arch, both centered on the Eighth Street axis. However, as a political strategy it becomes a high-rise sculpture subject to questions of style and scale compatibility. The controversial arch received initial tentative approval from the Washington Commission on Fine Arts but at the same time was subject to severe criticism from segments of the PADC and the National Capital Planning Commission. Eventually the opposition became so great that the plans were scrapped and Conklin-Rossant was asked to develop a new parti. Conceptually the new parti attempts to achieve the same site-presence as the arch but does so in a much less ubiquitous, more conservative way. A circular, horizontal form replaces the imposing vertical object as the mediator between opposing geometries on the site (fig. 5-48).

Western Plaza: The Flat Square

Several blocks from Market Square, near the President's House toward the west end of the avenue, is the recently constructed Western Plaza, a product of the firm of Venturi, Rauch, and Scott Brown (fig. 5-49). The design is a nonliteral representation of the form and intent of L'Enfant's plan. With their usual wit and inventiveness, Venturi's firm created a pastiche of the historic plan of Washington, playing with symbolic and formal elements in an ironic manner.

The physical containment and organization of the plaza is the minor order of grid streets. At the same time it straddles Pennsylvania Avenue—a location referring at once to the federal city and the local neighborhood. In symbolic miniature, the design is a metaphor for the city within a city, similar in concept but not in physical form to the firm's proposal for Copley Square (see fig. 3-25).

The plaza alludes to L'Enfant's plan in a parterre pattern of granite paving that represents at minute scale a map of the city's historic streets and blocks. The greenery of the Mall is reflected in a grassed-in area on the flat surface of the plaza. The design is basically a response to the two-dimensional plan as pattern rather than an expression of the three-dimensional articulation of space. It is ambiguous, representational design: "the plaza as ballroom within an embossed floor pattern. . . . Unity and clarity are harder to find."[81] A raised podium vertically separated from circumscribing roads and sidewalks, the plaza is not an enclosed square but a horizontal billboard laid flat, reflecting the uniformly low-rise character of the city. Western Plaza is successful as two-dimensional design in response to Washington's historic plan, but as three-dimensional space it lacks vertical edge definition of any consistency or meaning.

In the original design, two monumental, 86-feet-high pylons were placed on the plaza to acknowledge the major axis of Pennsylvania Avenue, framing the vista of John Mill's Treasury Building that juts out in front of the White House. Of the pylons Venturi says:

Figure 5-46. Conklin-Rossant. Preliminary Design for Market Square.
The preliminary Conklin-Rossant plan for Market Square called for a dramatic "Arc de Triomphe" oriented along the grid. This arch would serve as the backdrop for a band shell and house in its attic, ten stories above street level, the naval exhibition. The arch would help define an urban "room," enclosed to the north by arcaded buildings that are angled to create a forced perspective. (Courtesy: Conklin-Rossant Architects.)

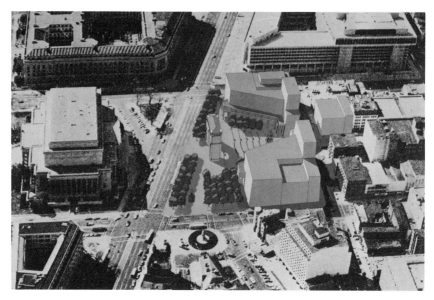

Figure 5-47. Conklin-Rossant. The "Arc de Triomphe," Market Square. The controversial arch was intended to bring the Archives Building into the square by framing its facade and responding to its architectural style. (Courtesy: PADC)

L'Enfant used the Baroque device of terminating his axes with statues or buildings, but there is another method in the Baroque tradition, that of André Le Nôtre in the garden side of Versailles. He placed nothing central at the end of the principal axis. But he made the combination of open space and bare horizon positive by framing the vista with two sets of trees. We have proposed two pylons to do the same thing at the end of our axis—to frame the scene, to make positive the otherwise amorphous combination of too little portico in clumps of trees. Our framed image is not so compelling as space articulated as infinity at the end of an axis in a

Figure 5-48. Conklin-Rossant. Current Design Concept for Market Square. The design concept as of this writing calls for an imposing public space framed by crescent-shaped buildings and a circular, dished plaza in the center designed as an inverted world globe. (Courtesy: PADC. Drawing by M. Brown)

Figure 5-49. Venturi, Rauch and Scott Brown. Western Plaza. 1980.
Also on Pennsylvania Avenue is the recently constructed Western Plaza, a product of the office of Venturi, Rauch and Scott Brown. Surrounded on all sides by roadway, the square is not intended as an intimate public space but as a symbol of L'Enfant's plan as a metaphor for the city. Although successful as a two-dimensional pattern, it lacks either enclosure or a vertical focal point. The intention was to include two tall pylons and scale models of the Capitol and the White House, but these proved too politically sensitive and were shelved. (Courtesy: Venturi, Rauch and Scott Brown)

French garden. But our framed image does not make a bad picture, and it is picturesque in several ways. It is an asymmetrical composition, a Romantic scene of a Classical portico in a rural landscape, whose prettiness Mills in mid-century might have appreciated. It is reminiscent of the oblique view of the portico of San Giorgio across the lagoon framed by the two columns on the piazzetta of San Marco, and it is a symbol of American pragmatism perhaps, framed in a Baroque plan and developed not by the authority of a prince but through the vagaries of cheques and balances.[82]

Venturi's arguments for the pylons, as interesting as they were from an intellectual point of view, were not convincing enough for the design-review committee, and they were eliminated from the plan. Paradoxically, the pylons as an expression of monumentality meant too many different things to too many people and lacked the political and aesthetic neutrality of the Roman Arch proposed in A. J. Downing's aborted 1851 plan for the avenue. Inherently the pylons of Western Plaza (or the arch of Market Square) cannot provide the legibility and clarity of the Arc de Triomphe on the Champs Elysées.[83] One of the intentions of the py-

lons, inscribed with quotations from the Constitution and Declaration of Independence, was to suggest a higher order of national and international values—an order expressed by their intentional overreaching of human scale.

In deliberate, even cheeky, contrast are the scaled-down models of the White House and Capitol buildings proposed by Venturi for Western Plaza. Twenty feet high, these models suggest the puniness, the human fallibility of institutions, anchoring the visitor to the space and giving a visual expression to the idea of democratic control of government. Politicians perceived the incongruity of scale; the high pylons of idealism versus the miniature representation of real government. Political process and the conservative nature of the design review committees shelved both ideas. However there has been recent pressure to revive Venturi's scheme. Plywood mockups of the models were even installed on a temporary basis to try to prove the point! They were an overwhelming success among users but still didn't convince the decision-makers.

Stripped of the pylons and scale models, the existing plaza (fig. 5-50) has lost much of its symbolic meaning, beauty, and relationship to the

Figure 5-50. Western Plaza. Ground-level View. Venturi's plan is inventive and elegantly executed, but is more interesting as a conceptual piece than as usable public space. (Courtesy: PADC)

broad context of Washington—a grim commentary on design by committee.

Intended to create a climactic public space—reclaimed from a snarl of traffic lanes—Western Plaza is a product of an exceptional design talent misapplied and brilliant ideas thwarted. Whereas the Plaza might have shown the amazing potential of Pennsylvania Avenue, its fate may well become a symbol of the watering-down, the compromises, awaiting the designers of this boulevard of monumental dreams![84]

On a block immediately west of the Plaza sits the contrasting world of Pershing Park (fig. 5-51) designed by M. Paul Friedberg. Compared to Western Plaza, which functions predominantly as a circulation space, Pershing Park provides quiet sitting areas protected from traffic. Friedberg uses devices typical of contemporary landscaping: we find a stepped-down amphitheater, sunken pool, and lush plant materials forming a cozy place—a withdrawn retreat from urban life. As in most of Friedberg's urban spaces, the descending terraces form visible stage sets for people and activities. Designed at the same time as Western Plaza, Pershing Park establishes a unified complex of open spaces within, but largely turns its back on the exterior city, becoming a square without context. Although it does not respond to the historic form of Washington, it is well detailed and extremely popular with the public, especially at lunchtime.

The assessment of these two very different urban spaces raises an important question: is it possible to have a contextually responsive space in Washington that is also a comfortable place? Must we continue to design spaces in isolation, even if they are next door to one another? John Morris Dixon, Editor of *Progressive Architecture,* writes about Western Plaza and Pershing Park: "Observers a few years hence will never believe that these motley fragments were all produced at the same time for one powerful public client."[85]

Master Plan for the U.S. Capitol

The idea of establishing the historic open-space system of Washington with background buildings that form squares is underlined by Patrick Pinnell in his review of the recent and very impressive master plan for the United States Capitol.

The various new House and Senate structures are intended to be functional but undistinguished "background" buildings. The buildings themselves are not its essence; instead, its series of public squares are primary. To put it another way, it is not the interior rooms which determine the proposed building shapes, but the exterior spaces, the regular courtyards, squares and street corridors.[86]

Five years in preparation by the office of the Architect of the Capitol, along with a broad-based team of notable consultants on everything from history to parking, the Master Plan encompasses 243 acres on Capitol Hill. The purpose of the plan is to try to reverse the decline in public appearance and image of the Capitol area while accommodating an expansion of government facilities. The plan (fig. 5-52) attempts to relate, in a direct sense, to the legacy of the Capitol and Capitol Grounds as well as the Capitol Hill Historical District to the east, a National Register–designated residential community. While satisfying numerous functional requirements of movement, access, and parking, the Master Plan acknowledges the natural form of the Hill by preserving existing open spaces, including Olmsted's landscape for the West Front Terraces of 1874. By this landscape-sensitive approach, a symbolic place reflecting nature in the city is achieved and the aesthetic relationship of the Capitol Grounds to its surroundings is established. "This Plan is not intended to be an imposition on the existing fabric of buildings and landscape in the area. Rather, it is the result of a search for a carefully defined relationship between the existing and the new, and between the built and the natural."[87] Probably the most significant aspect of the plan is that it establishes an environ-

Figure 5-51. M. Paul Friedberg and Partners. Pershing Park. 1981.
Adjacent to and contemporary with Western Plaza, Pershing Park represents a total contrast in design and intention. Providing a quiet retreat from Pennsylvania Avenue, the stepped-down amphitheater, sunken pool, and lush landscaping are deliberately removed from the surrounding city. Although it does not respond to the historic form of Washington, it is a well-detailed, extremely popular, and active public space. (Courtesy: PADC)

mental capacity for the Hill, recognizing the ecological limit to the number of people and bulk of buildings that the Hill can sustain in the future. This was an important step toward curbing the erosion on the Hill, the "gradual disappearance of the original image of the Capitol, due largely to extensive physical growth in the vicinity."[88] The plan restores a sense of order by putting into proper balance new buildings and natural landscape.

Figure 5-52. Capitol Master Plan. Model of Proposal (north is upward)
The current Master Plan accomplishes a number of important goals for the restoration of urban spaces in the city. It proposes new infill buildings forming a "senate square" to the northeast and "house square" to the south. Strengthening the linkages along major axes, it also provides for a hierarchy of more intimate enclosed spaces connected to the primary spatial structure. Formal plantings establish major directions while the looser, more intimate treatment introduced by Olmsted around the Capitol is respected. Above all, the plan responds to the special character of Washington—the monumental that gives it definition as a place. Also see fig. 5-38. (Courtesy: Office of the Architect of the Capitol)

The Capitol Master Plan is also exemplary for its successful urban-space design. The new Senate Square to the northeast of the Capitol is formed by two new buildings on the First Street axis. In similar fashion, proposed buildings to the south of the Capitol form a new House Square, framing a vista of the dome. In both of these areas, public space provides the driving force in shaping the site and architecture. Other critical urban-space features of the plan include the restructured Capitol Square, the transitional edge along Second Street between government and residential areas, and reforestation to screen the modernday intrusions of highways and parking lots. Overall, the plan is carefully arranged as a design unto itself, but more importantly it is a framework for future devel-

opment of the critical resource that reflects the symbolism, meaning, and historic context of L'Enfant's Washington as a whole. It represents an important step toward restoring the urban spaces and parklands in Washington, D.C.

Conclusion

This examination of spatial design in Washington shows how intimately related problems of linkage, figure-ground, and place ultimately are. The diagonal boulevards are potentially very strong linkages throughout the city. The structure breaks down, however, through poor definition along the edges of the street. At the same time, the city lacks the density and building coverage of figure-ground to provide the hierarchy of spaces needed in successful urban structure. The overriding character of the city is defined by its monumental plan and important public buildings. This character must be respected in the design of any new architecture or landscape architecture.

CASE STUDY 3: GÖTEBORG, SWEDEN

Some of the problems encountered in Göteborg are similar to those of Boston and Washington. Others are unique to its individual setting and historical evolution. It, too, however, requires the creation of structured urban spaces at specific sites, strong linkages through the city, and an awareness of its unique place characteristics in planning for its redevelopment.

Second in size only to Stockholm, and Sweden's only port on the Atlantic, Göteborg (population 500,000) is a city of major national importance. Like Boston it is a city of long evolution; like Washington it is a city with a tightly organized original plan. What we need to look at is the impact of the Modern Movement and the automobile on a cohesive, planned European city.

The forces at work in Göteborg duplicate the experience of many European cities. Some writers (such as Tom Wolfe) have treated the Modern Movement as basically a European import into America. From the European point of view, the high-rise building is equally symbolic of creeping "Americanization." Xenophobics aside, cities all over the world are suffering from the disregard of public open space that has resulted from the transformation of architecture to a form of personal artistic expression rather than a responsible urban contribution.

Like every city, however, Göteborg is not merely an example of tendencies. It has a unique history and character that need to be understood and used as the basis for restructuring the city.

As European cities go, Göteborg is a relative neophyte. Founded in the early 1600s under the aegis of Gustav Adolf II, its initial form (fig.

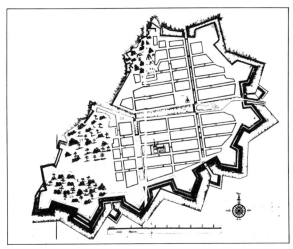

Figure 5-53. Göteborg. Plan. 1644.
The original plan of Göteborg was laid out by Dutch engineers for King Gustav Adolf II. The walled-city plan, with a grid of canals laid over rectangular urban blocks, reflects a number of ideal city plans of the Renaissance and Baroque. (Courtesy: Chalmers University of Technology)

5-53) was based on the ideal bastion city of the Renaissance. Low-lying marshlands on the Göta Älv River were protected by an impressive hemisphere of zigzag walls. Within this wide buttressing wall, a defense against the Danes to the south and the Norwegians to the north, the Dutch engineers hired by the king laid out a system of canals to give each part of the city equal access to the water. Over this they imposed a tight grid of streets. The original networks of canals and streets are still evident in today's Inner City (fig. 5-54), although some of the waterways have been filled in to make roadways.

Case-study analyses and spatial design suggestions in this section of the book stem from personal experience in working with the Göteborg City Planning and Development Office to mend five major sites of lost spaces in central Göteborg. These spaces resulted from several decisions that were either misguided or simply backfired through historic transformation. As a European city under growth pressure, Göteborg offers a fascinating laboratory for applying methods to restructure lost

Figure 5-54. Göteborg. Aerial View.
The original pattern of streets and canals is still very evident in the Inner City, although some of the waterways have
been filled. (Courtesy: Central Office of the National Land Survey of Sweden)

space in a setting where the historic framework is still unusually intact.

Göteborg's urban form consists of a pattern of distinct districts separated by green space and roads. The districts of Göteborg evolved over five definable periods in response to a number of influences.[89] The first, stretching from 1644 to about 1800, was heavily indebted to the Dutch Baroque. As suggested, the Inner Stad (downtown core or Inner City) was laid out by Dutch engineers on the ideal urban-fortress type of the Italian Renaissance. The pervasive canal system in the lowlands earned the city the nickname "Amsterdam of the North."

Historic Transformation: Five Periods

The first stage of development was a period of containment. The bastions defined the compact city to the east; the river defined its edge to the west and both provided a defensive barrier and a means of communication to the outside world. By water the main entry was the Stora Kanalen (Central Canal), where small rigs would transfer goods to and from larger ships, distributing them through the narrower canals that provided a hierarchy of access into the city. Three high points within the city were reserved as lookout points and royal preserves.

On the landward side, three major gateways penetrated the walls: Carl's Port, King's Port, and Queen's Port. These important points of penetration are still evident in the city fabric and, as we shall see, have become problem areas needing major restructuring.

As in most European cities, the internal streets and squares of the Inner City are well defined by consistent, even uniform, building heights of significant density. The figure-ground relationship of the Inner City reveals a density far more comparable to Nolli's Map of Rome than the stretched-out discontinuous coverage found in Washington. Because the mass of buildings in Göteborg is more compact with greater density, open areas become positive space and meaningful definitions of districts. As in Boston, however, the primary pedestrian connections between districts tend to be problematic. Positive urban space is concentrated within neighborhoods, and lost spaces are generated at points of pedestrian transition between districts.

One of the reasons for the lack of coherent connection was the decision to "leap the walls" in the early 1800s. This outward movement defines the second phase in the city's evolution (fig. 5-55). Under the influence of English town-country suburbanization, surrounding rural landscape was appropriated for residential neighborhoods. Between 1800 and 1870, the Inner City suffered several major fires, and a series of rebuilding programs contributed to the pressure to expand. Several waterfront sites were focal points for new growth (fig. 5-56).

When the walls were actually removed (ca. 1850), the city made a major decision, choosing to preserve a greensward around the urban core. In response to the English Park and Garden tradition, a linear park was established around the Inner City. The decision must have been controversial: in 1808 the City Architect, Carl Carlberg, had proposed a continuous pattern of urban blocks over this perimeter to extend the Inner City out-

Figure 5-55. Göteborg Plan. 1820.
In the early 1800s the need was felt to expand beyond the walls. Under the influence of English "town-country suburbanization," surrounding rural landscape was appropriated for residential neighborhoods. (Courtesy: Chalmers University of Technology).

Figure 5-56. Lagerberg. View of the Main Canal in 1820.
Throughout its history, the principal spatial corridor in Göteborg was the Main Canal. Although no longer at its prime, this waterway still dominates the visitor's image of the city. (Couresty: Göteborgs Historiska Museum)

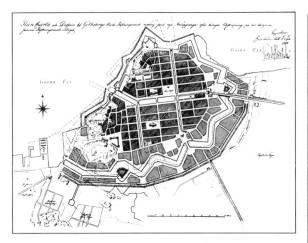

Figure 5-57. Carl Carlberg. Proposal for the Expansion of Göteborg. 1808.
One of the proposals for expansion across the walls was Carlberg's scheme for a continuous fabric of urban

ward (fig. 5-57). However, what was built and runs through this ring of green today is the Nya Allén, a roadway that has become a six-lane high-speed thoroughfare and a major barrier to pedestrian traffic between the Inner City and the outlying districts.

First crystallized in the 1863 Competition Plan for the city, the greenbelt concept became a determinant of urban expansion over the next one hundred years. The plan shows the outlines of the later, turn-of-the-century Stone Districts of Vasastaden as well as the new Kungsportsavenyn. This grand avenue extends from the former gateway of

blocks rather than a greenbelt between new residential areas and the old city. (Plan: Carl Carlberg)

King's Port to a major cultural focus at Göta-platsen, site of the art museum and performing-arts center. This avenue extends one of the major arteries through the Inner City, the Östra Hamngatan, formerly a canal, into the newly developed outlying districts.

Of major interest in this second period of the city's evolution is the manner in which it dealt with growing pains of expanding over its walls. This problem has been common to all European cities laid out on an enclosed, ideal plan, especially those with physical walls. For example, Bremen and Cracow preserved their greenbelts, but Florence and Vienna expanded with a continuous pattern of urban blocks, similar to Carlberg's 1808 proposal for Göteborg. Amsterdam, with an expandable system of concentric canals, had the flexibility within its original layout to grow with consistency.

An issue in Göteborg today is the function of the linear buffer around the old walls. This so-called Nya Allén, described above as a high-speed motorway blocking pedestrian links between the Inner City and outer residential districts, creates a heavy traffic burden at the edge of the central core. One of the questions posed is whether and how the pedestrian links can be reestablished.

The third identifiable period in Göteborg's evolution runs from about 1870 to 1910 (fig. 5-58). This time the influence was from the Neorenaissance Movement, particularly from French and German sources. The impact of this movement was less one of planning than of architectural style. As the Stone Districts of Vasastaden and Lorensberg outlined in the 1863 competition plan were actually constructed, they developed a uniformity of architectural style based on these sources. Construction was rapid, also contributing to the cohesive character of these districts.

The fourth period (ca. 1910–30), developed under the joint influence of Swedish Nationalism (sometimes referred to as Nordic Classicism) and the City Beautiful Movement, principally affected outlying districts such as Majorna and Kungs-ladugården. The new residential developments were obvious and beautiful expressions of a na-

Figure 5-58. Göteborg Plan. 1900.
In the third period of Göteborg's evolution, the green-sward along the old fortifications establishes a buffer between the Inner city and the new neighborhoods. The design of these neighborhoods was strongly influenced by the Neorenaissance movement, particularly from French and German sources, and were constructed with remarkable unity of architectural style and block pattern. (Courtesy: Chalmers University of Technology)

tional classical style influenced by the International Art Nouveau, as well as the Austrian Movement (Vienna Secession) headed by Camillo Sitte. Projects such as the Bagaregården Housing by the well-known Swedish architect Lillienberg (fig. 5-59) are important monuments of this period. Its peak was the 1923 National Exhibition held in Göteborg.

The most recent period of Göteborg's urban evolution is, as almost everywhere, the era of the Functionalist Movement. From 1930 to the present there has been an unprecedented expansion into the suburbs as well as extensive renewal of downtown sites. Large new communities have been constructed in Västra Frölunda, Kortedala, Angered, and other outlying areas on virgin territory miles from downtown (see fig. 1-1, fig. 2-3). Mistaken projections of regional growth dictated the

Figure 5-59. Architect Lillienberg, Housing at Bagaregården. 1915.
Impressive residential developments of the City Beautiful and Swedish Nationalist Movements are characteristic of outlying districts. The architectural style is distinctive, although reminiscent of the International Art Nouveau and the Vienna Secession. (Courtesy: Chalmers University of Technology. Photo by Jaan Tomasson)

size and locations of these developments. In general, such areas are characterized by high vacancy rates, social pathology, segregation, and uncomfortably long commuting distances typical of bedroom communities.

Within the central city, spheres of lost space have also been introduced in southern highlands areas such as Landala and Johanneberg. These new areas in the central core, and especially the bedroom communities outside, are persistent thorns in the sides of Swedish planners and architects. There have been serious recent proposals actually to dismantle the vacant housing blocks of the bedroom communities and move them, wall by wall, to downtown sites.

Threading through this evolution of districts there has been a vernacular architectural style that gives a special flavor to the city. ''Bohuslän Vernacular'' is a unique form of brick and wood construction, dating principally from about 1750 to 1900. This indigenous home-built construction is evident in collective harbor workers' housing (for example, Lindholmen), cottages at Slottsberg, and the Governor's Houses[90] of Haga, Gårda, Olskroken, and elsewhere. Most of this construction was

responsive to difficult rocky sites, economic concerns, and simple materials and ornaments.

Present-day Physical Form

Having discussed the evolution of the city and its indigenous vernacular, we need to summarize the distinct types of urban form in the central area (fig. 5-60), then to identify the problems within and between them.

1. The Waterfront Zone, consisting at present of underused residual space in the form of parking lots and through trafficways.
2. The Inner City, still dense and consistent, is the main commercial and employment center for the region.
3. The Nya Allén, or wide linear park encircling the landward side of the Inner City. The problem here is the expressway that runs through the park and cuts off pedestrian connections between the Inner City and the outlying areas.
4. The Stone Districts of turn-of-the-century

Figure 5-60. Figure-ground of the central core of Göteborg.
This figure-ground plan reveals five distinct patterns of urban fabric:
   1. The Waterfront. *At present an underused, residual space of parking lots and through trafficways.*

2. *The Inner City. The traditional core, still dense and consistent, retains its functions as the main commercial and employment center of the region.*
3. *The Nya Allén, or wide linear park along the old fortifications. The problem here is the major expressway that runs through the park and cuts off pedestrian connections between the Inner City and outlying districts.*
4. *The "Stone Districts" of turn-of-the-century mixed residential and commercial buildings immediately adjacent to the Inner City beyond the greenbelt.*
5. Residential communities on the hills, *consisting principally of midrise apartment buildings.*

mixed residential and commercial buildings immediately adjacent to the Inner City beyond the greenbelt. These areas have a cohesive architectural style and a rigid orthogonal block system.

5. The residential communities on the hills, consisting primarily of midrise apartment blocks. Steep topography has had a strong impact on the form of these areas.

These five areas of the city emerge in a series of views (figs. 5-61, 5-62). From the outlying hill districts there are wonderful vistas over the city, and the point-block towers complement the topography and clifflike punctuations in the landscape. A visual relationship between the crests of the hills is established by the midrise towers that appear to cling to the rock projections (fig. 5-63). Beneath these high areas there is a sea of metal roofs and treetops.

At the lower elevations of the Stone Districts, these rocky knolls become natural walls, sometimes part of the building form, sometimes part of the corridors through which buildings were carved—an impressive blending of natural and manmade elements that creates a unique character in this Bohuslän Region. In these upland areas the geometry of streets twists through the outcroppings, in contrast to the straight lines and right angles of the lowland region. These shifts in grid angle give the city a unique character responsive to its topography.

When Göteborg's fortifications were removed, the city fabric expanded from a closed to an open structure (fig. 5-64), with discrete districts somewhat disconnected from each other. As in Boston, problems of orientation arose in the areas between

districts, giving rise to the same issues of legibility and identity that Kevin Lynch addressed in the *Image of the City*.[91] Historically, as we have seen, the fortifications gave identity and visual definition to the city as a whole, complementing the water's edge to the west. Entrances from both land and water were articulated by elaborate gateways (fig. 5-65) that announced arrival to the old city. The gateways acted as doors to the city room, the plazas at these points as foyers between the Inner City and the world outside. One of the major focuses of the design proposals for Göteborg has been an attempt to restore the center and visual orientation that were lost with the original walls and gateways.

The Ring Road

Where the walls and the waterfront once stood, there has emerged a ring road around the old city (fig. 5-66). Like the central artery in Boston (but designed more efficiently and not elevated above grade), this highway system is necessary for traffic dispersal but also operates as a pedestrian barrier to the east and a blockage to the waterfront on the west—a marked contrast to the clearly defined and meaningful points of entry represented in the old gateways.

The ring-road system was developed about fifteen years ago as a traffic enclave, allowing the planners to create several important auto-free promenades within the city (fig. 5-67). Göteborg received international attention in the sixties as one of the first cities to implement such a traffic-management plan. The objective was to reduce automobile movement within the old city. In this the system was quite successful. What did not work

Figure 5-61. Facing page: *Aerial View of Downtown Göteborg.*
The aerial view shows Göteborg's waterfront in the distance, the Inner City surrounded by the Nya Allén in the center, and the Stone Districts in the foreground.

(Photo: © Bildservice, Jacky Leissner)

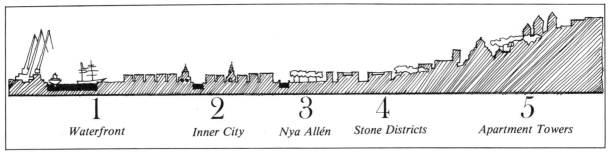

1	2	3	4	5
Waterfront	Inner City	Nya Allén	Stone Districts	Apartment Towers

Figure 5-62. Silhouette of the City.
The profile of the city shows an expansion inland toward higher topography. Residential communities on the hills consist principally of midrise apartment buildings closely adapted to their steep setting.

very well was the channeling of local and through traffic into the ring-route system, which increased its speed and volume and in doing so disrupted the parkland and waterfront. The city government is presently looking at ways of reducing the volume of traffic on the ring road and of reconstructing the waterfront highway (Göta Leden) so that certain sections could be built underground. These ideas should be pursued seriously and could create some important urban-design opportunities. Through-traffic on the waterfront could be moved across the river to Hissingen and the number of lanes on the Nya Allén reduced. Traffic problems at the entry squares of Drottningtorget, Järntorget, and Kungsportsplatsen should be reorganized.

Circulation, then, is one of the major issues in contemporary Göteborg. Another problem in common with Boston is physical connection be-

Figure 5-63. Hans Hedlund. Multifamily Dwellings at Kungshöjd. 1906.
This building offers a characteristic view of Göteborg's attractively detailed midrise dwellings that appear to cling to the ubiquitous rock projections of the residential areas. (Courtesy: Chalmers University of Technology. Photo by Jaan Tomasson)

Figure 5-64. The Street Patterns of Göteborg.
In the uplands, the regular grid of lowland streets gives way to curving, twisting patterns in response to topography.

Figure 5-65. The King's Gateway. 1820.
Elaborate gateways announced arrival to the old city and, together with the walls, gave clarity and spatial order to the inner core. Following the demolition of the ramparts, gateway areas have become major problems in the structure of the city. (Courtesy: Göteborgs Historiska Museum. Etching by Erik Dahlberg)

tween districts. As we have suggested, Göteborg's urban form in the center is relatively intact within a clearly defined border. Most of the city is contained within identifiable districts (fig. 5-68). The difficulty lies in the areas between districts, specifically along the waterfront and in the three major gateway squares. Design intervention is therefore focused on these points.

Lost Space Nodes

The five nodes of lost space we have identified will be the most important development sites in the core over the next two decades. As facades and gateways their significance to Göteborg is such that the city must lay down guidelines before handing them over to private developers. A public policy of open space, giving coherent form and meaning to the sites, must be established as a way of controlling and directing the physical structures that are built in the future.

The analysis of Göteborg (fig. 5-69) reveals two important realities in its present form:

1. A primary historic spatial structure internal to the core, consisting of three linear outdoor corridors. These are the Nya Allén (linear park), the grand avenue space created by Östra Hamngatan and Kungsportsplatsen, and the major canal still existing in the core, the Stora Hamnkanalan.
2. A current ring of space devoted to the automobile encircling the downtown core.

The points of intersection between these two systems reveal the five nodes of lost space that need restructuring: the two waterfront sites of Lilla Bommen and Stenpiren and the three gateway squares, Järntorget, Kungsportsplatsen, and Drottningtorget. In looking at these areas we developed recommendations for extending pedestrian space, rerouting traffic, infill building, definition of public spaces, and suggestions for arcades, bridges, platforms, plants, and water.

The proposals are at a conceptual level. The object was not to prescribe specific architectural forms or site plans, but to outline generally the shape and scale of the public space. Graphically the problem was how to express the minimum public framework or structure within which architecture, landscape architecture, and engineering can operate, but without drawing in the details necessary to program and implement the projects. These details are the product of continued interactions between the Planning Commission and developers of the sites in question.

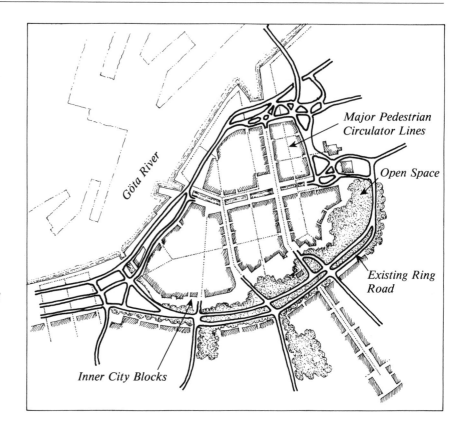

*Figure 5-66. Ring Road and
Pedestrian Circulation
Lines.
Diagram illustrating the
conflicts between the ring
road and desired pedestrian
connections across the
greensward and to the
waterfront.*

Lilla Bommen

The most important axis in Göteborg, the
"Champs Elysées" of the city, is formed by Östra
Hamngatan and Kungsportsavenyn (see fig.
5-61, boulevard on right side of photo). To the
south, the axis terminates symbolically in the Götaplatsen, a fine square formally enclosed on three
sides by major theater and museum complexes.
The cluster of buildings at this square focuses on
Carl Milles's famous Poseidon statue. On the
waterfront end, however, the axis has been cut off
abruptly 150 meters from the harbor, through
which a highway interchange creates a zone of lost
space (figs. 5-70, 5-71).

Our proposal was to redesign the interchange,
creating a square at Lilla Bommen that would be
a counterpoint in spatial clarity and symbolism to
the Götaplatsen. The space was to be continuous
with the enclosed street grid of Östra Hamngatan,
meeting the waterfront in a symmetrically shaped
public space that contained place but left open a
directed axial view (fig. 5-72). The formal spatial
geometry proposed for Lilla Bommen is similar in
plan to the main square of the Danish Fredenborg
Castle of 1720.

One way of dramatically reestablishing the connection of the city to its waterfront would be to
restore the Östra Hamngatan as a canal (fig. 5-73).
The bulkheads still exist under the pavings, and
excavation would be a relatively minor operation,
well justified by its benefits. It might even be possible to put back the original prefabricated bridges
of the early 1900s designed by the engineer Rick-
ert.[92] In its wisdom the city did not destroy the
bridges when they were removed, but stored them
for possible future reuse.

Figure 5-67. Auto-free Promenade within the City.
The ring road was developed to allow for auto-free promenades and to reduce traffic congestion within the old city.
However, the problem has been increased traffic pressure along the periphery as well as the destruction of connections
across the highway.

In the square itself the continuation of the urban fabric is technically achieved by attaching a building to the back of the Nord Stad Parking Structure, a multistory garage prominently located on the north end of Östra Hamngatan. The arcade, lined with shops, could be continued through the present garage one story above street level. A linked passage would thread through a series of buildings (hotel, retail, or housing) above the roadway. The climax would be a semienclosed city room at Lilla Bommen, which would be partially climate-controlled and would serve as the kind of glassed-in space that was developed in the nineteenth century, first in the Galleria Vittorio Emmannele III in Milan, then in the Crystal Palace that Thomas Paxton designed for the 1850 exhibition in London.

On the opposite side of the street at Torggatan a similar pedestrian connection is created, framing the end of the Östra Hamngatan and enclosing the Lilla Bommen. At this point the highway, Göta Leden, is redesigned to four lanes below grade to allow for a street-level platform at the end of Östra Hamngatan.[93] The idea is to restore the urban waterfront edge of 1820 and to create a framework into which individual buildings can be

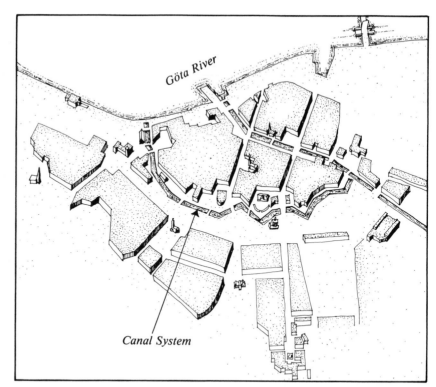

Figure 5-68. District Edges.
As in Boston, many of the problems in the spatial structure of Göteborg occur between relatively clearly defined districts. The focus of design should be to create links between these districts while preserving their distinct character.

Figure 5-69. Primary Spatial Structure.
An overlay of the principal linear corridors (the Nya Allén, The Main Canal, and the Östra Hamngatan corridor with the ring of lost space surrounding the old city reveals five principal nodes of critical importance in the reconstitution of Göteborg's spatial structure.

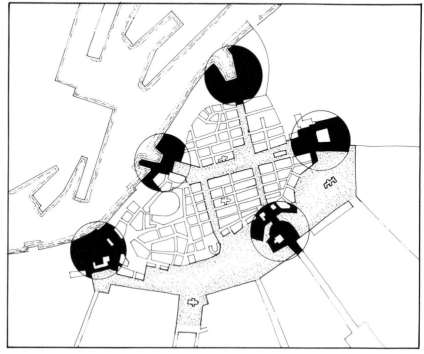

Key:
⊞ Existing Blocks
▨ Primary Spatial Structure
◕ Nodes of Lost Space

Figure 5-70. Lilla Bommen. Model.
At Lilla Bommen, the waterfront end of the Östra Hamngatan, the highway cuts the formal connection to the water-
front, which should be linked to the axis by an important public space. (Model: Göteborg City Planning Office.
Photo by Jaan Tomasson)

plugged, allowing for a variety of architectural styles and a variety of compatible uses. Within the proposed glassed-in colonnade and public square at Lilla Bommen, the visual amenities of sculpture and water features and the activities of boating, shopping, eating, browsing, sitting, and simply enjoying the sensation of urban life on the waterfront can occur throughout the year—major considerations, given Göteborg's northern location and harsh climatic conditions.

Järntorget

Järntorget, the "Worker's Square," is the point where the old city walls met the waterfront at the western edge of the Inner City. Today it is a shambles of roadways, parking lots, and missed opportunities (fig. 5-74).

There is a specific function to this area. As the site of the Folkets Hus (People's House), it has become a traditional rallying point for demon-

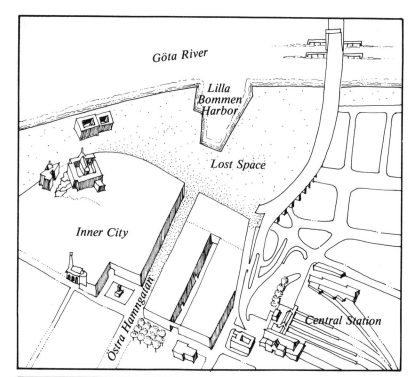

Figure 5-71. Diagram of Lost Space at the Lilla Bommen. The diagram illustrates the vast amount of lost space at this important node.

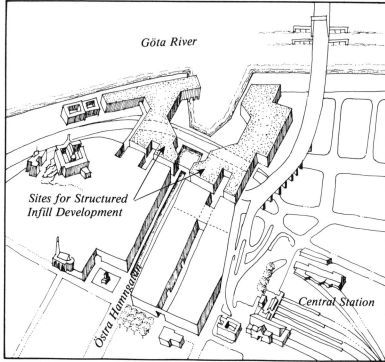

Figure 5-72. Proposed Infill Development at Lilla Bommen. Infill and restructuring of the highway at this point can create a counterpart to the important public space at the Götaplatsen. If the highway were dropped below grade, a symmetrical structure could bring the avenue to the water's edge, creating an enclosed place but leaving open an axially directed view. The important concept is to impose a framework of public space into which individual buildings can be plugged.

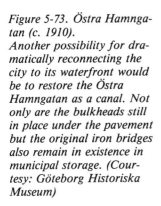

Figure 5-73. Östra Hamngatan (c. 1910).
Another possibility for dramatically reconnecting the city to its waterfront would be to restore the Östra Hamngatan as a canal. Not only are the bulkheads still in place under the pavement but the original iron bridges also remain in existence in municipal storage. (Courtesy: Göteborg Historiska Museum)

strations against capitalist inequities and the conflicts between city and state government—especially on May Day. As in all public-space design, the traditional uses of an open area need to be taken into account before specific design decisions are made.

Whereas the meaning of the square is clear, its physical form is not. Large areas of lost space (fig. 5-75) float through the district. The Folkets Hus itself, which should be the focal, organizing building, is a freestanding element that does little to clarify the structure of the space. Without a clearly defined front and back and without a connection to exterior space, the building is unable to do what it should for its square.

Another problem is a lack of connection with the waterfront. In the square, one is surprised to realize how close one is to water. Nothing in the site reflects its proximity to harborfront. To the southwest is a major car ferry (Stena Line) linking Göteborg with Denmark and Germany, a function that has produced a huge area of paving along the waterfront. The spread of its facilities has been uncontrolled and disorganized, and a staggering amount of hardtop covers this important site. The city and the ferry company must reassess their pol-

icies—physically and politically—at the Worker's Square.

We proposed several methods of restructuring this area (figs 5-76, 5-77):

1. A deliberate drawing-in of the linear park into the square, bisecting the square by market stalls that define clear zones for pedestrian uses and the trolley station within the site.
2. A continuous walk to the water along the major entry, the Järnväggatan, from the south. At this point the highway should be dropped below grade to allow for a public-space link to the harborfront. The highway and local streets reemerge to the east to allow automobiles access to the area.
3. A new building complex on the vacant site behind the Folkets Hus. This complex would link the government building to the squares—it could function as a parking garage and office space with street-level shopping.
4. A new marina at Skeppsbrokajen. This is an area to the northeast of the square, along the riverfront that should be injected with a new level of activity.

Figure 5-74. Järntorget, or Worker's Square. Aerial View.
Another important waterfront node, the Järntorget is currently a jumbled array of randomly placed buildings, parking lots, roadways, and interrupted pedestrian sequences. As a site it has a special function as the traditional rallying point for political demonstrations. (Courtesy Göteborg City Planning Office. Photo by C-G Johansson)

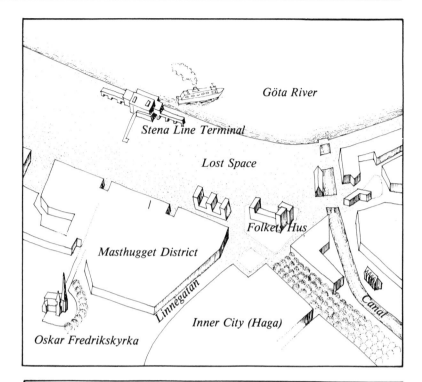

Figure 5-75. Diagram of Lost Space at the Järntorget. Axon. The new buildings fail to provide the enclosed structure and new figure-ground relationships needed to hold the space together. Nothing on the site responds to the waterfront. The ferry terminal to the southwest has engendered a huge area of paving along the water's edge through an uncontrolled and disorganized spread of facilities.

Figure 5-76. Proposed Infill at the Järntorget.
Judicious infill at this site could restructure the space as a series of "urban rooms" and reestablish the links to the waterfront. The linear park could be drawn into the area. A continuous walk to the water could bridge over the highway (dropped below grade at this point), and a new complex behind the Folkets Hus would link the government buildings to the squares. Infill blocks could extend the architectural integrity of neighboring areas into the square. Finally, the functional requirements for vehicular ferry service should be accommodated farther down river, retaining facilities for pedestrians at their current location. These proposals would restore lost spatial definition and disrupted connections to the riverfront.

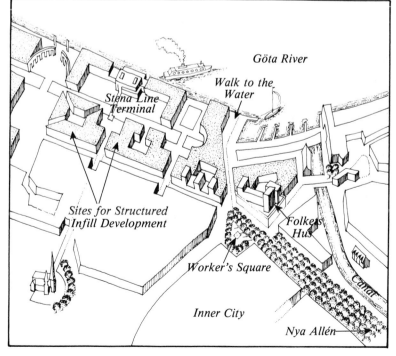

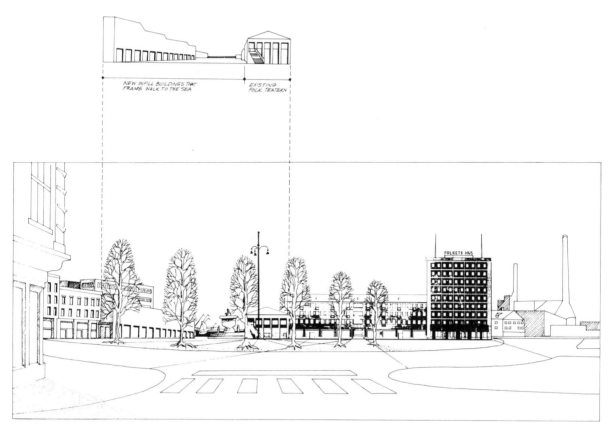

Figure 5-77. Perspective of Proposal for the Järntorget.
A new building complex could link the existing Folkets Hus to the proposed new sequence of squares.

5. The infill of urban blocks at Masthugget in a configuration that preserves the integrity of the existing physical patterns stretching from Masthuggtorget, Värmlandsgatan, to Oscar Fredrikskyrkan and Nordhemsgatan.

6. Sufficiently contained sites for an expansion of the Stena ferry line. Heavy trucking and large-scale vehicular transportation should also be removed to a point further down river, closer to the open sea. This move is inevitable anyway because of shipping requirements. The ferry service should continue, but principally for pedestrians, since it functions both as an important downtown activity and a link to other European countries.

Kungsportsplatsen

Kungsportsplatsen, the original king's gateway plaza, now poses a major problem of lost space. Instead of being the grand entrance to the city, it is an amorphous zone (fig. 5-78) with Kungstorget and Bastionplatsen, two ill-defined plazas, on the Vallgraven Canal. The central monument in the space is the Stora Teatern, one of the city's main theaters and a beautiful building in its own right. Sadly, it sits among parking areas that not only detract from the building but also destroy the important gateway function of the space (fig. 5-79). A major bridge across the Vallgraven canal provides access to the Inner City at this point, but the whole announcement of entry is destroyed by the

Figure 5-78. Kungsportsplatsen. Aerial View.
The third key node of lost space in Göteborg occurs at one of the traditional gateways into the old city. No longer a grand entrance, it is now an ill-defined zone occupying important sites along the canal that follows the outline of the former ramparts. Parking lots take up areas that need to reinforce the gateway function of the site. (Courtesy: Wezäta Förlag. Photo by Bertil Wahlin, HT Bild)

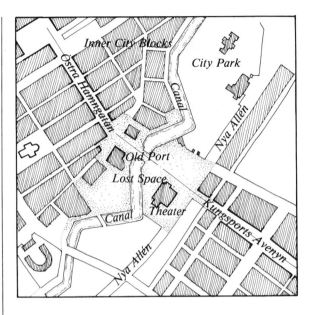

Figure 5-79. Kungsportsplatsen. Diagram of the Spatial Structure.
The central monument in the site, the theater is isolated among poorly defined residual spaces that detract from its architectural and functional importance. Although the strong form and attraction at the canal at this point could be an important amenity and gateway to the old city, the potential is destroyed by the weak spatial definition.

vast expanse of paved surfaces.

In order to create both a fitting frame for the theater and an effective expression of entrance, our proposals included wiping out the parking lot and roadway in front of the theater and creating a formal Baroque garden in this place, together with a system of linear pedestrian spaces (fig. 5-80). A semitransparent colonnade, extending the rhythm of the theater, could provide the connection between the avenue and the bridge, wrapping around the formal garden (fig. 5-81). An additional advantage of the colonnade would be to provide shelter in inclement weather. It would also be a means of incorporating the Lawn Area, a locally famous place for spring sunbathing, into the plan.

Another recommendation was to infill buildings

(fig. 5-82) at the triangular Kungstorget or "King's Square" an area to the west of the Kungsportsplatsen, formed by the original bastions and the canal but currently given over to surface parking. We proposed removing parking from this square, the canal edges, and the similarly shaped Bastionsplatsen to the northeast. Existing streetcar lines and stops would be retained in the area as part of a system that allows for a public-transportation connection between the Kungsportsplatsen and the rest of the city.

We put forth these ideas in response to and with an understanding of the political and emotional issues at hand. In 1976, there was a massive demonstration and actual occupation of Kungstorget to halt new building and parking on the site. Huge

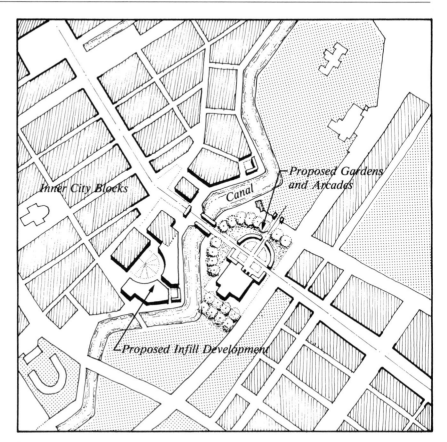

Figure 5-80. Proposed Restructure for the Kungsportsplatsen.
In this proposal, emphasis was placed on creating a setting for the theater, on reinforcing the strong triangular forms of the original bastions, and on restoring the sense of arrival to the Inner City.

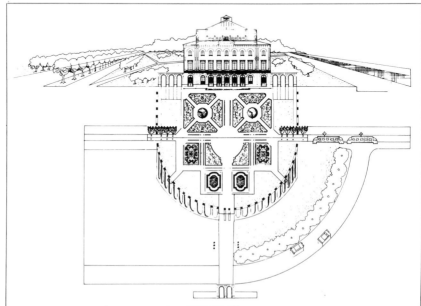

Figure 5-81. Theater Square, Kunsportsplatsen.
In order to create an appropriate frame for the Stora Teatern, a formal Baroque garden was proposed as a forecourt, surrounded by a semitransparent colonnade reflecting the rhythm of arches on the facade of the building. This arcade would wrap around the formal garden and link it to the main axis leading into the central city.

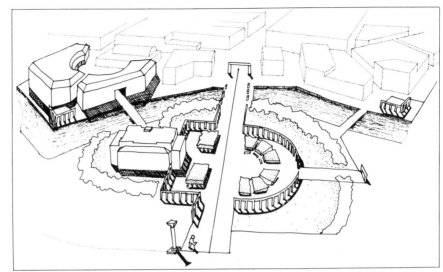

Figure 5-82. Diagram of Proposed Infill Buildings. Another proposal was to replace the surface parking lots at the key site of Kungstorget across the canal from Kungsportsplatsen. Proposed infill buildings would respond to the original outline of the canals and bastions, creating a strongly defined entry.

parking lots are clearly inappropriate and would only add to the congestion and circulation problems of the inner core. If necessary, additional parking could easily be accommodated at Heden, a large open space and existing parking area a minute away by foot.

Our proposal is for a sensitively designed structure for the square that would provide the spatial and visual qualities that would make it a useful and attractive pedestrian front door to the old city.

Stenpiren

Another gateway from the water is Stenpiren, a large stone pier at the entrance to the main canal (figs. 5-83, 5-84). For many visitors to Göteborg the most memorable image is that of the main canal. However, as at Lilla Bommen and Järntorget, traffic is a major barrier between this site and the river. Furthermore, there is no way to depress the roadway at this location since boat access must be retained. Hence a proposal for this area (figs. 5-85, 5-86) was to create spatial definition by densely packed bridges over the surface roadways—street bridges like the Ponte Vecchio in Florence (see fig. 6-4) or the original London bridge. These bridges would extend the walls of the Central Canal, linking a series of public spaces

with office and retail uses. We also suggested a large marina as the waterfront focus of this area to give new vitality to the district. Floating piers could easily be added to the existing structure to increase usable ground area.

To the north, the street continues along Postgatan and Kronhusgatan to a public plaza. Behind this corridor is a handsome row of characteristic buildings on St. Ericksgatan. Any building along these blocks should be low enough to reveal this attractive architectural ensemble.

Another important historic building in this area is the old Toll House. Our proposal is to recycle the building as a mixed-use shopping complex in which the facades and basic framework of the buildings are retained, but the interior space is reorganized as a series of courtyards around a central arcade. The main traffic intersection would be at the foot of Smedjegatan—the major grid street parallel to Östra Hamngatan—providing highway access to the local street system of the district.

Drottningtorget

The Queen's Square (fig. 5-87) is the last lost-space node addressed in this case study. The most important function of the site is as a focal point for transportation into the city. Except for air traffic,

Figure 5-83. Stenpiren. Aerial Photo.

Another major entry point from the waterfront is Stenpiren, a large pier at the end of the Main Canal. Once a focus of urban life, this area also suffers from the disruptive effects of the automobile. Unfortunately, the highway cannot be dropped below grade at this point, as boat access must be maintained. (Courtesy: Göteborg City Planning Office. Photo by C-G Johansson)

everything from international and local trains, regional and local buses, city streetcars, private automobiles, pedestrians, and even canal barges converge at this center. The square is ill-formed amid the Central Train Station, Main Post Office, canals, and several dispersed retail office buildings (fig. 5-88). The city's major park (Trädgårdsföreningen) lies to the south of the square. In this confusing space transportation systems wind around the center from all directions and the pedestrian is at a complete loss.

Our concept for restructuring the Queen's

Figure 5-84. Diagram of the Spatial Structure at Stenpiren.

The area adjacent to Stenpiren consists of compact blocks cut through by the main canal. The highway and parking lots, however, create major problems of lost space.

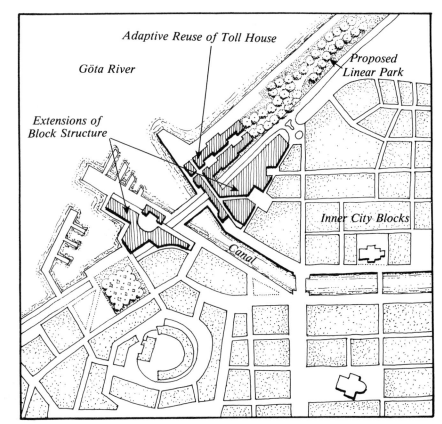

Figure 5-85. Proposal for Infill at Stenpiren.
The area could be reincorporated into the city by bridge buildings across the roadway. These structures, similar in function to those of the Ponte Vecchio in Florence (see fig. 6-4), would extend the walls of the canal and could contain public spaces as well as private office and retail facilities.

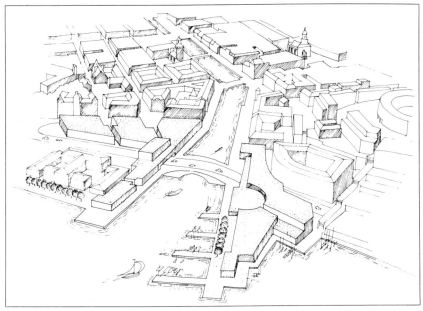

Figure 5-86. Aerial Sketch of Proposed Development. In conjunction with the bridging structures, a marina would give new vitality to the district and create a link between the canal and the waterfront.

Figure 5-87. Drottningtorget. Aerial Photo.
The final major entry point to the old city, the Queen's Square is particularly plagued by conflicting traffic systems and poorly defined edges. Trains, buses, trucks, automobiles, canal barges, and pedestrians converge at this point, which lacks strong architectural enclosure or perceivable spatial structure. (From S. Schånberg, Vägen Till Göteborg*)*

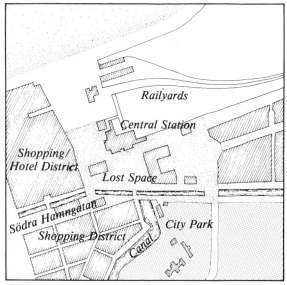

Square is to carve out a pedestrian sanctuary with major plantings in the center of the square, essentially creating a "square within a square" (figs. 5-89, 5-90). Layers of localized activities would be superimposed over a reorganized and more rational transportation network. The idea for the new transportation plan (fig. 5-91) is to use a street-level "ladder system" to channel autos, trains, and buses.

Figure 5-88. Spatial Diagram of Drottningtorget.
The major buildings around the square do not provide sufficient enclosure or consistency of alignment to define the edges adequately.

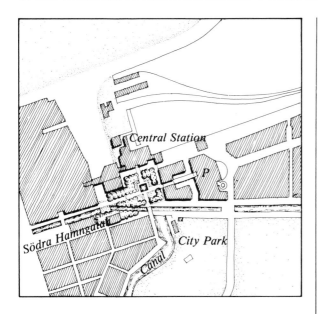

Figure 5-89. Proposal for the Restructuring of Drottningtorget.
The main concept is to carve out a pedestrian sanctuary
in the center of the square, thereby creating a square
within a square. Transportation lines would be reorganized and additional buildings added to close off the
edges and corners.

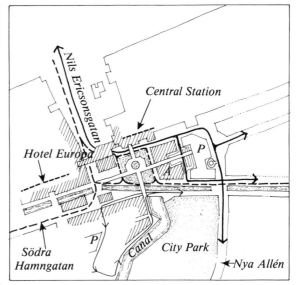

Key:
A. Old Post Office
P. Parking Structure
--- Streetcar Lines
——Major Through Traffic

Figure 5-91. Diagrams of the Proposed "Ladder System" for Transportation.
By separating traffic types, a viable pedestrian zone
could be created at the center of the square.

Fgure 5-90. Perspective
Sketch of the Restructured
Drottningtorget.
Layers of activity and major
plantings would be superimposed over a reorganized
and more rational transportation network.

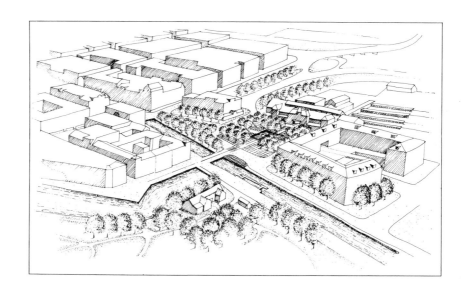

After reordering the traffic systems, a cruciform pedestrian layout is imposed. The longest axis beginning at the main entrance to the train station and extending to the edge of the canal at Nygatan. At right angles about one-third of the way from the station is the cross-axis linking the Norra Hamngatan to the square itself centering on the post office building. We envision a grand staircase leading into the center of the post office building with a passageway through to a parking garage behind. The post office has in fact an excess of floor area and the square in front badly needs a focus from the main canal. Creating a pedestrian axis to this facade could give an exciting and dramatic new face to the Queen's Square. With the main floor of the post office one level above grade, a pedestrian walkway and raised buildings could bridge the main thoroughfare to the train station and define this northeast corner.

Behind the Hotel Eggers another bridge building could be constructed to connect the Hotel Europa and the shopping center to the train station, giving closure at this corner. Colonnades and planting could complete the other two corners to create an identifiable square within a square (fig. 5-92).

At present there are several dingy underground pedestrian tunnels running through this district. These should be eliminated, placing all pedestrian traffic at street level and above. An added feature would be to incorporate the 1952 proposals of City Architect Tage William Olsson, to bring in "water parterres" from the canal to the center of the square, further enhancing its interest and human focus.

Conclusion

What has been important in looking at these five squares (fig. 5-93) is the wide variety of solutions that the combination of historic meaning and current uses suggests. Even though these squares share

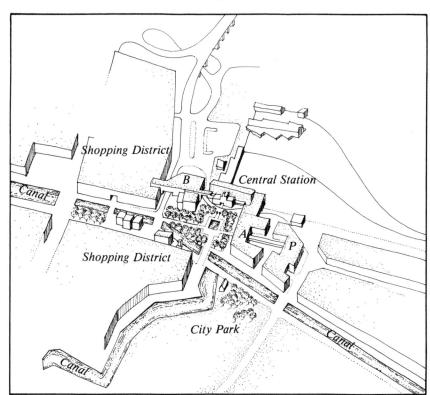

Figure 5-92. Drottningtorget. After Reconstruction. Axon.
The proposed reconstruction creates strong axial relationships to tie the buildings into a coherent space and provide a strong central focus.

Key:
A. Old Post Office
B. Hotel Europa Addition
P. New Parking Structure with Office and Retail

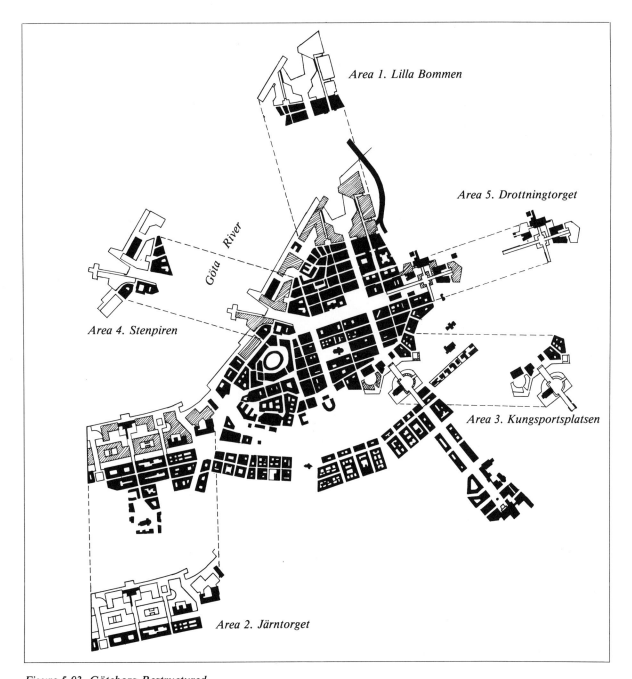

Area 1. Lilla Bommen

Area 5. Drottningtorget

Göta River

Area 4. Stenpiren

Area 3. Kungsportsplatsen

Area 2. Järntorget

Figure 5-93. Göteborg Restructured.
Each of the five areas of concern had different functional and traditional significance, and each had its individual problems. The solutions, however, can respond to both small-scale and large-scale factors. Linkages between important axes would be established, while weaknesses in the figure-ground of defined urban space would be corrected.

a common characteristic in redefining entry into the city through either the waterfront or old city walls, no single solution is applicable to all the sites.

In the case of the Lilla Bommen, we felt that its role as a terminus of the major axis on the waterfront was most important, and that it could function best as a mixed commercial/retail center. Its prominence on the waterfront justified depressing the highway below grade and perhaps even excavating the Östra Hamngatan and reinstating it as an historic canal.

The Worker's Square, although also an important entrance to the waterfront, had different needs. Its political importance as a rallying point for dissent is more significant than any other use. At the same time it is an important transportation center spilling out into the ferry to the south. What we proposed for this area was a continuation of the park into the space and a pedestrian link to the harborfront. Infill buildings necessary for spatial definition are also proposed, but their specific use is perhaps less important than their defining function.

At Kungsportsplatsen the issue was how to create an effective gateway and an appropriate set-ting for the Central Theater. In this area we suggested creating a formal garden in what is now a parking lot in front of the theater. A colonnade would form a pedestrian link to a new gateway across the bridge from King's Port.

Stenpiren's problems involved the junction of two incompatible traffic systems: the main canal and the Göta Leden highway. We attempted to resolve this conflict by creating densely packed bridges over the canal and by giving a strong water focus to the district with a large marina.

More than at any other site in the city, traffic plagues the Drottningtorget, the convergence point for all systems of travel to and through the city. Amid a confused attack from all sides, the pedestrian doesn't know where to turn. What we proposed for the Queen's Square was a pedestrian sanctuary, a square within a square.

These restructuring proposals (figs. 5-94, 5-95, 5-96) are intended to give order to the urban-development process by establishing plans and strategies for future investment in the core of Göteborg. They illustrate development-infill ideas that the city can promote in attracting investment to the downtown without jeopardizing its historic integrity.

Figure 5-94. Plan of the Waterfront after Reconstruction.
The highway is at points dropped below grade, at others buildings bridge over it to reestablish connection to the waterfront. The urban fabric is extended to form a consistent edge to park land and activity areas along the waterfront. The waterfront edge is defined by infill parcels in white.

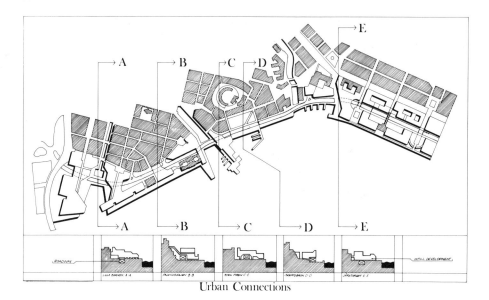

Urban Connections

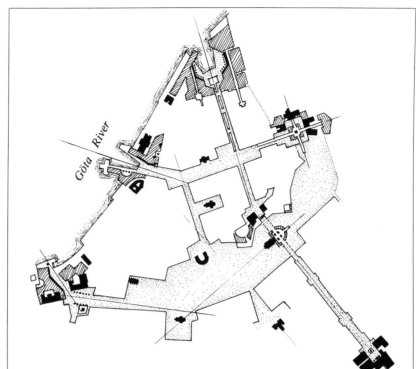

Figure 5-95. New Public Space Extensions and Visual Relationships.
The various restructuring proposals are intended to give order to future urban development by establishing priorities for investment that will contribute to the physical and visual linkages and structural space of the city.

Key:
▨ *Infill Development*
✠ *Important Public Buildings*
▱ *Structured Open Space and Visual Relationships*

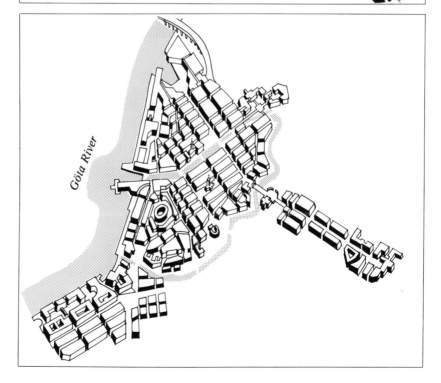

Figure 5-96. Axon of Göteborg's Core in the Year 2000.
Through a judicious planning of the spatial organization of development, the historic integrity of the city can be maintained and strengthened, and the destructive potential of random investment directed into publicly desirable channels.

CASE STUDY 4: BYKER, NEWCASTLE, ENGLAND

If the issues in Boston, Washington, and Göteborg are how to provide an integrating structure to urban form at the large scale, the problem at Byker was how to preserve the unique qualities of a distinct neighborhood within the broader community. Ralph Erskine, the designer for Byker, felt that the preservation of neighborhood identity was more important than the creation of connections to or homogeneity with the surrounding city. This is therefore a very different kind of case study, one that suggests that urban design is concerned not only with the order of the whole but also with the integrity of the parts. The redesign of Byker is a study in how historic and community continuity can be maintained even when a physical fabric must be almost entirely replaced (fig. 5-97). In contrast to the wholesale and often disastrous demolition projects of urban renewal in the sixties, the Byker redevelopment retained the scale, density, and important landmarks of the existing neighborhood and invited the active participation of residents in its design. More than in any of the case studies, ''place'' was the overriding concern.

Within a very closely knit traditional community, Ralph Erskine experimented with methods of relocating a population of 10,000 with minimal disruption to their cultural, social, and physical lives. Nearly complete at this writing, this unique housing scheme is a profoundly successful effort at rebuilding a neighborhood and saving it at the same time. The process was a social and educational experience for both the designers and the users and a dramatic statement about the political

Figure 5-97. Byker, Newcastle. Ralph Erskine, Architect. 1976.
Erskine's experiment in rehousing the community of Byker without disrupting its social cohesiveness is an important case study in the place theory approach to spatial design. Through careful phasing, community participation, and the preservation of fragments of the past, the urban designer avoided the pitfalls of most renewal projects. This 1976 Christmas card illustrates the villagelike atmosphere he conceived for the new Byker and the site office he set up in the former funeral parlor to invite resident input. (Courtesy: Ralph Erskine)

Figure 5-98. Byker before Redevelopment.
The existing neighborhood consisted of grim nineteenth-century Tyneside Flats in appalling condition. High density
and economic hardship had, however, fostered strong community feeling and close personal ties. The preservation
of these values was a primary concern in the reconstruction of the district.

form of urban transformation in low-income neighborhoods.

Byker is a working-class community in the center of Newcastle, England. In 1968 the local authorities decided to rebuild Byker under the political banner of "Byker for the Byker People." The existing neighborhood (figs. 5-98, 5-99) consisted of rows of rather grim 1880 Tyneside Flats in appalling condition, without indoor bathrooms, hot water, trees, or outdoor space. Living conditions were extremely congested, but high density and economic hardship had developed a strong community feeling and close personal re-

lationships. Over the years, Byker had become virtually a self-contained enclave within the larger city.

The proposal to rehouse the residents was initially met with skepticism and suspicion, largely because of a general lack of confidence in the ability of the city authorities to respond to the desires of the community. On the other hand, an extensive opinion survey of the residents showed that 80 percent were in favor of tearing down the old housing and rebuilding the neighborhood. Recognizing the urgency of the situation and the rapid deterioration of both the physical structure and

Figure 5-99. Byker after Reconstruction.
The density and intimate scale of the old Byker were retained in reconstruction, together with traditional focal points and landmarks. At the same time, however, new amenities, architectural forms, and landscape elements enchanced the identity and positive self-image of the community.

community spirit of Byker, the authorities established a resettlement policy and hired Ralph Erskine to implement it. Erskine's reputation as a socially responsive architect made him an appropriate choice.

Erskine arrived at Byker with a commitment to architecture as a means of bettering the lives of ordinary people and a belief that the forms of architecture should respond to the vernacular and the picturesque. His approach departed significantly from that of the first generation of Modernists, particularly in his concern for the integration of activities instead of their segregation and in his ability to become involved in the "dreams, personal details and minutiae of his clients."[94] Especially at Byker, his work demonstrates an extraordinary capacity to give equal weight to aesthetic and social factors and to experiment with the forms of late Modernism without sacrificing humanism. He was able to produce low-cost housing that retained traditional elements of the region—elements that gave scale, texture, and color to an otherwise bland, minimum-budget environment (fig. 5-100). This kind of ar-

Figure 5-100. View of Byker Low-rise Area.
Erskine's commitment to architecture as a means for bettering the lives of ordinary people has made him a specialist in providing low-cost housing that creates a framework of community identity but allows individuals to adapt and alter their personal environments. In Byker, referential fragments from the past have been incorporated into new architectural forms.

chitecture, combined with organic villagelike exterior spaces, encourages users to become involved in and to manipulate their surroundings. From a practical point of view, Erskine combined these principles with a response to the realities of climate and site, at the same time retaining his own architectural poetry.

Before accepting the terms of the Byker contract, Erskine sent two members of his staff from Sweden to live in the area for several months in order to establish design concepts and processes for approval by the Housing Authority before the final agreements were signed. It was a move intended to gain political leverage, win the confidence of the community, and protect the architect from future veto of his plans. In the agreement, Erskine writes:

> At the lowest possible cost for the residents and in intimate contact with them particularly, and with relevant authorities generally, [we shall set out] to prepare a project for planning and building a complete and integrated environment for living in its widest possible sense. This would involve us in endeavoring to create positive con-

ditions for dwelling, shopping, recreation, studying and—as far as possible—working in near contact with the home. It would involve us in considering the wishes of the people of all ages and many tastes.

> We would endeavor to maintain, as far as possible, valued traditions and characteristics of the neighborhood itself and its relationships with the surrounding areas and the centre of Newcastle. The main concern will be with those who are already resident in Byker, and the need to rehouse them without breaking family ties and other valued associations or patterns of life. We would endeavor to exploit the physical character of the site, more especially the slope towards the south, its views and sunny aspect.[95]

At the very outset, then, Erskine laid the ground rules for the design of this new community as an extension and continuation of historic traditions, social relations, and physical site of Byker (fig. 5-101). Ultimately the genuine working partnership between designer and residents reinforced the particular attributes of place in a reconstructed Byker.

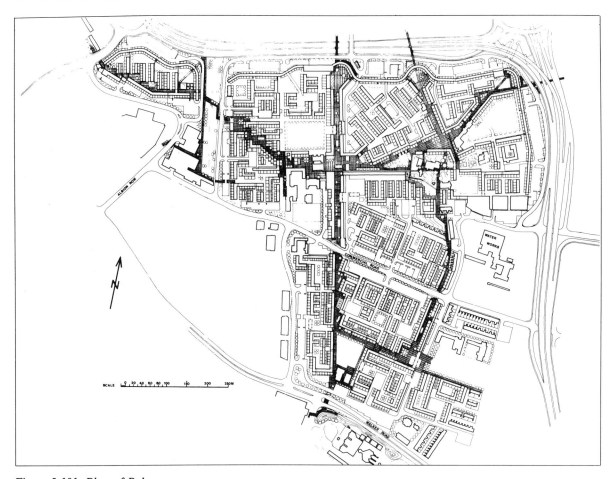

Figure 5-101. Plan of Byker.
The plan of Byker was generated by climate and site factors as well as the need to preserve traditional monuments and landmarks. To the north a perimeter wall cuts out noise from the highway and minimizes heat loss; to the south, exposure to the sun and views outward were major design considerations. A system of well-defined pedestrian connections based on the old pattern of streets and squares gives internal order to circulation systems. (Courtesy: Ralph Erskine)

Tenant Involvement

There were several important physical and institutional procedures that led to success in the recreation of space as place at Byker. One of the most important was the involvement of the tenants—an approach that started with the establishment of a local on-site office in an unused funeral parlor. The open-door policy of this office and the participatory workshops held for residents of all ages met with enormous success: from the beginning a relationship of mutual confidence between users and professionals was established. This approach also served to reduce the apprehension that previous encounters with the Housing Authority had produced in the community.

Perhaps one of the most unusual aspects of tenant involvement in the Byker project was the pilot project involving some forty six recruited families who were intensely engaged in the planning and design of the first phase of cluster units in the New Byker. Although the feedback from this experiment was of no immediate benefit to the first group of residents, it was immensely beneficial in the design of later clusters, correcting deficiencies in the layout of units and public spaces. Throughout the phased sequences of development (fig. 5-102), each consisting of 250 unit clusters, tenant feedback was solicited in designing the next phase—an iterative process to respond to the real needs of the clients.

Even though people were moving within the same community, Erskine recognized the trauma of family relocation and managed to implement a new procedure known as "forward allocation." This procedure meant that a family would be told in advance of the location of their new house and those of neighbors and close friends, as well as the arrangement of interior rooms, entrances, and gardens in relation to the path of the sun. In this way a sequence of clearance, rebuilding, and rehousing (now in its tenth year) has proceeded with

the involvement and collaboration of tenant-management groups, which has succeeded in preserving the social unity and fabric of whole neighborhoods. Although the units are rented and not owned, the approach has given the tenants of Byker an unusual and highly meaningful responsibility in the shaping and maintenance of their urban district and a political control over their social and cultural future. It has made a major contribution toward weaving together architecture and society, too often divorced, and incorporating established personal and communal habits into new patterns of living.

Retaining Physical Fragments of the Past

The continuity of place in Byker was supported by certain key decisions to retain significant fragments from the past. The New Byker was not a tabula rasa bulldozed urban-renewal project but a reconstruction in which socially important structures were preserved to give historic continuity to the community. Raby Street, the main thorough-

Figure 5-102. Byker under Construction. Aerial Photograph.
One of the most important contributions Erskine has made to the architecture of social commitment has been his careful phasing of construction. After the building of each 250-unit phase, he consulted tenants for suggestions to improve the design of future unit clusters. Tenants were also informed ahead of time about where they, relatives, neighbors, and friends would be rehoused. (Courtesy: Ralph Erskine)

Figure 5-103. Raby Street, St. Michael's Church Area.
To preserve the historic and social continuity of the community, important urban spaces such as those along Raby Street (one of the main thoroughfares) were maintained as structuring elements. Fragments of old walls, steps, and pavingstones either remained intact or were incorporated into new structures.

fare (fig. 5-103), pubs, churches, open spaces, cornerstones, pieces of old walls, steps, pavingstones, statuary friezes, and reliefs remained intact or were incorporated into new structures. Sometimes old community monuments such as Grace Street or Priory Green were given new and heightened importance in the neighborhood as focal points of axes or as monuments enclosing a square or creating an edge (fig. 5-104). Furthermore, new monuments and community facilities were consistent with the spirit of the old. Although the area is almost totally redeveloped, older elements coexist

happily with newer, and the spirit of the industrial past has not been destroyed as it was in the urban renewal of Boston's West End.

Urban design at Byker has been a response to complex circumstantial forces rather than a "knee-jerk" fixed system of rational order. The lack of obvious logic in layout reflects the true nature of the history of city development, with its sedimentary character and its ability to accommodate changes within a pattern of space that gives coherence to alterations. Byker will always remain unfinished. Residents will always be able to mod-

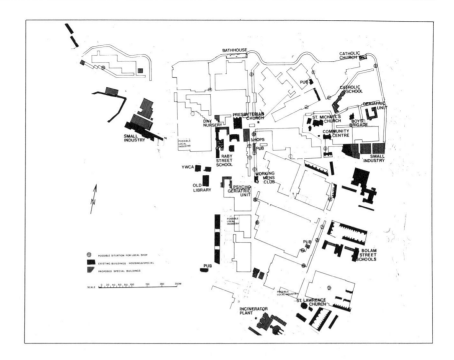

Figure 5-104. Plan Showing the Location of Retained Structures and New Special Buildings.
Existing and new special buildings and spaces were given heightened significance as focal points of axes, monuments enclosing square or edge-defining structures.

ify their environment as the community evolves into the future.

Byker's New Physical Form

So far we have discussed the social context of Byker from the point of view of maintenance and reconstruction of the community; we have not discussed the actual design. The New Byker consists of two very different physical forms: a mile-long perimeter block—"the wall" along the northern edge—and a "carpet pattern" of blocks of low-rise housing spreading over the site to the south.

The wall (fig. 5-105), initially conceived of as a noise barrier between the community and the highway, has become a billboard for Byker, a colorful mural reminiscent of a Paul Klee collage that announces the edge and entry points to the district. The wall articulates the scale of the new community. Varying from three to eight stories, the wall is virtually windowless on the highway side, but on the community side, facing the southern view (fig. 5-106), the facade explodes into a spat-

tering of large windows, attached balconies, pergolas, and galleries of wood and plexiglass. As Reyner Banham describes it:

> At Byker it looks as if a tidal wave of sheddery and pergolation had broken over the lower terraces and splashed as far up over the Wall as it could reach, leaving balconies and flower boxes and pigeon lofts clinging insecurely all over the facade.[96]

One of Erskine's successes was in applying the Team 10 concept of city wall as definer of place in a truly effective way, in contrast to the Smithsons' Haupstadt project (see fig. 4-22). Erskine was a member of Team 10 and used the wall idea in several other major projects. The reason for his success lies in his skill in breaking down scale with textural elements and in tying the wall to the low-rise community with rich detail and linking buildings. Many architects and planners have used ideas of "community within a community" and "social identity" based on the walled cities of the past, including Le Corbusier in his 1930 plan for Algiers

Figure 5-105. The Physical Form of Byker.
Byker has two contrasting architectural characters. To the north a mile-long undulating perimeter wall of varying height defines the edge of the community. A barrier against traffic noise and a colorful banner for the new Byker, the wall illustrates Erskine's concept of creating a special place, rather than integrating the district with the outside urban fabric.

Bay. This project referred to by Le Corbusier as "shrapnel" was designed to break through administrative red tape and establish a new dimension in city planning in response to contemporary realities. At Byker the wall serves the multiple purposes of defining the psychological edge between outside and inside, capturing sun, blocking highway noise, offering distant views, and defining the process of exit and arrival. Perhaps most importantly it acts as a banner for Byker's tenet of architecture for the people.

Within the wall and inside the neighborhood a different atmosphere dominates (see fig. 5-100; fig. 5-107). The interior blocks have the low-rise character of a village. Patterns of irregular public spaces respond to the topography of the site, preexisting streets and landmarks, spatial sequences, and sight lines. Appropriately, Erskine took an urban approach to the integration of automobile and pedestrian traffic but in this fusion gave precedence to the pedestrian. Parking is contained in small covered and open courtyards integrated into the urban form.

Figure 5-106. The Byker Wall from the South. Virtually windowless to the north, the wall breaks down on the south in a series of balconies, pergolas, and galleries. Town squares are formed at gateway sites leading into the neighborhoods within the wall. Exaggerated mechanical systems punctuate these entry spaces.

Conclusion

The traditional richness and variety of the streets of Byker have been reinterpreted and formalized in an organic way: as a sign of its success as an urban place, visitors are often confused by the complexity of the scheme. The richness is carried into detail—the lampposts, bollards, trellises, fences, detachable canopies, cobblestones, bright colors, and lush landscaping. In summer the narrow lanes become tunnels of flowers and vines,

Figure 5-107. Transition from Wall to Mid-rise Buildings.
The inner wall is an example of design that is responsive to climate and site but at the same time provides a series
of transitional layers between high and low elements where villagelike spaces dominate. Interior blocks are low-rise,
responding to topography, preexisting streets and landmarks, spatial sequences, and sightlines.

creating the feeling of an urban garden. To provide an instant garden city, a tree nursery was established as a source of mature plant material to be moved to the clusters as they were built. In such small but meaningful ways, Erskine has been enormously successful in reinforcing the character of the community, making Byker one of the few important responses to place in contemporary design. Physical space has become an expression of the society and particular life-styles of the people of Byker, who are overwhelming in their support and enthusiasm for their revitalized neighborhood. Instead of becoming just another housing project, Byker has retained its indigenous identity through a process of reconstruction with tenant involvement and the incorporation of historical continuity into a wholly new urban area. The residents were rehoused with minimal dislocation, and traditionally significant buildings were reinforced and given new meaning. The design and construction of Byker are virtually complete, but as a place it will continue to change in response to the desires of the residents.

6

TOWARD AN INTEGRATED APPROACH TO
URBAN DESIGN

In this last chapter we will discuss an integrated approach to urban design, drawing from the theories, cases, and precedents presented in the text. This approach is by no means exhaustive, but is meant to serve as a starting point for further exploration by the users of this book.

The chapter begins with an overview of the important ingredients of an integrated approach, clarifying and summarizing principles of design that can be used to achieve *integration*. It then defines the role of the designer and the nature of the design process. Strategies for implementing the integrated approach are then described, concluding with a statement of the responsibilities of the designer to larger societal concerns in the years ahead.

As we have stated, an integrated approach must combine the spatial definition of the figure-ground theory with the connective qualities of the linkage theory and the social responsiveness of the place theory (see chapter 4). An integration of these theories can greatly improve our chances for successful urban design. The approach must not, however, be merely conservative or myopic. The designer should integrate new elements with old in order to express the concept of time. An integrated approach is not static but must incorporate

change and innovation to give added meaning for contemporary users.

Integration can also be achieved by incrementalism. In many cases small-scale steps toward the renewal of an urban landscape are more effective than total redevelopment, which, as we have seen, often segregates the patterns of urban space. Through gradual selective infill, new pieces can be effectively brought into harmony with existing spaces and architectural forms.

In the *use* of urban space, integration is also desirable. Spaces that can accommodate mixed or integrated uses have much greater richness and vitality than single-use spaces, which are often static and remain lifeless for substantial periods of time. Design must respond to the dynamics of social uses in its physical form.

It is also desirable that new ways of integrating the automobile into the urban landscape be found without destroying the quality of outdoor space for the pedestrian. Although automobile-pedestrian separation may be appropriate in certain instances, most spaces in cities and towns will have to accommodate a mix of people and cars.

In most modern cities, areas for work and living are widely separated, creating tremendous transportation problems and a downtown deserted at dinnertime. A goal of the integrated approach should be to promote closer proximity between housing and employment, a goal that will also help eliminate wasted land in the city core.

A further objective should be the integration of regional character into the design of urban space. This regional character lies not only in indigenous architectural forms but involves a broader concept of environmental identity that includes the natural forms of the land and plant materials characteristic of the area.

Finally, it is imperative that a concern for design quality be integrated into the political decision-making process. Too often, functional and economic considerations override those of design. Part of the designer's role is to influence policy makers and the public in order to ensure that the quality of the public environment is not compromised.

With these objectives of the integrated approach in mind, we now turn to a summary of specific design principles that can help achieve these goals.

PRINCIPLES

The five physical design principles that follow are key concepts for the creation of integrated urban space. Summarized from the study and documentation of theories, precedents, and case studies, these principles are illustrated by prototypical and well-known historical models. Each of the models combines the creation of a strong spatial configuration with concerns for linkage, integration, and the specific place characteristics of the surrounding environment.

Principle One: Linking Sequential Movement

The historic models that we need to look at most closely for inspiration in restructuring modern urban spaces are those that have successfully solved problems of connecting existing structures into a sequential, unified space. One of the finest of all historic models is the tripartite plan of the Place Royale at Nancy, France, built in 1752–55 (fig. 6-1). Three interrelated squares at Nancy form a sequential composition linked by transitional features. Starting at Place Royale square, one moves across a bridge, through a triumphal arch and a rococo wrought-iron gate to the Place de la Carrière, an elongated symmetrical square that leads to the elegant, colonnaded hemicycle at the Goverment Palace with gardens behind. The sequence is an exquisite progressive layout that ties together the halves of Nancy: the medieval city to the north and the Ville Neuve to the south. In describing the squares at Nancy, Giedion says, "new elements were used in these squares to bring already existing features into a new inspiring and vital spatial unity."[97] The directed continuity of public space at Nancy is a stellar example of the importance of the pedestrian experience of moving between districts and buildings—an experience that should not be compromised for the sake of the automobile. Therefore, the important urban-design principles in the Nancy example that can be applied to contemporary design have to do with the exterior landscape acting as a link between buildings and directing sequential movement through a series of spaces. We can apply the linkage principles to knit together discontinuities by infilling directional pedestrian space. The sequences of spaces in Nancy stress the movement and transition from one space to the next, in contrast to the static quality of many historic and modern compositions.

Principle Two: Lateral Enclosure and Edge Continuity

In today's cities we must often create new frontage onto public space by filling in the gaps that break up the consistency of the urban wall facing streets and squares. Continuity of the wall is important for achieving lateral enclosure and creating a setting for street-level activities appropriate to the area being redesigned. The success or failure of public space depends largely on the character of its frontage and the continuity of its walls. Ma-

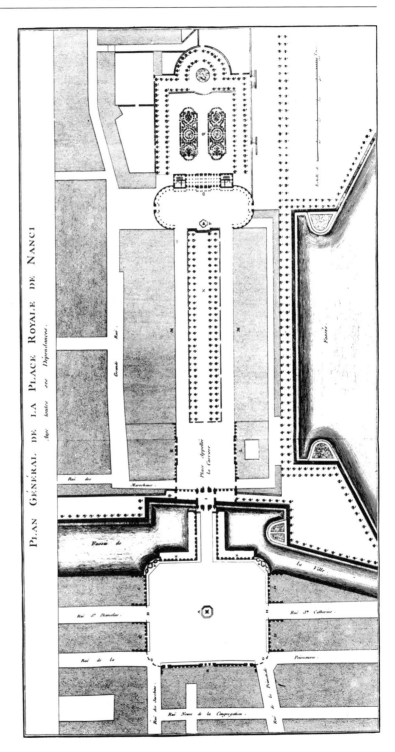

Figure 6-1. Hèrè de Corny. Place Royale. Nancy, France. 1752–1755.
The Place Royale at Nancy is one of the finest of all historic models for linked sequential movement through space. Three important squares are connected by transitional features that unite the medieval city to the eighteenth century city: Place Royale square at the bottom, the elongated Place de la Carrière in the center, and the Government Palace spaces flanked by curved colonnades at the top. Buildings and landscape direct sequential movement through spaces that are self-contained but part of a larger composition. (Courtesy: Cornell University Archives)

terials, ornamentation, and the rhythm of openings (doors and windows) are as critical as the height of the wall in relation to the scale of the outside space. The articulation of the wall—the bays, crenelations, stoops, colonnades, plantings—should respond to the needs of the interior as well as the exterior, since it is an edge that separates the public and the private realm through varying degrees of transparency and opacity.

A good example of this principle of spatial design is Ragnar Ostberg's City Hall in Stockholm, 1913 (figs. 6-2, 6-3), where the buildings shape open space by creating squares, visual landmarks, and a marvelous arcaded landscaped edge to the waterfront. In the original scheme, of which only a portion has been implemented, the urban architecture of Stockholm's city hall serves as a magnificent frame for outdoor space. Rather than the negative exploitation of a site and surroundings that happens when buildings are designed as objects unto themselves, this example makes a significant contribution to both *immediate* and *distant* space in Stockholm. The main principles that Ostberg successfully applied in his response to immediate space were lateral enclosure and edge continuity to direct the flow of voids in the courtyards and around his buildings. He was also most successful in articulating the spatial walls through the use of arcades and a sensitivity to surface materials and details of the ground plane. In response to distant space, Ostberg shaped his building mass to act as a base for the omnipresent spire. Ostberg's spire serves as an important visual landmark and citywide focal point that can be seen from many different locations in Stockholm.

Principle Three: Integrated Bridging

Another design principle that can be applied to today's urban landscape is illustrated in the Ponte Vecchio in Florence. The Ponte Vecchio (fig. 6-4) is best described as a building that is a bridge and a bridge that is also a building. The two functions are successfully integrated into one form. This principle can be applied when blockages or bar-

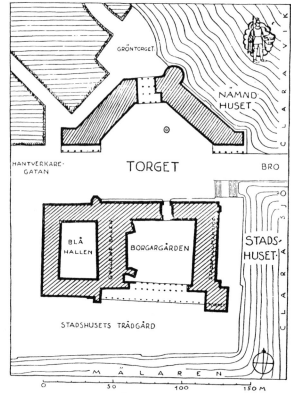

Figure 6-2. Ragnar Östberg. City Hall. Stockholm, Sweden.
Östberg's design for the Stockholm City Hall is an example of an effective use of building to frame exterior space. The architect applied principles of lateral enclosure and edge continuity to respond to "immediate" space. (Drawing by Östberg, 1929)

riers in the city's fabric needs to be overcome, and when elevated pedestrian platforms and bridges are necessary to retain spatial continuity. An example of the use of bridging to overcome the barrier of a roadway was illustrated in the case study of Göteborg. The principle can also be applied to reclaim leftover space between districts that segregates continuity in urban form. By integrating buildings and activities through this bridging it is possible to design continuous pedestrian spaces without the negative gaps that often disrupt the spatial flow. We should strive for an uninterrupted mesh of activities in public spaces, such as occurs

Figure 6-3. Ragnar Östberg. City Hall. Stockholm, Sweden.
At the same time, the vertical accent of the tower responds to the distant surroundings
of Stockholm, providing an important visual landmark for the city. (Photo: © *Lennart*
AF Petersens)

Figure 6-4. The Ponte Vecchio, Florence, Italy.
A building that is also a bridge, a bridge that is also a building, the Ponte Vecchio built during the Renaissance by Neri di Fioravanti illustrates the possibility of using bridging devices to overcome gaps in the city fabric. In the modern city, elevated passageways integrated with buildings can, like the Ponte Vecchio, serve as a link between disconnected urban areas. (From Benevolo, History of the City. *Courtesy: MIT Press)*

at Ponte Vecchio, where the bridge becomes an armature of connections or a coherent system of pedestrian ways onto which buildings can be glued. In this manner, separated buildings and activities can be integrated with coherent public space defined by architectural and landscape elements. Often these can take the form of enclosed, climate-controlled passageways that are covered to the sky. The caution, as previously expressed, is that this armature of urban spaces support the street and not run counter to it, as happens in the mall examples (see Renaissance Center and Eaton Centre, figs. 2-26, 2-27).

Principle Four: Axis and Perspective

A further model that is applicable to present conditions is the symmetrical hierarchy of urban space laid out along formal axes, as illustrated in André Le Nôtre's plan for Versailles, L'Enfant's Washington, or the Eiffel Tower in Paris. This type of organization can set up a system of visual orientation (fig. 6-5), connecting disjointed elements through lines of sight. The use of axis and perspective establishes a datum and order of organization and can be applied when an overriding image is needed to subordinate as well as coordinate existing spaces that are undistinguished and randomly disposed. As significant urban-design principles since the Renaissance, axis and perspective can greatly help in designing hierarchies of spaces based on levels of visual and functional importance and can be used to clarify block patterns. Since block patterns give shape to streets and squares, which in turn provide directional guidance for movement, their layout should invariably be based on simple, fundamental geometries that link elements at the macroscale. Axis and perspective are tools for creating such clear, organizing geometries.

Principle Five: Indoor/Outdoor Fusion

In all urban design the transition between indoor and outdoor space is of great importance. Some powerful examples of welding the two include Joseph Paxton's Crystal Palace of 1850, Gunnar Asplund's transparent architecture for the Stockholm exhibition of 1930, and the GUM Department Store in Moscow (fig. 6-6). These glass-enclosed spaces are particularly important in northern climates, where it is desirable to extend the use of public space over the twelve months. The principle of indoor/outdoor fusion has enormous potential for creating new types of urban spaces in the future—spaces that are responsive to energy needs (passive-solar, climate-control systems, and the like), spaces that take greater advantage of the potential of year-round usage, spaces that integrate landscape and urban gardens, and spaces that also explore new architectural possibilities with the use of advanced materials,

All of the above design principles are representative of urban designs composed of spaces and buildings that are more than freestanding objects. Instead of being isolated icons, the buildings and sites in these examples generate successful collective space. We do not propose adopting an historically static image of the city (a dead city) but suggest that we take into account typologies evolved through history and endow them with poetic expression in transforming them. Awareness of history allows us to build upon the memory of the city and its constituent elements in a way that can give us the vocabulary for a contemporary language of urban space. Each project demands that we look at context and program separately before integrating them into a final design.

THE DESIGNER'S ROLE

Before looking at the strategies available to the designer for implementing these principles, we should first discuss the designer's role and the design process itself.

Design is the fundamental skill required to restructure urban space—a skill that distinguishes it from other activities of planning and engineering the built environment. Without design, the mod-

Figure 6-5. The Eiffel Tower, Paris, France.
A strong use of axis and perspective can set up a system of visual orientation, registering disjointed elements through sight lines and providing an overwhelming image that will subordinate and coordinate otherwise undistinguished and randomly disposed spaces. At the Eiffel Tower in Paris, for example, the strong verticality of the landmark is linked to the city by an equally strong horizontal axis.

Figure 6-6. Facing page: *GUM Department Store, Moscow, U.S.S.R.*
An important example of the principle of outdoor/indoor fusion, the GUM Department Store in Moscow provides a protected, glass-enclosed place for year-round activity in a northern climate. This principle has enormous potential for urban spaces of the future.

ern landscape would evolve in the absence of judgments on aesthetics, visual quality, and social concerns. Design strives to create order, beauty, and scale: *order* concerns the logical, comprehensible arrangement of separate elements, including the disposition and relationship of one element to another; *beauty,* the quality that delights the senses or exalts the mind, the aesthetics and outward visual impression; and *scale* concerns the proportion of elements to the human figure that gives a sense of well-being and comfortable spatial relationship to the environment.

Through artistic inquiry the designer states a position, describes a philosophy, explains a set of values. The primary medium of this act is drawing—a language for analyzing and revealing the order of things. Through drawing the designer strives to simplify complexities and, by simplifying and diagramming, to express essential sensory relationships in the form of design. The process of analyzing and interpreting the parts of a problem is prerequisite to reassembling the parts into a whole. While the process remains the same, the factors in each situation are variable, unique to each site.

Urban spatial design is an environmental art. Beauty is measured by how well the components fit into a larger spatial structure—a structure that provides the gestalt for design. Contextual design looks first outward, then inward. The broader and more cultured the outlook, the richer and more delightful the solutions. The way to achieve integrative, contextual design is not to start from scratch but rather to reassemble known components into new combinations to express a particular condition.

THE DESIGN PROCESS

As we have stated, all urban projects are different, requiring unique formal responses to the conditions inherent in a place in time. We have also discussed why this approach to urban spatial design was absent in Modern Movement thinking. The process of arriving at solutions—the way the problem is looked at—is very much a part of the final, built product, and it is necessary to look at this process in somewhat more detail.

Step One: The Study of Place

The first step in the urban spatial design process is to study the evolution of the structure of a place by developing descriptive biographies of growth and change. In such studies, major events that have influenced historic urban patterns are analyzed, including the definition of important growth periods, planning proposals, and possibly design competitions that have guided the development of urban form. It is important to gather historic maps in order to look at the previous relationships between streets and block patterns, districts and their edges, green systems, and waterways. Extensions and infill of the urban core should be assessed in comparison with the growth of other cities. Historic images of groups of buildings and spaces, with consideration of their mass, shape, and character of facade as well as patterns of human activity, should be examined in order to determine the unique regional characteristics of a place. A study of resident needs and perceptions, the cataloging of environmental elements, and the documentation of institutional goals are necessary in order to make informed design decisions.

Step Two: Spatial Analysis

The next step is to analyze the existing physical form of the city. In planimetric format, urban solids and voids are mapped through figure-ground drawings that simplify masses, allowing the designer to distinguish between buildings, landscape, and other district patterns. Isolated buildings that are not tied into the larger context become obvious. Similarly, diagrammatic cross-sections, axonometric drawings, and aerial photographs reveal the vertical dimensions of the site. Three-dimensional scale relationships and opportunities offered by topographic grade changes and other landscape features can now be assessed. Exterior space systems and linkages—the network of streets, walkways, squares, and parks—are mapped and photographed for visual quality, taking into account view corridors, vistas, and visual axes. Patterns of use and activity are also recorded.

Step Three: Identification of Lost Space and Restructuring Opportunities

The first two steps of the urban-design process, which in fact are not linear but cyclical and iterative, provide the basic data for restructuring. The next phase is to analyze the problems and opportunities, a phase that begins by identifying the primary spatial structure. Typologies and adjacencies of the urban fabric are diagrammed to allow for the study of street and block patterns and places where connections between districts are confused or unstructured. Lost spaces, land that is vacant or underused, is delineated. Traffic patterns are examined to determine where they create barriers impeding continuous pedestrian flow along desired paths between and within districts. Political and economic development policies are looked at in order to evaluate redevelopment sites where change is inevitable. The fixed, unchangeable sites in a district, the important historic resources and newer buildings to remain, become the cornerstones around which the restructuring framework is put in place.

Step Four: Design Intervention

By overlaying these highly valued spaces with areas of lost space, the designer can pinpoint major gaps in urban continuity and establish priorities for design intervention on a site-by-site basis. Through comparison with relevant historic precedents, ideas for spatial restructuring can be generated. By following this procedure, the designer can achieve an overlapping of time and space that responds to the history of a site, user aspirations, and provides a strategy of physical connection in urban design. The massing of buildings and distribution of land uses are informed by these strategies. This approach preserves the richness of the context, retaining the identity of the place and offering the public a functionally connected system of exterior space. The fundamental rule is that no buildings or spaces are to be designed without reference to the overriding spatial structure. Effective urban-design guidelines for promoting a fit between new and old will emerge from the process described above. In summary, the more important guidelines to keep in mind are:

(1) maintain continuity of the street wall
(2) respect the existing silhouette of buildings and landscape
(3) prevent building masses that are out of scale
(4) match and/or complement materials
(5) respect existing rhythms of facades and spatial elements
(6) enhance patterns of public space usage

Design Strategies

The steps in the design process represent an overlay of the figure-ground, linkage, and place approaches. Together with the structuring principles outlined at the beginning of the chapter, this process should supply the designer with a method of providing integrative solutions to problems of urban spatial design. However, solutions are futile without strategies for implementation. After a design has been generated, the designer must know how to put it into effect. This will almost invariably require flexibility, collaboration, the ability to look for incremental actions, and the willingness to accommodate modifications and change.

There are various strategies associated with the integrative approach to design. These include infill and modification of existing structures, the generation of alternatives, collaboration with other professionals and the public, and persuasion of economic and political interests.

Infill, Modification, and Recycling

For the current urban environment, infill, modification, and recycling of existing structures are major strategies for the creation of successful public spaces. Rather than demolishing buildings and spaces and starting over, we can infill, modify, and recycle these environments by adding missing urban elements based on the historically sound principles of mixed-use streets, enclosed squares, and connected places. Instead of trying to design the complete environment at once, we can work on separate parts within an integrated plan, an incremental approach to planning and design in keeping with the conflicts and diversities of our period.

Richard Sennett, in *The Uses of Disorder,* states cogently that:

> The "Urban Whole" is a myth of purity. . . . in Haussmann's Paris the ideal was planning the parts from the nature of the whole. This metaphor of planning is an expression of the technology by which modern machines are constructed. The parts of the machine are different, to be sure, but these differences exist to create a simple function; any conflict between the parts, or even the existence of parts working independently of the whole, would defeat the purpose of the machine. In planning cities on the machine model, an urbanist is trying to integrate these needs, and for the purposes of this integration conflict and pain between the parts are viewed as bad qualities to be eliminated. . . . freedom and diversity [are] taken to be less important than the creation of a community that is conflict free.[98]

So, as urban designers we must work as surgeons or auto mechanics and repair the diverse broken parts of the city rather than trying to manufacture a completely new, self-sufficient, conflict-free urban machine. We must reorient our thinking toward centralization rather than dispersion, integration rather than segregation, and urban space that expresses its setting rather than superimposing order from outside. Incremental plans and piecemeal intervention will inevitably provide greater flexibility for growth and change than was possible in the holistic, rigid Functionalist city.

The integrated approach recognizes that the city is a continuum, that it will change over time as a result of a multitude of public and private decisions. There is no master plan cast in stone. Rodrigo Perez de Arce, in his *Urban Transformations and the Architecture of Additions,* writes:

> Additive transformation ensures a sense of continuity in the construction of a town, and a sense of place in both historical and spatial terms: in historical terms, because it is in this way that the city builds upon itself, and buildings become repositories of successive interventions; and in spatial terms because a true complexity and a meaningful variety arise from the gradual accumulation of elements which confirm and reinforce the space in an incremental process.[99]

Transformation of unworkable environments by adding elements is a much more satisfying approach than that taken at Pruitt-Igoe (see fig. 1-17). De Arce, for example, proposed a scheme for the additive transformation of Chandigarh involving extensive infill (fig. 6-7). Leon Krier wrote of this scheme:

> By reurbanizing this "earthly paradise" with Corbusian urban blocks, Rodrigo de Arce formulates an extremely powerful manifesto; he demonstrates that the Capitol would indeed become a real city, with its busy shadowed and colonnaded streets, its monuments and urban fabric, this time put in correct relationship and proximity.[100]

In the history of urban design the American contribution has been embarrassingly negative: the strip as a devastated wasteland at the fringe and the high-rise tower at the city core. These urban landscapes of "spare parts" rather than ordered patterns need an urbanism of additions—the establishment of hierarchies of public spaces and rules for connecting them. Rules should be developed slowly and incrementally to avoid the trauma of violent, holistic reordering as in the blight-

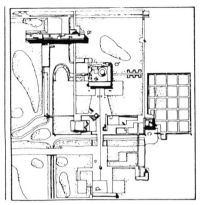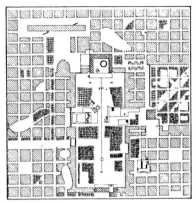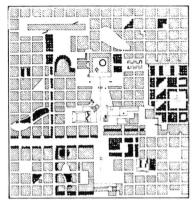

Figure 6-7. Rodrigo Perez de Arce. Scheme for the Transformation of Chandigarh.
De Arce's drawings for the reconstruction of Chandigarh demonstrate the possibility of restructuring an environment through infill and modification rather than demolition. His proposal draws on principles of enclosed urban space, human scale, and linked sequence in order to "reurbanize" an unworkable environment. (Courtesy: Rodrigo Perez de Arce)

clearance project. Strategies include combinations of additive and subtractive transformations: the infill or removal of buildings or fragments of buildings (fig. 6-8) in order to reinforce or recreate the street and the square as fundamental components of exterior space, or the positive reinforcement of nature in the city.

Generating Alternatives

Another strategy of the integrative approach to urban design is to generate alternative solutions within a strong conceptual structure set by the designer. Alternatives without a strong design and programming concept behind them result in weak, compromised solutions. But rarely is it possible to see all elements of a design realized in its entire ideal form. The final solution will always be a trade-off between cost, user needs, and aesthetic criteria. The goal is to adjust design elements within an overall structure to accommodate these considerations without losing the essence of the initial idea. The best way for a designer to retain the basic concept while allowing for modifications is to develop a range of alternative intervention strategies within an overriding structure that covers various contingencies, offers choices, and is flexible to change.

Collaboration

The designer must also recognize the limits of personal influence. Urban design is a hands-on experience that seldom occurs behind closed doors. It requires multidisciplinary teamwork at the professional level, exposure to community groups and users at the social level, and often involvement with governmental institutions at the political level. Tools and experts from fields outside pure design, such as law, finance, sociology, ecology, and psychology, should be involved in the design process and its implementation. The particular expertise of the designer, however, is in understanding the principles of urban open space and the way in which these should be used to govern the communal spatial structure.

Economic and Political Factors

The designer's goal of establishing the physical character and public uses of restructured urban space is an important means not only of improving environmental quality but also of creating incentives for private investment.[101] Private investment, in turn, can be a major contributor to the goals of design. In other words, when private investment is guided by a strong public policy for

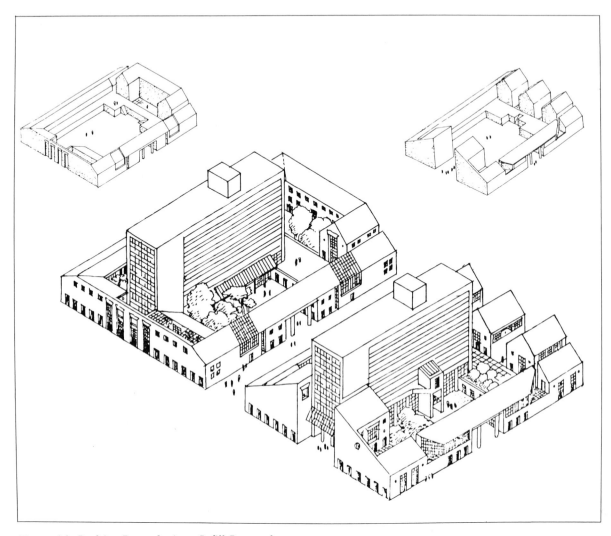

Figure 6-8. Rodrigo Perez de Arce. Infill Proposals.
De Arce's proposals for transforming slab apartment blocks into housing areas of mixed residential types, enclosed courtyards, defined entryways, and varied scale show how modification can transform an inhuman, lost environment into an environment for living. (Courtesy: Rodrigo Perez de Arce)

urban space, it can help shape this space in a positive way. The practice of urban design is founded on the assumption that the public sector can provide opportunities that stimulate, influence, and guide the actions of the private sector—the so-called public/private marriage. One of the strategies of urban spatial design is to promote this interaction of public and private interests.

The public sector has the strongest control where market forces and investment incentives already exist. Here urban design can have the most influence. However, design can also implement strategies to stimulate change in stagnant, underdeveloped areas or to intervene to prevent or alter the rate of change as a means of preserving important buildings, sites, or resources.

TOWARD THE YEAR 2000

These principles and strategies of urban design will become increasingly important over the next two decades. The 1980s are unmistakably a period of resource consciousness and economic restraint, especially in the public sector. Although certain private sectors of the American economy are improving, as of this writing we will probably never again see the massive construction that occurred in urban-renewal days. This is a blessing rather than a cause for regret. It gives us an opportunity to be more sensible about preserving history and valued traditions as we renew our urban environments.

What the present situation seems to indicate is that countries throughout the Western World have undergone a major transition from an era of seemingly limitless resources for new construction to an era of scarcer resources and slower construction. As the technological leverage of large oil companies declines, engineering and biological approaches will emerge that will allow us to benefit more from the renewable energy of natural systems. By necessity, buildings and cities will take on new forms to integrate more closely the production and consumption of energy—food, water, wastes. An ecology-based architecture founded on natural and cultural determinants will emerge. In order to prepare ourselves for this challenge we must begin an urgent search for new criteria to govern future urban form. Politics and economics will undoubtedly continue to present challenges, but many problems can be overcome by creative environmental planning and design.

Urban design that responds to indigenous context must be open to community participation, design-review boards, and other public organizations that infringe on professional prerogatives. Like designers of houses, we must meet the client when designing cities and learn how to use community participation as a positive factor in the creation of urban form. As the feeling for localism grows, so will public sophistication and knowledge about the development process. Architects, landscape architects, and town planners must learn the art of politics in order to arbitrate between clients with conflicting criteria and demands. More and more decisions are being made outside the architect's office. Training will be required to develop techniques for matching professional expertise with the needs, wants, and desires of people affected by community design. Architects, landscape architects, and planners who write legislation, draft zoning ordinances, and conduct public reviews of proposals will have a profound effect on the future quality of the urban landscape. We must develop the patience and sensitivity to work creatively with environmental rules, codes, and restrictions. We must learn to operate within bureaucratic structures and to manipulate them rather than succumb to or deny them.

The fruits of indigenous urban design do not appear overnight. We must think ahead, develop a fluid system for phasing, remain flexible about programmed use, and target design interventions where they will have the greatest effect. And we must keep in mind the fact that minimal intervention is sometimes more effective than overdesigning but that solutions inspired by strong ideas and philosophical ideals will always prevail.

The theoretical analyses and practical applications discussed in this book have been attempts to focus on the urban spatial problems that the current and rising generation of architects, landscape architects, and planners will have to face in the 1980s and 1990s. The principal problem that we have identified is how to restructure lost space in modern cities. From the beginning our goal has been to take the discussion beyond academic criticism and the simple identification of the problem into an exploration of how the urban landscape can be restructured to help solve future urban problems. Our cities have enormous potential; if we look at possible infill sites, we can probably find enough acreage in the core to satisfy growth needs for twenty to thirty years. We can ill afford, therefore, to continue to expand the city outward into the suburban fringe and must direct our attention to improving the quality of life within our urban centers. To achieve this we must bridge the gulf between urban design theory and practice.

The future of Western society is inextricably linked to the quality of its cities. Urban environments that fail in functional and human ways foster hostility, anxiety, and social disruption. The prophets of our profession foresee a future of more collective and compact urban patterns as diminishing resources require more efficient use of urban land. The need for reusing vacant urban land will permeate most if not all environmental planning and design in the years to come. The Western World is witnessing a new form of urban community shaped by recycling measures. This will require inventing alternative structures and forms to make best use of what already exists. The preservation of historic and special places in the urban landscape has also become an increasingly powerful public demand, and planners will have to respond to the desire for a restored social fabric and neighborhood identity.

By necessity, a greater percentage of the population will live in urban settings in the future as housing becomes denser and community services more concentrated. The revitalization of the existing city to accommodate greater density will be accomplished largely through the adaptive reuse of existing structures and incremental infill projects on a much smaller scale than occurred over the past two decades. The movement toward preservation, permanence, and new systems of property ownership will force those who shape and run the city to become more responsive to social concerns. Creative programs for transferring revenues from downtown development to the residential neighborhoods will make it possible to better the urban living condition. This is another form of the *linkage concept,* where private parties pay for the strain on public resources produced by their developments.

There are three major issues that will dominate postmodern city design in the 1980s and 1990s in the quest for our lost space tradition.

Context

It is incumbent upon designers of the modern city to find the inherent relationship between form and purpose that has evolved through local tradition and regional context. The International Style and Modern Movement models of urban space must be replaced by a respect for the indigenous nature of the city. Responsiveness to the historic evolution of a place will avoid superficial repetition and a retrogressive, cosmetic treatment that does not respond to the spirit of the times. In the process, the common denominators of time and place will knit together the fabric of the city: *time* in the sense of understanding and responding to the process of change, and *place* through a conscious respect for local values and traditions when planning something new.

Incrementalism

A piecemeal reconstruction of and addition to the parts of the city will become increasingly more important than the creation of complete, self-generated environments. The leftover lost spaces between buildings, districts, and neighborhoods will become desirable properties as land and resources grow scarcer. Undoubtedly, national, public, and private planning decisions will continue to result in spaces that require remedial intervention. Automobiles will continue to play an important role in American life, but constraints must be imposed in order to reclaim lost space given over to the automobile for more useful urban development. Urban design during the last two decades of this century will require strategies for conservative intervention tailored to a reduction in public funding. In fact, the incentive to initiate urban design will increasingly shift to the private sector.

Integration

Finally, an integrated city will prevail if, in the process of transforming wornout urban areas, we bring infill development into harmony with the predominant existing pattern. An integration of living and work places in the urban core can stimulate a functional yet cultural city of mixed uses, in which lost exterior spaces become new arenas for social and physical interaction.

NOTES

CHAPTER 1

1. Urban Design International Conference Syllabus. Pittsburgh, Pennsylvania, Oct., 1984.
2. Stanford Anderson, ed. *On Streets*. (IAUS Demonstration Project). Cambridge, Mass.: MIT Press, 1978, p. 341.
3. Steven Kent Peterson, "Space and Anti-Space," *Harvard Architectural Review: Beyond the Modern Movement*. Cambridge, Mass.: MIT Press, 1980, p. 89.
4. Jaquelin Robertson, Harvard University GSD Lectures, Dec. 4, 1981.
5. Harry Cobb, Harvard University GSD Lectures, Dec. 4, 1981.
6. Tom Wolfe, *From Bauhaus to Our House*. New York: Farrar, Straus & Giroux, 1981, pp. 80–82.
7. James Stewart Polshek, Preface in Deborah Dietsch and Susanna Steeneken, eds. *Precis: Architecture in the Public Realm*. Columbia University Graduate School of Architecture and Planning, New York: Rizzoli International Publications, Inc. Vol. 3. 1981, p.3.
8. Ada Louise Huxtable, "The Troubled State of Modern Architecture," *AD*. 1/2, London, 1981, p. 16.
9. Charles Jencks, *Modern Movements in Architecture*. New York: Doubleday, 1973, p. 299.
10. Robert Campbell, "The Choice: Learn from the Past or Fail in the Future," *The Boston Globe Magazine,* Nov. 11, 1984, p. 35.

CHAPTER 2

11. Moshe Safdie, "Private Jokes in Public Places," *The Atlantic Monthly,* Boston, December, 1981, p. 65.
12. Anderson, p. 341
13. Sigfried Giedion, *Space, Time and Architecture*. Cambridge, Mass.: Harvard University Press, 1980.
14. Rob Krier, *Urban Space*. New York: Rizzoli International Publications, Inc., 1979, p. 81.
15. Christian Norberg-Schulz, *Genius Loci*. New York: Rizzoli International Publications, Inc., 1979, p. 189.
16. Wolfe, pp. 23, 76.
17. Anderson, p. 341

18. Anderson, p. 341.

19. Gaston Bachelard, *La Poétique de l' espace (Poetics of Space).* Paris: Presses Universitaires de France, 1967.

20. Frederick Gutheim, "Urban Space and Urban Design" in Lowdon Wingo Jr., ed. *Cities and Space.* Baltimore: The John Hopkins Press, 1963, p. 120.

21. Christian Norberg-Schulz, *Meaning in Western Architecture.* New York: Rizzoli International Publications, Inc., 1975, p. 205.

22. Deborah Dietsch, "Public Life," p. 7.

23. Ann Kaufman, "The Vision of American Urban Parks," in Dietsch, p. 25.

24. Leon Krier, "Urban Transformations: The Blind Spot." AD. 4/78, London, p. 219.

25. Robert Venturi, *Complexity and Contradiction in Architecture.* New York: Museum of Modern Art, 1966, p. 16.

26. Colin Rowe and Fred Koetter, *Collage City.* Cambridge, Mass.: MIT Press, 1978, p. 50.

27. Norberg-Schulz, *Genius Loci,* p. 189.

28. Francois Barré, "The Desire for Urbanity," *AD* 11/12, London, 1980, pp. 5–7.

29. Daralice Donkervoet, "The Malling of the Metropolis," in Dietsch, p. 65.

30. Donkervoet, p. 65.

31. Robert Hughes, *The Shock of the New.* New York: Alfred A. Knopf, 1981, pp. 164–65.

32. Ebenezer Howard, *Garden Cities of Tomorrow.* Cambridge, Mass.: MIT Press, 1965, p. 29.

33. Lewis Mumford Introduction, in C.S. Stein, *Toward New Towns for America.* Cambridge Mass.: MIT Press, 1966, p. 16.

34. James Rouse interview, *Time Magazine,* Aug. 24, 1981, p. 45.

35. Van Eyck caption, in Alison Smithson, *Team 10 Primer.* Cambridge, Mass.: MIT Press, 1968, p. 44.

CHAPTER 3

36. Jean Paul Carlhian, "Guides, Guideposts and Guidelines," *Architecture Old and New.* Washington, D.C.: National Trust for Historic Preservation, 1980, pp. 49, 66, 67.

37. Huxtable, p. 13.

38. Venturi, p. 80.

39. Peterson, pp. 89–90.

40. *The American Heritage Dictionary of the English Language.* New York: Dell Publishing Co., 1979, p. 667.

41. Camillo Sitte, *City Planning According to Artistic Principles.* London: Phaidon Press, 1965.

42. Norberg-Schulz, *Genius Loci,* pp. 58–59.

43. Moshe Safdie, *Form and Purpose.* Aspen Colorado: International Design Education Foundation, 1980, pp. 107–11.

44. Steve Carr and Kevin Lynch, "Open Space Freedom and Control," *Urban Open Space.* New York: Cooper-Hewitt Museum, the Smithsonian Institution's National Museum of Design, 1979, p. 9.

45. Rob Krier, pp. 67–68.

46. Anderson, p. 273.

47. Susana Torre, "American Square," in Dietsch p. 32.

48. Gerhard Kallmann and Michael McKinnell project description.

49. Architect: I.M. Pei; Landscape Architect: Hideo Sasaki.

CHAPTER 4

50. Steven Kent Peterson, "Urban Design Tactics," *AD.* Vol. 49, No. 3–4, 1979, p. 77.

51. Eric Adlercreutz, "The Fall and Rise of Public Space," *Seminar on Architecture and Urban Planning in Finland.* SAFA, Helsinki, Finland, 1984, p. 31.

52. Torre, p. 31.

53. Norberg-Schulz, *Genius Loci,* p. 176.

54. Oscar Newman, *Defensible Space: Crime Prevention Through Urban Design.* New York: Macmillan Company, 1972.

55. Fumihiko Maki, *Investigations in Collective Form.* A Special Publication, No. 2., St. Louis: Washington University School of Architecture, 1964, p. 29.

56. Norberg-Schulz, *Genius Loci,* p. 7.

57. Martin Heidegger, *Poetry, Language, Thought.* Albert Hofstadter, ed. New York: 1971.

58. Norberg-Schulz, *Genius Loci,* p. 5.

59. Smithson, p. 86.

60. Van Eyck in Smithson, p. 89.

61. Statement often made by the late American architect Louis Kahn of Philadelphia.

62. Herman Hertzberger, "The Building as an Instrument for Its Occupants." Architect's description of the Centraal Beheer office building in Apeldoorn, Holland, 1982.

63. Peter Smithson, from urban-design research report by Bengt Edman, School of Architecture, Lund University, Sweden, 1981.

64. Kevin Lynch, *What Time Is This Place?* Cambridge, Mass.: MIT Press, 1972, pp. 99, 241.

65. Leon Krier, Harvard University GSD Lectures, Oct. 31, 1984. Reviewed by Mary E. Dolden of *GSD News* 1/2 1985.

66. Peterson, *Harvard Architectural Review,* p. 93.

67. D. Deshouliéres and H. Jeanneau, *AD Profiles: 15.* Vol. 48, No. 8–9, London, 1978, p. 16.

68. Hans Hollein, Harvard University GSD Lectures, Nov. 14, 1984.

69. Gordon Cullen, *Townscape.* New York: Van Nostrand Reinhold Co., 1975, p. 17.

70. Donald Appleyard, *Liveable Streets.* Berkeley: University of California Press, 1981.

71. Herman Hertzberger in *Architecture for People,* Byron Mikellides, ed., New York: Holt, Rinehart and Winston, 1980, p. 40.

72. Lucien Kroll, "Architecture and Bureaucracy," in Mikellides, p. 166.

CHAPTER 5

73. Lewis Mumford, Boston College Citizen's Seminar, Dec. 11, 1951, Boston, Mass. (NB: This theme has appeared in at least seven books by Mumford on the future of cities and urban development issues.)

74. A statement often made by architectural critics of the Boston Urban Renewal Program of the 1960s and 1970s.

75. *Downtown By Design* and *Harborpark* are reports prepared by the Boston Redevelopment Authority, 1984.

76. Edward Logue's address at Harvard University's Eighth Annual Urban Design Conference, Cambridge, Mass., May 3, 1964.

77. Patrick Pinnell, "U.S. Capitol's Master Plan: The Missing Link," *Federal Design Matters.* NEA, 1981, pp. 1–2.

78. J.L.S. Jennings, "The Washington Landscape," *LA Magazine,* Nov., 1981, p. 723.

79. Discussions with Architect Ron Eichner and others at the Pennsylvania Avenue Development Corporation.

80. Paul Spreiregen, ed., *On the Art of Designing Cities: Selected Essays by Elbert Peets.* Cambridge, Mass.: MIT Press, 1968, p. 71.

81. Robert Venturi, "Western Plaza," London: *AD* 1/79, p. 31.

82. Venturi, p. 31.

83. Suzanne Stephans, *Progressive Architecture.* 5:79, p. 113.

84. John Morris Dixon, ed., *Progressive Architecture.* 10:81. "News Report,", p. 17.

85. Dixon, p. 17.

86. Pinnell, p. 1.

87. Architect of the Capitol, *The Master Plan for the United States Capitol.* Washington, D.C., 1981, p. 1.

88. Architect of the Capitol, p. 3.

89. Historic periods defined through discussions with Professor Ursula Larsson, Chalmers University of Technology, Göteborg, Sweden.

90. "Governor's houses" are unique to Göteborg—a building type found all over the city that responds to the governor's mandate of the 1800s for reducing the risk of fire by setting height restrictions on wooden construction. The builders responded by constructing a full one-story masonry cellar above grade with wooden construction on top as a means of getting around the governor's law and increasing floor area within the restriction.

91. Kevin Lynch, *Image of the City*. Cambridge, Mass.: MIT Press, 1960, p. 2.

92. Source of information: Professor Elias Cornell, Chalmers University of Technology, Göteborg, Sweden.

93. Source of technical information: C-G Johansson, traffic engineer for the city of Göteborg. The Lilla Bommen scheme is not contingent upon sinking the highway, as the proposal spans over surface roads. If the highway were taken underground, vertical grades could be met at the bridge (Göta Alvbron).

94. Ralph Erskine, architect; quote from *AD* 11–12, 1977, p. 839 (Erskine memorandum, 1968).

95. Erskine, p. 839.

96. Reyner Banham, *AD* 11–12, 1977, p. 840.

CHAPTER 6

97. Giedion, p. 145.

98. Richard Sennett, *The Uses of Disorder*, New York: Vantage Books, 1970, p. 97.

99. Rodrigo Perez de Arce, "Urban Transformations and the Architecture of Additions," *AD* 4/78, p. 237.

100. Leon Krier, "Urban Transformations: The Blind Spot," *AD*, 4/78, p. 221.

101. John Kriken, "Urban Design," in *The Practice of Local Government Planning*. International City Management Association and American Planning Association, 1980, p. 354.

GENERAL REFERENCE BIBLIOGRAPHY

The books and articles in this general reference bibliography have been alphabetically listed in four categories:

principles and theories of space
modern movement attitudes
history of spatial design
design methods

DESIGN PRINCIPLES AND THEORIES OF SPACE

Alexander, Christopher. The Oregon Experiment, New York: Oxford University Press, 1975.

Anderson, Stanford. *On Streets.* Cambridge, Massachusetts: MIT Press, 1978.

Arce, Rodrigo Perez de. "Urban Transformations and the Architecture of Additions. *AD.* 4/78, p. 237.

Ashihara, Yoshinobu. *Exterior Design in Architecture.* New York: Van Nostrand Reinhold Company, 1970.

Banham, Reyner. *Theory and Design in the First Machine Age.* New York: Praeger Publishers, 1960.

Barré, Francois. "The Desire for Urbanity." *AD 11/12,* London, 1980, pp. 3-7.

Carlhian, Jean Paul. "Guides, Guideposts and Guidelines." *Architecture New and Old.* New York: National Trust for Historic Preservation Publication, 1980, pp. 49-68.

Columbia University. *Prècis: Architecture in the Public Realm.* New York: Rizzoli International Publications, Inc., 1981.

Cullen, Gordon. *Townscape.* New York: Van Nostrand Reinhold Co., 1975.

Hall, Edward T. *The Hidden Dimension.* New York: Doubleday Anchor Books, 1969.

Krier, Leon. "Urban Transformations: The Blind Spot." *AD 4/78.*

Krier, Rob. *Urban Space.* New York: Rizzoli International Publications, Inc., 1979.

Lynch, Kevin. *The Image of the City.* Cambridge, Massachusetts: MIT Press, 1969.

———. *What Time Is This Place?.* Cambridge, Massachusetts: MIT Press, 1972.

———. *A Theory of Good City Form.* Cambridge, Massachusetts: MIT Press, 1981.

Maki, Fumihiko. *Investigations into Collective Form.* St. Louis, Missouri: Washington University Publications, 1964.

Newman, Oscar. *Defensible Space.* New York: Collier Books, 1973.

Norberg-Schulz, Christian. *Genius Loci.* New York: Rizzoli International Publications, Inc., 1979.

———. Meaning in Western Architecture. New York: Rizzoli International Publications, Inc., 1975.

Peterson, Steve. "Urban Design Tactics." *AD* Vol. 49, No. 3-4. 1979, pp. 76-81.

Rasmussen, Steen Eiler. *Towns and Buildings.* Cambridge, Massachusetts: MIT Press, 1969.

Reps, John W. *The Making of Urban America*. Princeton, New Jersey: Princeton University Press, 1965.

Rowe, Colin, and Fred Koetter. *Collage City*. Cambridge, Massachusetts: MIT Press, 1979.

Safdie, Moshe. *Form and Purpose*. Aspen, Colorado: International Design Education Foundation, 1980.

Sennett, Richard. *The Uses of Disorder: Personal Identity and City Life*. New York: Vintage Books, 1970.

Sitte, Camillo. *City Planning According to Artistic Principles*. London: Phaidon Press, 1965.

Smithson, Alison. *Team 10 Primer*. Cambridge, Massachusetts: MIT Press, 1968.

Sommer, Robert. *Personal Space: The Behavioral Basis of Design*. Englewood Cliffs, New Jersey: Prentice-Hall, 1969.

Trancik, Roger. *Restructuring Anti-Space: With Applications in Göteborg's City Core*. Göteborg, Sweden: Chalmers University Press, 1981.

Venturi, Robert. *Complexity and Contradiction in Architecture*. New York: Museum of Modern Art, 1966.

———. *Learning from Las Vegas*. Cambridge, Massachusetts: MIT Press, 1972.

Whyte, William H. *The Social Life of Small Urban Spaces*. Washington, D.C.: The Conservation Foundation, 1980.

MODERN MOVEMENTS IN ARCHITECTURE, LANDSCAPE ARCHITECTURE, AND PLANNING: CRITICAL ASSESSMENTS

Blake, Peter. *Form Follows Fiasco: Why Modern Architecture Hasn't Worked*. Boston: Atlantic Monthly Press, 1977.

Brolin, Brent C. *The Failure of Modern Architecture*. New York: Van Nostrand Reinhold Company, 1976.

Frampton, Kenneth. *Modern Architecture: A Critical History*. London: Thames and Hudson, Ltd., 1980.

Gropius, Walter. *The New Architecture and the Bauhaus*. London: Faber and Faber, Ltd., 1935.

Harvard Architectural Review. *Beyond the Modern Movement*. Cambridge, Massachusetts: MIT Press, 1980 (see especially articles by Steve Peterson and Jaquelin Robertson, pp. 89, 115.).

Hughes, Robert. *The Shock of the New*. New York: Alfred A. Knopf, 1981.

Huxtable, Ada Louise. "The Troubled State of Modern Architecture," *AD* 1/2 . 1981, pp. 9–16.

Jencks, Charles. *Modern Movements in Architecture*. New York: Anchor Books, 1973.

Koolhaas, Rem. *Delirious New York*. New York: Oxford University Press, 1978.

Wolfe, Tom. *From Bauhaus to Our House*. New York: Farrar, Straus & Giroux, 1981.

HISTORIES OF EXTERIOR SPACE

Adams, William Howard. *The French Garden 1500–1800*. New York: George Braziller, Inc., 1979.

Benevolo, Leonardo. *History of the City*. Cambridge, Massachusetts: MIT Press, 1980.

Fox, Helen. *Andre le Nôtre, Garden Architect to Kings*. New York: Crown Publishers, 1962.

Howard, Ebenezer. *Garden Cities of Tomorrow*. London: Faber and Faber, 1951.

Jellicoe, Geoffrey and Susan. *The Landscape of Man*. New York: Viking Press, 1975.

Marx, Leo. *Machine in the Garden*. New York: Oxford University Press, 1964.

Morris, A. E. J. *History of Urban Form*. New York: John Wiley and Sons, 1979.

Zucker, Paul. *Town and Square: From the Agora to the Village Green*. New York: Columbia University Press, 1959.

ENVIRONMENTAL DESIGN METHODS

Appleyard, Don. *Livable Streets.* Berkley, California: University of California Press, 1981.

Bacon, Edmund N. *Design of Cities.* New York: Penguin Books, 1978.

Barnett, Jonathan. *Urban Design as Public Policy.* New York: Architectural Record, 1974.

Brambilla, Roberto. *For Pedestrians Only.* New York: Whitney Library of Design, 1977.

Clay, Grady. *Close-Up: How to Read the American City.* Chicago: University of Chicago Press, 1980.

Cooper-Hewitt Museum. *Urban Open Spaces.* New York: Cooper-Hewitt Museum, The Smithsonian Institution's National Museum of Design, 1979.

Fein, Albert. *Fredrick Law Olmsted and the American Environmental Tradition.* New York: George Braziller, 1972.

Giedion, Sigfried. *Space, Time and Architecture.* Cambridge, Massachusetts: Harvard University Press, 1980.

Halprin, Lawrence. *Cities.* Cambridge, Mass.: MIT Press, 1972.

Hapern, Kenneth. *Downtown USA.* New York: Watson-Gaptill, 1978.

Jackson, J.B. *American Space.* New York: W.W. Norton and Co., Inc., 1972.

Jacobs, Jane. *Death and Life of Great American Cities.* New York: Random House, 1961.

Laurie, Michael. *An Introduction to Landscape Architecture.* New York: Elsevier Publishing Company, 1975.

McHarg, Ian. *Design With Nature.* New York: The Natural History Press, 1969.

Mikellides, Byron, ed. *Architecture for People.* New York: Holt, Rinehart and Winston, 1980.

Newton, Norman T. *Design On The Land.* Cambridge, Massachusetts: Belknap Press of the Harvard University Press, 1971.

Rudofsky, Bernard. *Streets for People.* New York: Doubleday, 1969.

Spirn, Anne W. *The Granite Garden: Urban Nature and Human Design.* New York: Basic Books, 1984.

Spreiregen, Paul. *Urban Design: The Architecture of Towns and Cities.* New York: McGraw-Hill Co., 1965.

Whyte, William H. *The Last Landscape.* Garden City, New York: Doubleday, 1968.

INDEX